FAMILY HOUR

FAMILY POWER

Order this book online at www.trafford.com
or email orders@trafford.com

Most Trafford titles are also available at major online book retailers.

Note for Librarians: A cataloguing record for this book is available from Library
and Archives Canada at www.collectionscanada.ca/amicus/index-e.html

Printed in Victoria, BC, Canada.

ISBN: 978-1-4251-8848-1

Library of Congress Control Number:

*Our mission is to efficiently provide the world's finest, most comprehensive book publishing
service, enabling every author to experience success. To find out how to publish your book, your
way, and have it available worldwide, visit us online at www.trafford.com*

Trafford rev. 09/25/09

 www.trafford.com

North America & international
toll-free: 1 888 232 4444 (USA & Canada)
phone: 250 383 6864 ♦ fax: 812 355 4082

Parents who disown their young-adult children offer a variety of reasons for this drastic action. Their rationales include unacceptable choices by young folks as to lifestyle, marriage, politics, religion, career, etc. But one factor appears to weigh heavily in all these parent-child divorces. The truth is that parents disown their grown-up offspring because they cling onto the mistaken concept that they owned them in the first place.

FAMILY HOUR
FAMILY POWER

THE ROAD TO FAMILY UNITY

James T. Barry, MSSS
Lois P. Krop, EdD, MSW

This work is dedicated to parents everywhere who wish: *to give* their children the best possible start in life; *to enjoy* the child-rearing years exercising self-confident leadership; and *to experience* rewarding friendships in the future with their former little ones.

CONTENTS

SECTION I

FAMILY HOUR: AN IDEA WHOSE TIME HAS COME

SECTION II

FAMILY HOUR LEADERSHIP

SECTION III

FAMILY HOUR TODAY KEEPS DISASTER AWAY

SECTION IV

ENRICHING YOUNG LIVES THROUGH FAMILY HOUR

SECTION V

LONG-TERM BENEFITS OF FAMILY HOUR

HELP SECTION

ACKNOWLEDGEMENTS

We are most grateful to our loving spouses, Juanita and Michael, for their consistent support and patience. Our combined eight prized progeny--Pamela, Kenneth, Daniel, Raymond, Judith, Marcelina, David, and Dawn have shared a great deal of love with us, taught us numerous valuable lessons, and permitted us to play a crucial supporting role as they have undertaken and continued with their chosen journey. We will cherish their friendship always. Without them, this book could never have been written.

Great thanks also goes to the many counseling clients and workshop attendees with whom we have been associated in our fascinating careers. Their dedication to overcoming obstacles and enhancing their lives and the lives of their loved ones has been a source of great satisfaction to us; and they have taught us much about ourselves. We also owe a great deal to the kinfolk, friends, teachers, and associates who have inspired us, extended a helping hand when needed, and pointed us in the right direction when we were feeling unsure of our way.

Also, a very special thank you to Dr. Benjamin Spock, who chose not to curse the darkness, but instead chose to light a candle. The light from this candle has now spread to every corner of the world, and the authors are grateful to be able to bask in it.

INTRODUCTION

Some parents and their now-adult youngsters engage in heated political debates or a rehashing of old family issues, and then they go right back to being good friends. That's just fine, you think, but wouldn't it have been nicer if they had been able to deal with such touchy issues so candidly when they were living under the same roof? Yes, some of these families had been mired in a combat zone or in an ice age when their offspring were teens; but quite a few other families were in truth able to remain on friendly terms during no-holds-barred discussions all throughout the years. How did these parents do this? To some it came naturally, having been raised in a similar climate; and others had a harder journey-- getting raised in emotionally restrictive circumstances, and later on learning to loosen up. Yet no matter how they get there, "emotional freedom" parents all realize that openness is the ideal scenario toward resolving most issues of everyday living. They are not likely, however, to have found much mention of or enthusiasm for family dialogue in the parenting literature.

The parenting scene these days is awash with strategies like time-outs, deal making, threats, incentives, grilling, grounding, hounding, shielding, etc.--all aimed at evoking desired behaviors and discouraging contrariness. What's so terrible about that, you ask? In small doses it's O.K., but when strategies dominate your scene, trouble lurks not very far behind. First of all, a "take action right away" approach to problems, even when successful, tends to keep family members from dealing with conflict below the surface; and it also stifles the natural flow of ideas and feelings, which in turn fosters an emotional distance. Then to make matters worse, it casts a gigantic shadow over the blossoming out of youthful self-reliance--a process that does not suddenly materialize as graduation time draws near, but takes shape gradually from the time of the first steps in toddling around.

Books and articles on effective communication show folks how to talk and listen in a focused, thoughtful way to sort out conflicts with colleagues, spouses, friends, and other adults. Thus if bosses and their staffs can benefit from open-ended talking, can't family leaders and their "followers" do it too? Ah, but most parenting writers remain deafeningly silent on the subject; and many advise dishing out punishments for those who erupt verbally, viewing this "lack of respect" as an assault on parental authority. Now are grown-ups really all that vulnerable? Absolutely not! In our judgment, parents who keep their cool as they tolerate, contemplate, and then hopefully learn from opinions and spontaneous expression they don't relish hearing are in reality demonstrating maturity and strength of leadership.

Now here comes the big question: how can you allow little ones--or even worse, teenagers--to express themselves openly without having the floodgates of chaos open up? It's not difficult at all, as you will see in the chapters up ahead. And be assured that, while parent-child dialogue is really golden, it gets rendered useless when your little rowdies are running roughshod over you. Have you ever gotten acquainted with or had the good fortune to work under a boss who is willing to hear out an employee's gripes, discuss them thoroughly, and then act confidently? It goes without saying that they command a great degree of respect from all who work under their auspices.

Ah, but contending with growing little ones is different, you insist. Surely there are differences; but dialoguing parents learn to differentiate between spontaneity on the one hand, and manipulation and harassment on the other. They welcome the former while slamming the door on the latter, and then firmly lay down the law when the occasion demands. But then, where dialogue flourishes, situations that call for handing out consequences tend to be relatively rare. Now is this all beginning to sound like pie in the sky? Well in fact, legions of parents have raised their children this way from time immemorial. These are the "really lucky" parents we all have heard about; but they usually let their children do the boasting for them--like "My mom and dad were really terrific. I always knew I could talk to them."

Oh by the way, we are not bragging about the benefits of free-flowing communication in a vacuum. This is a truly complex society we reside in, and quality time can run in scanty supply in modern-day households. Therefore, we present to you a realistic way to safeguard this precious time--the weekly family meeting. Now family meetings are by no means a novel idea in the parenting literature, but most writers cover it in a paragraph or two and recommend a limited range of structured formats for your discussions. We, on the other hand, urge you to customize your family hour style and to experiment with agendas as much as you wish. Furthermore, we go from A thru Z in showing you how to succeed at family hour, which mostly involves keeping dialogue from drifting off course. And no, dialogue is not a step-by-step, how-to-do process, but rather a how-to-stay-out-of-trouble one.

The longer you continue with family hour, the more you will get from it; and in order to succeed you don't need a stratospheric IQ, a charismatic personality, or a salesman's gift of gab. The big secret, rather, lies in keeping steady at the wheel in facilitating the agenda, while at the same time flexible about shifting gears when needed; being diligent in keeping the discussion moving along, but quick to step in to shortcircuit destructive interaction; and staying in touch with your sense of humor, especially the ability to laugh at yourself. What is more, faith in the long-range benefits that await household members will strengthen you with perseverance. There no doubt will occur rough moments as you move along, but for the most part your sessions should be really interesting, and hopefully loads of fun. We wish you much success and good fortune in the weeks and months ahead.

FOREWORD

The authors met at Barry University School of Social Work in Miami, where they were both clinical faculty. Before long they discovered they had a few things in common: they were engaged in raising four children apiece, shared a like parenting philosophy, and had undertaken family meetings on a regular basis with their families. When they began sharing stories about the amazing and amusing things going on in the weekly family sessions, it was not long before they concluded that word about "family conferencing," as they called it at the time, needed to get out to families all over. At that juncture each one knew what was on the other's mind, and thus began their dedication to seeing it become a reality.

From that day onward, the authors set out to train parents in counseling sessions and in parenting workshops to function as family hour leaders. They also spread the word in newspaper and magazine articles, on radio shows, and at nationwide symposia, among other places. Their ideas were invariably greeted with enthusiasm, and the query they heard again and again was "When will your book be coming out?" Well, the book has taken a wee bit longer than originally had been anticipated, as it has gone through many revisions and rewritings along the way. At one point a publishing contract loomed nigh on the horizon, but that was not to be. Then after further reworking, the same process got repeated. But things always appear to fall into place in their own time; and now, happily, that time is here.

ABOUT THE AUTHORS

Jim Barry has a master's degree in social service. A long-timer in foster care, adoptions, and also family agency and private practice, he has throughout the years been engaged in individual and group therapy, marriage counseling, and family therapy. He has formed and led parenting classes, supervised social work interns as well as clinical staff, trained indigenous community leaders, and served as a Spanish language interviewer and translator. In addition, Jim has written, produced, directed, and acted in several stage plays, has written extensively in the field of human behavior and in other areas, and has obtained credits as a free-lance editor. He calls Gainesville, Florida his home.

Lois Krop obtained a master's degree in social work and a doctorate in educational psychology. Through the years she has worked as a marriage counselor; educational psychologist; therapist working with children, adults, and family groups; and a trainer for master's degree candidates in the social service field. Widely known as an organizer and leader of parenting classes in South Florida, Lois has also provided expertise to nationally syndicated parenting columns, recruited for and conducted stress-management seminars, served as consultant to major corporations, and hosted call-in radio talk shows that have interpersonal relations as their focus. She resides in the Miami, Florida area.

SECTION I

FAMILY HOUR:
AN IDEA WHOSE TIME
HAS COME

CHAPTER ONE

THE CONFIDENT PARENT:
AN ENDANGERED SPECIES

We all sat around the living room for our first family meeting, and 6 year old Samantha began asking as to why we were here. So I went into a long explanation about family hour's significance and what I wished to accomplish. Then I inquired about her thoughts, and she said "No, mom, I only wanted to know why we aren't in the family room where we always hang out." Laughter followed, and I got all red-faced, but that loosened everybody up and we had a very enjoyable first session.

Insurance agent, mother of 3

When my oldest was born I wept buckets, then it all happened again next time around. My wife, who has a sense of humor like mine, never forgot this; and when we sat down for our first family hour session, she said "You're not going to start crying, are you?" So I replied "No, but I'm thinking of sending you to bed early." We have been at it for about 8 months now, and--needless to say--our meetings get raucous at times. The kids are usually the worst offenders.

Inventor, father of 4

Anxiety is a warning signal that calls for decisive action-- fight or flight. But flight is just not an option when it comes to contending with your little ones; and if you let anxiety keep on building up, you run the risk of turning into a nervous wreck. Thus the only alternative, unless you give in to the prospect of spiraling on down into a depression, is for you to prepare for the battle. Far, far too many parents, however, end up fighting the us-against-them fight, which leads to their looking upon the children as adversaries. But it need not be like this. Yes, you must sometimes get tough; but as long as you are looking out for your own best interests as well as for theirs, you will feel secure in your position, and your youngsters will be your staunch allies in the child-rearing odyssey. We will show you how to accomplish this.

Parents these days have so much to fret about. Potential ecological and nuclear disasters loom around the bend; and closer to home parents stew about youthful drinking and drug use, gang involvement, pregnancy, AIDS, and suicide. They worry their six-year-old starting out school won't have any friends; and then when she gets into high school they worry about her having too many of the wrong type friends. And what always bedevils parents is the question of whether they are making the right decisions. Even the most rock-solid types radiating self-assurance in their professional dealings and social relationships find themselves nagged over and over by child-rearing questions such as:

☐ I've tried everything. Why don't they obey?

☐ Did I react too harshly after she made me angry?

☐ Why do I feel so guilty when he looks at me that way?

☐ How can I avoid the mistakes my parents made?

☐ Why don't they appreciate everything I do for them?

☐ I'm trying to be nice; so why won't she talk to me?

☐ Is all my work really going to influence their lives?

The insecurity of modern-day parents has lots of origins, one of which dates back to the earliest times of the enlightenment era. Parents were offered valuable insights into children's needs, but before long they began worrying about whether they were attending properly to all these needs. Then we have the lapsing into disfavor of corporal punishment. At one time it was a simple matter of "Give 'em a whack when they answer you back." Nowadays parents grope after alternative modes of enforcement; and when all else fails, their resorting to smacks on the rear end and slaps in the face might create spasms of guilt. Parental insecurity is also rooted in the dazzling array of options our complex, sophisticated society affords us. The more choices on our plates, the more we fret over choosing incorrectly. Then too, parental self-confidence is not helped by pressure-packed schedules and a hectic pace of living, which makes it harder for parents to keep tabs on their little ones' physical whereabouts and emotional wherewithal.

There are still other factors that have played havoc with the stability of parents' self-esteem, but we suspect that you might be more interested in finding out about remedies. In this regard we have both good news and not so good news. The less-good news is that your parental doldrums cannot get remedied with step-by-step management formulas, repeat-after-me phrases, or making bargains and contracts with youngsters. Indeed, there aren't any quick fixes--at least ones that don't do more harm than good. In taking the right road, you may need to rethink certain of your approaches to maintaining youthful decorum, get everybody to agree to a few adjustments in household routine, and persevere through a few rough spots here and there.

Now here is the good news. There does exist a system for child-rearing that keeps parents and youngsters alike on an even keel throughout the normal ups and downs, and it lies within the reach of everyone--and it will prove both enjoyable and enlightening. So is this beginning to sound like a pipe dream? Have no fear; it is in fact a time-tested yet also woefully under-appreciated approach to parenting; and as you read on, you will see how it all works--and you already may be doing a lot of it.

So now we present to you our four precepts that shore up the underpinnings of parental self-esteem in our present-day society. We refer to them as:

THE CORNERSTONES OF CONFIDENT PARENTING

1. **Pursue your own and your children's needs equally.**
2. **Propagate free-flowing communication in the home.**
3. **Promote a cooperative spirit among family members.**
4. **Preserve blocks of quality time for family togetherness.**

The Cornerstones of Confident Parenting all sound simple enough in their outline form; but to be sure, there is a catch to it-- that you need to put consistent effort into the particulars that move them on toward fulfillment. Delightful results, however, show up early on; then the longer you work at incorporating these corner- stones into your parenting routine, the more you will get rewarded with success and the self-confidence that goes along with it. Then again, everybody struggles through off days, and you will no doubt make mistakes. When you adopt the Cornerstones of Confident Parenting, you will no longer find yourself becoming exasperated by seeing your youngsters:

- ☐ Wear you down until you finally give in.
- ☐ Be evasive regarding their whereabouts and activities.
- ☐ Do exactly the opposite of what you suggest.
- ☐ Pretend they don't hear you when you talk to them.

❑ Give you hateful looks as they slam doors behind them.

❑ Make you feel guilty for reprimanding them.

The following is a capsule summary of each one of the four cornerstones:

1. Pursue your own and your children's needs equally.

Which should be given a higher priority, children's or parents' needs? There is no correct answer to be sure, as giving the nod to one implies that the other is of lesser importance. Youngsters' and parents' needs alike call out for attention on a regular basis, one never needing to get shunted aside for the sake of the other. And when these needs appear to clash, you must not allow the nagging magnet of guilt prevent you from looking out for your own welfare. Indeed, parents have to temporarily postpone some needs, such as for sleep when newbies are in full voice for half the night; but that, contrasted with the self-sacrifice of long-suffering parents, is a normal phenomenon. Young ones place the lion's share of their energy, as indeed they must, into pushing their own agenda; while *you* carry the burden of looking out for their welfare as well as for your own. And since you must serve as your own advocate, it is very crucial that you approach this chore diligently, but in a loving manner.

Attending to your own needs can mean finding quiet time for reading, splurging with a night on the town, or pursuing a desired hobby; but it is also a matter of how you take good care of yourself in your direct dealings with youngsters. It involves listening to your feelings, watching out for signs of indecisiveness and self-criticism, and giving yourself pats on the back for a job nicely done. What is more, it calls for perseverance in your search after alternatives to any child-management tactics that prove to be unproductive. In short, it is a matter of being helpful to yourself *while* you help your youngsters. Unfortunately, the road to parental self-advocacy tends to get all strewn with obstacles. For one thing, we resist the verbal abuse from others more so than we do the abuse we direct inward with unspoken words. Questioning your methods of parenting can be productive; but if it spirals you into mental tor-ture and self-loathing, a broad range of self-destructive behavior can follow in its wake. Thus if you fail to listen to your own needs now, you will for sure wind up searching for relief later--not in self-protection, however, but in recovery.

Today's parents are keenly aware of the impact that psy-chological trauma has on early-stages development, and this can lead to another self-confidence stumbling block. As they strive to shield infants and toddlers from insecurity and frustration, parents quite easily become insecure and frustrated themselves. But in-stead of hastening to their own rescue, they begin to accept their misery as simply an occupational hazard--a big mistake, since the psychological well-being of *parents* is way high on the list of items children need for making a healthy adjustment.

Another danger is that child-rearing information is focused more on your youngsters' thinking and behavior than on your own. But child raising is every bit as much about you as it is about your offspring. One of our aims, therefore, is to encourage you to be-come more "selfish" in a self-helping context. While young people are known to grumble about parents being unfair or saying "no" to requests for freedom, they get really frightened from seeing them get all unglued, chronically anxious, or downtrodden.

One additional booby trap threatening parental self-help is the trend toward behavior-management strategies for every occa-sion. These tools work best when used only sparingly, and their excessive use sabotages communication and undermines trust, thus creating an emotional distance between parents and children.

When your action strategies hit the mark, you feel like you've won a huge chess match; and when they fail, you feel like a clever opponent has stolen your thunder, sending you frantically searching for new tactics.

Formulating unharried, unhurried parenting decisions is indeed vital to taking outstanding care of yourself. But youngsters, armed with guilt-tripping, hollow promises, pressure tactics, blame shifting, and sneakiness, are always on the ready to overturn your applecart. Threats to lucid thinking also spring up when you feel pressured for time, in a grumpy mood, or frazzled about finances, among other things. So making careful decisions can at times seem well-nigh impossible. Yet there exist methods for overcoming or circumventing every obstacle to careful decision making. Even on their very worst days, self-assured diamond cutters still do competent work; and so do confident, capable parents. They both take extra time to get focused, and then they call upon their tested-and-true skills. Getting work done "from memory" is surely not your most desirable scenario, but it is undoubtedly far superior to doing it out of the frustration of the moment.

Looking out for yourself can feel stressful on occasion, but don't let the agony linger on very long, and never let yourself slink into the role of put-upon victim. And most important of all, please don't start fretting over every self-interest item at this point in the game. The more you cozy up to and stay on board with our program, the more automatic it will become. You shall discover that doing right by yourself and by your youngsters at the same time is bound to develop into a truly satisfying experience.

2. Propagate free-flowing communication in the home.

When families suffer from garbled up communication, the blame seldom lies with stunted talking skills. Toddlers present one question after another, offer opinions freely, and let their emotions fly--and we were all toddlers at some time in the past. Obviously then, free-flowing communication is not a how-to-do thing; rather, it is a how-to-stay-out-of-trouble thing. We compare it to learning how to drive. You might master driving mechanics quickly, but this in no manner makes you an expert behind the wheel. You reach that level only after learning to anticipate and deal with all manner of dangers on the road. Only then do you get prepared to take the precautions or evasive actions needed for avoiding fender-benders and bone-crushing crashes.

Mastery in the field of communications is not unlike expertise behind the wheel in that vigilance is required for dealing with verbal hazards coming at you from every direction. You can engage in a "routine" discussion, and then suddenly you find yourself caught up in a verbal jousting match, a going-in circles argument, a crossfire of hurtful insults, or the huge frustration of finding an otherwise chatterbox family member, just when you most need a response, assailing you with icy silence. The danger from these verbal potholes is that when they jar your journey along the conversational highway on a regular basis, they tend to put the kibosh on more enjoyable and productive types of verbal interactions.

No family is immune to occasional hiccups in household routine such as misunderstandings, forgetfulness, wrangling over clashing desires, and nasty-mood grumbling. So running to great lengths to ward off any and all communication problems is not realistic. The sensible approach is to hop-step out of the way whenever you notice trouble brewing; and if that fails to work, to learn to resolve or sidetrack it in the early stages. The chapters up ahead are replete with practical advice on how to get this done.

When you become highly skilled at getting beyond momentary setbacks and at guiding communications back onto the track, misunderstandings invariably begin clearing up and compromises and other formal solutions start taking shape. Also, resentments gradually diminish once family members release pent-up emotions and experience satisfaction out of obtaining an attentive ear from others. When discord proves particularly stubborn, however, one life-preserving option is to place the matter on a back shelf for the time being; and we will show you how it gets done. It is amazing to see how much steam can be taken out of burning hot issues as soon as they get a chance to cool down.

Getting communication moving again following temporary interruptions is seldom easy, and at times can run sharply against your grain. It is not at all simple to break or even put a good sized dent in old habits such as getting in the final word, striving to make others listen when they are simply not in the mood for it, defending yourself against criticism, and straining to be proven correct. But letting go of these ego strokers in truth becomes a large pleasure once you see how rich become the rewards for doing so.

Free-flowing communication in the household offers you a double helping of satisfaction as both a feel-good thing and a do-good thing; and it is also the most powerful vehicle, hugs and gestures of support notwithstanding, available to you and your loved ones for the purpose of conveying caring involvement. Infatuated couples may allow their adoring gazes to do much of the talking at the start, but the deepening of their bonds relies on learning to express needs and to negotiate over scheduling conflicts, room temperature, preferences in music, and yet other burning or flickering issues of everyday living.

3. Promote a cooperative spirit among family members.

Everybody favors cooperation--on the part of the other guy! But real cooperation, the mutual type, dwells on the wrong side of the tracks in our winning-is-the-only-thing social order. Business operations routinely get to be dog-eat-dog competitive; the pursuit of money, power, and prestige is never ending; and some folks live by the popular phrase, "only the strong survive." Our families too have been deeply affected by the modern-day triumph of competition over cooperation. Family members no longer run to one another's aid in time of trouble like they used to do, nor do they pitch in together as before in work-together projects. But this trend can begin shifting into reverse, as you will see a little farther down the line. It takes time, but every step along the way will be wonderful.

Frustrated parents often ask, "How can I get my obstinate youngsters to meet me at least half way? The answer lies in your conjuring up an atmosphere conducive to a spirit of cooperation-- genuine cooperation being voluntary in nature. We all know that youngsters require some cajoling at times when you want them to get to bed, gather up scattered toys, and put in an appearance at the doctor's office. This, to be sure, is completely normal. A co-operative spirit doesn't guarantee compliance all across the board, but it does provide a predominant inclination; and exceptions, for parents as well as children, will always be apt to enter the picture whenever strong feelings become involved.

Little ones are naturally communicative, and it may appear that they are naturally contrary as well. Not so. The "terrible twos" are known for vigorously resisting curbs placed on their behavior; but they begin to conform pretty quickly, and with a sense of relief, as soon as they get used to reasonable limits applied consistently and in a kindly manner. The desire to cooperate is in fact deeply ingrained into human nature. Preteens are widely known for their enormous capacity to adapt to rigorous, exacting training routines; and multitudes of "rebellious" teenagers conform consistently, and oftentimes robotically, to peer-group expectations. And--surprise, surprise--adolescents will also conform to the major share of ex-pectations around the house as long as they view parents as allies rather than as adversaries as they journey toward a self-sufficient life in the grown-people world.

Give-and-take skills aren't mastered from sitting in a class, nor do they spring up from brief chit-chats or when T.V. programs take over center stage. Cooperation flourishes when family members interact with one another--e.g., conversing, collaborating over projects, and having fun. Even family feuding--the round-in-circles type excepted--can help in kindling the spirit of togetherness. And when dissension gets resolved, familial bonds grow ever deeper. When you and your youngsters can iron out contentious issues, your need to lay down the law gets drastically diminished. So if you can picture yourself working more agreeably with a boss who keeps his big-old stick in the closet than you would with one who goes around waving it in the air, bear in mind that youngsters find themselves in the exact same situation.

Another key to imbuing youngsters with a spirit of cooperation is the element of fairness as you exercise your authority. To be sure, differences in values and beliefs may strongly influence the way fairness is measured; but two factors narrow things down considerably. First is deliberation--taking all the time you need to gather up the facts and listen to the arguments from all sides. The practice of deliberation finds you refraining from ill-informed snap judgments and wave-of-emotion pronouncements. This will allow you to weigh various pros and cons. The other factor is flexibility. If you at least on occasion 'fess up to mistakes in judgment, allow yourself to be persuaded by your little ones' arguments, and agree to make compromises, you are to be congratulated on your having passed the course in healthy bending.

Youthful cooperation is further promoted by keeping your system for behavior management as simple as possible. Ponderous bureaucracy has long been associated with governmental operations; but now the bureaucratic red tape, minus the big piles of paperwork, has gained an increasing foothold into the parenting scene. Cooperation also thrives when behavioral consequences correspond to infractions.   Making "the punishment fit the crime" may call for some extra initial effort, but it pays big dividends later on.   Certain judges have garnered accolades for their common-sense innovations in sentencing, and you can achieve similar re-sults in your household (accolades optional).   A simplified system of management featuring related-to-deeds consequences is easy to establish once you get into the swing of our system.

4. Preserve blocks of quality time for family togetherness.

Ensemble dancers and team-sport competitors spend end-less hours practicing the skills required for their big performances. Individual talent is a great asset, but personal bonding, a natural byproduct of performers' striving all together toward team-member goals, has proven itself a major component in achieving success. The cheering and applauding from the audience fade away pretty quickly, but not so for the powerful camaraderie which grows and flourishes from working together over time.   This continues to go on and on.   Then when team members leave these groups, tears can be seen flowing in great profusion.

While emotional bonding in performance groups serves as a means to an end for the organization, it stands in center stage in helping programs such as therapy, support, and encounter groups. Therapists are keenly aware that the concern and support shared by all in attendance, therapists themselves included, substantially accelerates group-member emotional healing and growth; hence they actively encourage it.   And as is also true with performance groups, the sense of kinship continues on long after group partici-pants go their separate ways.

The family, a bohomoth among all groups, shapes our lives through its nurturing, instruction, and guidance.   But unlike groups we join into for a short or a long while, the family gives us a strong feeling of belonging for an entire lifetime.   Swimming in the same gene pool, adventuring all together through the child-raising years, and being joined in legal rights and responsibilities make family-member bonding quite powerful. Parents need not attain the professional expertise of a group therapist, nor must they endure the slightest pressure to meet competitive goals. What is more, family members need not become single-minded in regard to goals as do performance and helping-group members; but they do need some measure of quality time in one another's company if they hope to keep their bonding from feeling like bondage.

Every one of the cornerstones speaks to all parents from all around the world, past and present. But a century back, the wording of Cornerstone #1 might better have been reversed in order to read "Attend to your *children's* and to your own needs with equal vigor." This is because parents way back then didn't have an access to our wealth of information on childhood development. But this final cornerstone calling out for the preservation of blocks of time for family togetherness might not have needed a great deal of emphasis a few generations past. In those times, members of the household spent oodles of naturally occurring quality time in one another's company, and this generated an abundance of the communication and cooperation that have become so endangered in our modern, off-in-all-directions era.

Modern technology has made our home life more pleasant in so many respects, but it has also contributed to the erosion of family togetherness, highlighted by a sharp nose-dive in communication and cooperation in the home. It isn't that today's parents have become wearied of the family-group undertakings familiar to their ancestors; it's simply that most of them are no longer needed since our society is now highly urbanized and dependent on technology. However, you can overcome this obstacle without the use of a time machine, and your work toward this vital end will in many cases be a lot of fun. In upcoming chapters, and particularly in the next one, we'll take an extensive look at a broad range of family-together activities.

As you have most probably noticed, none of these corner-stones touches directly on the exercise of authority--devising and defining rules, dishing out consequences for unacceptable behavior, etc. This is because these prime concepts provide the *foundation* upon which parental authority stands. The simple fact is that when parents' and/or children's needs go begging, when communication is weak or convoluted, and when a cooperative spirit and quality time are in short supply, an army of skilled behavioral managers would not be able to bring into the household the sense of order that springs naturally from loving, harmonious relationships. But when these cornerstones stand strong in your corner, you will notice yourself hardly ever needing to bring out your whip. For the instances in which whip-cracking may be needed, however, we do offer a wide variety of practical information in the chapters ahead. (Only the softest of whips are recommended.)

The Cornerstones of Confident Parenting go way beyond the surface and get to the essence of healthy, harmonious family relationships--the true key to parental self-confidence. Satisfying working relationships in the household absolutely depend on your paying heed to your own as well as your children's needs and on your having a reasonable supply of family-together time--time in which communication and cooperation naturally flourish. There shall be no timetable for your accomplishing this, no pass-or-flunk grades, and no finish line to cross; just the prospect of your making progress and then still further progress. You will, however, be requested to roll up your sleeves and work--no drudgery involved. Our role is simply to point you in the proper direction, make some practical suggestions, and help you get back on the track after you meander off into a few or more than a few temporary detours.

The Four Cornerstones may sound just great in theory, but they crack and crumble when quality family time is in limited supply. But since we are too busy these days to even sit down as a group for dinner, the time you hope to nail down for family togetherness might very well prove to be illusory. This brings us now to the centerpiece of our book--the weekly family meeting, or family hour. In an era where important activities are routinely placed on your schedule, the practical approach for you is to *schedule in* a regular time for your family to talk and do activities together.

> *My neighbor and I often met in the laundry room, and one day she started telling me funny stories about the weekly meetings that took place in her home. What I felt was really strange that she was willing to take on yet one more thing to organize. Like me, she already managed a full-time job and two small children, plus an overworked husband. She got me thinking about how our family had gotten too busy to talk much lately.*
>
> *Working mother of 2*

You will very likely agree that holding regular family meetings seems like a nice idea, but of course many nice ideas remain forever on the drawing boards. Keeping this in mind, we have anticipated thinking you might entertain with relation to not following through. Here are just a few:

- ☐ I could never convince them about sitting down together.
- ☐ Where will we find the time for this extra activity?
- ☐ Getting everyone together at one time is too big a hassle.
- ☐ In my spare time I just like to sit down and relax.
- ☐ Guess who will get to do all the work? Yours truly.
- ☐ The kids are mortal enemies--they don't need immortality.

If you don't see any particular reason to set aside time for conversation and shared activities, please withhold your judgment until you have carefully gone over the first three chapters. Then if you remain convinced that your family spends sufficient time talking, working, and playing together, it would appear that scheduled sessions are not necessary for you and yours. But keep in mind that if your offspring brood is composed mostly or completely of toddlers and/or preteens, quality time will undoubtedly shrink to a substantial degree when they move into adolescence. But in any case, please give thought to the possibility that, regardless of the amount and quality of your family's be-together time, family hour might succeed in ushering in fresh and enriching experiences for everyone in the household.

For those of you concerned about a lack of time for weekly meetings, we again beg your indulgence. What gets placed onto or left out of schedules is determined by priorities. If we can convince you that spending one hour per week together will ultimately save you time and bring you great benefits, then you *will* assign it a high priority and etch it into your agenda. Then as your enthusiasm muscles up, you will conjure up the patience to work through your inevitable trouble spots, thus keeping family hour ensconced firmly in household routine. A limited availability of time rightfully keeps various activities off our dockets, but fears about not having sufficient time for everyone to be together for *just one hour* a week is a sure sign of the need to do exactly that.

Getting family members all corralled for their group experience may be a big challenge, particularly when teenagers are involved; but then again if your house suddenly caught fire, everyone would quickly drop what they were doing to become a volunteer emergency working force. So if you come to see family hour as even a teensy bit urgent, you will look upon your chores of organizing as a small price to pay for getting householders molded into a lesser-emergency work brigade. Also, successfully clearing this hurdle fosters your leadership skills.

If you fear that you might not be up to the chore of leading your weekly sessions, rest assured that all parents are capable of assuming the mantle of leadership, given help in areas of need; and abundant guidance will be found throughout the chapters and in the Help section. Furthermore, you can and should orchestrate matters according to *your* whims and needs, as your family's style of interacting differs from everybody else's. We therefore suggest that you to adopt an approach to your family meetings that is both comfortable and workable for your own family. Toward this end we offer various suggestions as to the mode of conducting sessions and to the content you may wish to consider--and we urge you to become flexible and creative in the process.

> *When I was little we had problems like everybody else, but what made us different was that we had "family time" every week. I didn't always enjoy the meetings, but they did allow us to say what was on our minds--or at least some of it. Now I'm so glad that my two girls are getting a chance to do like- wise, and I'm trying to be a tad more open-minded than my parents were. But--bless their souls--they were way ahead of their time.*
>
> *Homemaker in blended family*

How Family Hour Cements the Cornerstones

Family hour makes efficient use of quality family time.

As we noted in Cornerstone #4, quality family time tends to become scarce even in the sturdiest of modern-day households. The practice of family hour comes to the rescue by guaranteeing that family-together time will always be available, and then it goes one step further by obtaining outstanding mileage out of that time. Group interaction is more economical than the one-on-one variety, and keeping distractions and interruptions to a minimum makes it more economical still. Then your family hour time becomes highly productive when family members share personal news, arrive at family-related business decisions, vent pent-up feelings, grapple with burning or even luke-warm issues of daily living, and enjoy a few lighthearted moments.

When you all sit down together, information can be shared quickly and accurately, thus helping you to avoid the can-of-worms of one person's informing another (details usually changing along the way), who then tells--or forgets to tell--still another. Then too, minor annoyances get thrashed out during the sessions, keeping them from escalating into a major cacophony. Thus time is saved by the efficiency of the communication in your sessions, and then more time gets saved by your not having to struggle later on with misunderstandings and escalating conflicts.

Family hour helps generate and maintain dialogue.

"Dialogue" is a distinctly ponderous sounding word. A dialogue that at long last opens up in the halls of political summitry or at the labor-negotiating table indicates that all the involved parties have become prepared to listen with open minds and to nudge the crucial issues toward resolution. Yes, dialogue is a powerful tool, but it somehow seems to be beyond the average person's reach-- until now, that is.

Ah, but productive talks between world leaders are no different from your trudging through and working out conflicts with an alienated friend or a recalcitrant youngster, where bellowed accusations might get the proceedings going, but then the underlying issues emerge, often tearfully. Thus dialogue is simply dialogue, whether it takes place in the rarefied air of political summitry or in the nitty-gritty world of everyday family living. And it goes without saying that the spontaneous communications featured in Cornerstone #2 are dialogue as well.

> *Paulette was the only one of our four who gave us any trouble when we started our weekly meetings, sitting there time after time with that sullen look on her face, never saying a word. It finally got on my nerves to the juncture where I chastised her about spoiling the experience for the others. So she immediately launched into a tirade over not wanting to be there, and I instinctively yelled at her to shut up. She sat stunned for a moment, and then began to cry, saying "See, that's why I keep quiet all of the time." That's when we started to communicate like we never had before. Over the next few sessions we learned about a few instances where she had been wrongly blamed for things she had not done, and how some other kids at school ragged on her and called her "miss hand-me-down." We went out shopping pretty soon after that.*
>
> *Data processor, mother of 4*

Dialogue, excellent for resolving snarled communications but even better for keeping matters unsnarled to begin with, is the sine-qua-non of rock-solid family relationships and is the very lifeblood of family hour. But this precious commodity, sad to say, gets short-circuited again and again in our rush-about parenting scene, and gets the short straw from today's action-first parenting writers. The unfortunate upshot is that so many parents, not viewing dialogue as an option, dread the prospect of their youngsters speaking their minds, fearing that it may unravel their authority and their decision-making resolve. Thus, angry outbursts come to feel like a bursting of the dam, and tearful pleadings soon appear too powerful to resist.

In Chapter 6 we'll study dialogue in depth, and throughout the book we'll show how family-generated dialogue helps prevent and/or resolve scads of problems without your needing to initiate formal action. Talking solutions are in almost all cases superior to action-taking ones because they tend to be simpler, more satisfying, less likely to fan the flames of escalating conflict, and far better at bolstering parental self-confidence.

Family hour enhances parents' leadership skills.

Just as the term "dialogue" is not often used in the household context, the term "leadership" is similarly neglected in reference to the parenting role. But the most important leadership role in all the world is the one you stride into when your little ones arrive onto the scene, and one you hopefully exchange for a role of mutual friendship twenty or so years later. Effective leadership in every arena flows out of skillful management, especially the kind that elicits admiration from others. As we'll observe in Chapter 5, parents stand as the most natural of all leader types--and the most powerful of all role models. Not only are you given admiration and trust from simply doing a workmanlike job, but in truth you need to strive especially hard over the years in order to *lose* your youngsters' respect, even in the face of all the family-alien undercurrents in today's world. Obviously then, you require neither genius nor charisma in order to soar up to the pinnacle of leadership in your home; and your leadership work naturally engenders the cooperation we studied in Cornerstone #3.

Conducting family hour sessions boosts leadership skills in ways both obvious and subtle. To begin with, everybody's gathering together provides the perfect backdrop; and then your leadership decisions, including the use of toughness when needed, help keep the discussion moving along smoothly. You will want to keep your sessions interesting, informative, and enjoyable; and you will also want to keep an eye peeled for signs of creeping boredom or chaos. But do not stew about making a few or even more than a few missteps; you can stumble over and over again without suffering a fatal wound. Just maintain flexibility and patience, and bear in mind that there are countless correct ways to plan and lead the sessions--even ones nobody else yet knows about.

True self-confidence in the parental role springs from your balancing your own needs with the needs of others; and in family hour, everyone's thoughts, feelings, and desires deserve proper recognition. This distinguishes you from professional therapists, who put their own needs way in the background--a balancing act that is sometimes a factor in professional burnout. So taking care of your own needs gets to feel truly satisfying, and then experiencing success at the helm of the family hour ship-of-household gives you even greater satisfaction.

Family hour paves the way for family unity.

All parents dream of family unity, but some of them later on suffer the agony of watching this dream spin out into a nightmare. Household unity is, nonetheless, a reachable goal for all--and one that will come into view as long as everybody's feelings and needs receive attention, communication and cooperation stay at reasonably high levels, and family members spend at least a modicum of quality time together. Devoting one hour per week to family hour strongly promotes this dream. It's just that simple.

As oldsters look back to the bygone years, they cherish the memories of groups that gave them a sense of belonging and of a purpose-- e.g., the scout troop, the Peace Corps unit, the political campaign contingent, or the therapy or support group. When your time arrives, you will look back fondly upon your family hour experiences as a bastion of mutually supportive and nurturing kinship, and then your little ones will do the same a generation later.

I shall never forget the therapy group I joined many long years ago. There was the social worker who showed zero capacity to deal with her own feelings, the business mogul who had a lowly status in the group because of his surface involvement, and the nurse who was afraid I would get "slaughtered" because I looked so young and innocent. Yes, I really learned to speak my mind there, and that was such a wonderful experience. They were like family for me, and I truly wish I could have felt like that when I was growing up.

Retired college professor

CHAPTER TWO

QUALITY FAMILY TIME:

ANOTHER ENDANGERED SPECIES

Our house is a non-stop merry-go-round of coming and going, and then some going and coming. After school enrichment programs, little league, dancing classes, shleps to the mall--you name it. Our fourth grader wrote a poem recently, and the first I heard of it was when her teacher gave it a rave review at our PTA meeting. Of course I had to act like I knew all about it the whole time. That was pretty embarrassing. Now we routinely "grill" all the kids about what they have done in school each week.

Realtor, soccer mom

Quality time. Everybody loves it, and nobody seems to get nearly enough of it. We cherish it for the opportunity it offers us to share "the moment" with family and friends, and further because it enables us to place energy into activities we so greatly relish. But sadly, we seldom get an ample supply due to our hectic schedules and the countless items clogging up our "must-do" lists, much of which feels rather like sheer drudgery and somehow doesn't seem really vital in the grand scheme of things. Now while quiet relaxation and solitary hobbies are quality time as well, our focus here is on the people-to-people variety of quality time.

Quality time among family members takes on many forms. We share highlights of the day's happenings, work together stitching a quilt or tuning up an old car, debate the political headlines or the true meaning of life, or design and carry out weekend outings. Even a knock-down-drag-out registers as quality time as long as pent-up emotions find a release and issues get resolved or eased up. Then again, watching prime-time T.V. as a family group is way down the lower end of the quality scale, as conversational tidbits tend to be superficially chatty and an element of working together is absent; and casual badinage while on the way in and out of the kitchen suffers from this same deficiency.

A shortage of quality time in the home leads to a broad assortment of stresses and strains, as you will note in the chapters ahead. But when family members assemble together in a relaxed, essentially distraction-free atmosphere, all manner of benefits get set into motion. The information shared tends to be more accurate and complete, family business decisions appear to work out better, words get spoken from the heart, and spasms of laughter may now and again break out. These and other such features all contribute to greatly needed nurturing, or emotional feeding--the most important of all benefits accruing from the family group.

The word "nurturing" brings to the mind infants getting fed, cuddled, and comforted. But infant care is only a part of the total nurturing picture. Sure, newborns need massive amounts of love and attention as the foundation for an enjoyable, productive future. Yet your independence-bound teens need it as well, their disdain for the label of "mama's pet" notwithstanding. And as parents you crave it also--not just from physical tenderness and caring words, but also in more indirect ways such as being given a helpful hand, a proper dose of sympathy, a show of appreciation, and a spell of badly needed peace and quiet. As a matter of fact, emotional nurturing can be found in almost all routine dealings in the household. As parents you naturally become the primary nurturers, but tender loving care, once it gets initiated, tends to flow uninhibited in every direction--a beautiful thing to see.

As family nurturers you have no need of special talent, nor must you go through formal, supervised training. This is in contrast with professional and volunteer nurturing specialists such as special ed teachers, big brothers and sisters, social workers, and scout leaders. These folks are carefully screened as to aptitude and attitude, and must earn degrees, certificates, and/or workshop credits. As parent nurturers your credentials consist merely of a loving nature, some common sense, and the dedication to helping your little ones grow up to become nicely-adjusted, self-sufficient adults. Your care-providing skills get sharpened through the use of the old-reliable trial-and-error method; and there is no need at all to become motivational experts, as growing children respond to tender words and gestures like ducks take to water.

Emotional feeding grows out of interpersonal contacts in any setting, but your home has always been and shall forever be the ideal environment for it. The nuclear family, where a sense of belonging originates and then continues along through life's ups and downs, is in essence a cradle-to-grave nurturing system. And so much of what we do as family members, such as earning an income, paying the bills, cooking, overseeing chores, taking care of home repairs, providing transportation, and attending to the inevitable larger and smaller emergencies, plays a complementary role, one of protecting and supporting the people-nurturing unit.

Because nurturing is the family's primary purpose, oodles of time and energy need go into activities that promote it. After all, if you crave highest academic honors, you must burn up gallons of midnight oil; if your fondest dream is for sports accolades, endless practice is the best route to get there; and if your goal is prosperity in the dog-eat-dog world of business, workaholic devotion keeps you competitive. But these days, sad to say, so much of the family's nurturing--neonatal and toddler care the exceptions--is left to chance. Helping professionals make use of formal routines like teaching schedules or blocks of uninterrupted time for seeing patients or clients. Quality time in the family, however, doesn't wind up on the calendar. Instead, it flows naturally from our day-to-day activities. Yet even the most dedicated of parents nowadays, who juggle busy schedules, find the paucity of built-in structure stretching their nurturing capacity to the limit and beyond.

A few generations ago, when modern machines and gadgets existed only in our creative imaginations, quality family time in most households got taken for granted. Then it began slip-sliding away gradually as we got ever more engrossed in high-tech conveniences. We have now come to realize that pollution of the air, soil, and water is a big price we are paying for the fruits of modern technology; but "pollution" of quality family time appears to be an equally unfortunate side effect of the very same process. People do not simply turn their backs on emotional intimacy because they have had their fill or don't think it's worth the bother. In truth, old and young alike seem to be ever on the lookout for a listening ear or a caring response--in therapy and support groups, sibling-type friendships, romantic liaisons, club affiliations, peer groups, etc. Also, we mourn when family members or pets pass on, a love relationship falls apart, or a close friend moves out of town.

The ebbing of quality family time is not unlike the gradual loss of air from a slowly leaking automobile tire. Drivers paying no mind to tire pressure may fail to notice the problem until they become startled by thumping sounds from below. In a similar way, quality time in the home has slowly leaked away, and our societal "vehicle," the family unit, has likewise started seeing its underpinnings get weaker. Loss of automobile tire pressure is rather easy to detect, whereas the slipping away of quality family time tends to be more shadowy. Then again, we all know of families who return back to nature to experience a simple life. But lots of these latter-day pioneers give up the ghost, and even their successes may be questioned due to the inevitable "outside world" encounters. Thus going back to revisit the past looks like a rocky journey.

Modern technology may at this point look like the big bad villain, but we in no way advocate turning back the calendar. After all, the "good old days" featured legalized slavery, company-store servitude, child labor, high infant mortality, rampant illiteracy, anarchy, plague and pestilence, religious persecution, and other "delights." Modern technology has allowed us to live a more comfortable, informed, and sophisticated lifestyle; and it has bestowed on us limitless options for going places and doing things. Terrific new opportunities now abound everywhere, and we should enjoy them to the fullest. But when a society experiences rapid changes, certain things usually get thrown out of balance--and the solidarity of the family's structure is proving vulnerable in this modern epoch. So we, beginning with each family's individual effort, now face the task of working to get that balance restored.

When I was coming up, my grandmother lived with us, and she had so many stories to tell. Her folks worked hard scratching out a living on a farm, but they seemed to have lots of fun too. At times when grandma got all sleepy we would ask her for more stories anyway; and she never turned us down My mom now lives over on the other side of town, and when we go and visit I ask her to write down some of her own stories. I'm thinking about compiling a family history some day when I find the time for it.

Interior designer, mother of 4

In order to bring this situation into sharper focus, let us now compare yesterday's families with those in our modern era.

Quality Time in the Family: Past and Present

Nuclear and extended family

In an era when divorce was rare, family members had lots of time to spend together and their relationships held greater continuity. In yesterday's larger households, the sibling group resembled a sub-family, the older ones providing care and guidance for the later arrivals, and everyone standing unified against outside threats. Then there were grandparents, maiden aunts, and other relatives who lived either in the home or around the corner. These kin, through the caregiving, teaching, and tough times, were a key to family solidarity with their much needed help and support.

These days two-income families are quite commonplace, single-parent homes are almost the rule rather than the exception, step-parents and step-siblings arrive and depart, and many non-custodial parents live a plane ride distant. All this results in more fragmentation for togetherness time. Furthermore, many modern day grandparents living with grown children are either functionally impaired or housed in separate quarters, and thus play only a minor role in family nurturing. The more self-sufficient elderly as a rule either stay in the old home town or migrate to sunbelt, adults-only communities, thus reducing family get-togethers to holidays and special occasions. Grown siblings and extended family tend to be scattered all around the globe.

Neighborhoods and schooling

The small towns and rural areas that were home to the majority of our ancestors had family-together activities; and neighborhoods tended to be close-knit, in a sense serving as an extension for the extended family. So the wider community helped rein-force the nuclear family's already powerful social network. In the one-room schoolhouse of a bygone era, siblings of different ages often learned together, and lots of youngsters apprenticed from an early age into farming, crafts, or the trades, oftentimes joining with their parents and older siblings in family-run operations or in ones that accommodated several family members.

Three out of every four modern-day families live in or close to a city, where a smorgasbord of programs, not a great number of which are family-oriented, are made available to every age group. In the grassy stretches of suburbia, families tend to dwell in isola-tion, next-door neighbors are merely chit-chat friendly, and family members routinely go off in different directions with their own inti-mates. Today's schools, even ones in the local region, are not as knitted to the community as were those of our forefathers. Across-town busing is common, and a substantial number of teens and tweeners attend boarding schools. Many college students pursue their degrees out of town or state, and more often than not settle down into careers their parents only vaguely understand.

The workplace

Yesteryear's railroad workers, prospectors, and other far-flung laborers were far away from loved ones for lengthy periods; those toiling long hours at nearby factories and stores had at least some evenings and weekends as family time; but farmers, crafts-people, and trades pliers often had some family members, most likely sons, at their side. And women rarely worked in the market-place, instead toiling from sun-up to sundown at home--in cooking, canning, sewing, weaving, candle making, and in mother-daughter projects of all types. All this hands-on work, as period-piece films give testimony to, lent itself to spirited interaction among members of the household.

Nowadays both parents often hold down one or more jobs, the lion's share of the work taking place away from home. And for the many parents away on business trips, contacts with family are limited to phone calls, text-messaging, etc. Moreover, the technological nature of this work yields scant grist for the household discussion mill. Labor-saving contraptions have long since put the kibosh on the more interesting in-house chores; and the cooking, cleaning, laundry, bookkeeping, and yard work done by modern parents and youngsters are mostly solitary drudgery.

Travel and transportation

In a bygone era of limited traveling choices and a simpler way of life, family members stayed a lot closer to home than they do now; and as they strolled all together or rode on horse-drawn conveyances to school, church, friends' houses, the general store, and the old swimming hole, animated conversations and interactions flourished along the way.

Modern transportation has made a massive, although unintended impact on the family unit. We log trillions of motor-vehicle miles every year in the U.S.A., and a large measure of this has no relation to family activities. To be sure today's families do travel as a group in cars, buses, trains, and planes; but as a result of traffic concerns and crowded conditions, the atmosphere in most cases is far from conducive to relaxed communication and interplay. And while it is a fact that modern transportation allows us to visit loved ones in distant places, let's not forget that these same transportation systems gave them (and us) the opportunity to move so very far away in the first place.

Leisure-time activities

Our forebears used leg power to travel to festivals, dances, religious services and social programs, and to guild and town hall assemblies--activities which were often oriented to and organized by parents. Also, village pubs catered to the entire family, as they still do in some parts of the world. Today's young folks can't imagine how people managed to survive before the invention of radio, T.V., and computer. But history teaches us that they not only survived, but they indeed thrived. Stories filled the air at the supper table, on the front porch, and around the fireplace; creative crafts, music ensembles, and parlor games kept everyone involved; and yes, there were more than a few fights, but in the process scads of issues got alleviated that might tend to go on festering indefinitely in today's dialogue-deficient households.

These days we have a greatly varied menu of educational, social, religious, and recreational programs available in our communities. The entire family can participate all together in certain of these settings, but the great majority involve specialties that group people according to age, talents, interests, etc. This means that time spent in all these activities, more often than not, is time spent away from other family members. The latest in high-tech devices manage to consistently snuff out in-depth communications in the household. Television watching tends to restrict family-member interactions to surface banter; the headset radio keeps listeners in their own solitary world; and the telephone and computer permit users to remain in the home as they communicate with friends and acquaintances on the outside.

I won't buy those electronic toys that self-destruct after a week or end up on the shelf when the next new thing comes along. I held onto all my blocks and legos (actually my mom did) from when I was small, and Danny keeps going back to them again and again. I also saved a little toy soldier from my late brother's "army" with the name "Greasy Green" taped to the back. It is a flat piece of metal with the bottom bent back so it can stand up. I shall pass it

down later to Danny with the express instructions
that he keep it in the family. He also enjoys empty
cartons and pots and pans. We love to see him
using his imagination--and he has a vivid one.

At-home mom expecting again

Creations from modern technology have arrived in a rapid-fire stream, and have been welcomed again and again with open arms. The scientists and engineers driving this revolution would shudder over the least hint that they were helping downgrade the quality of family life--innovators being inclined to see only the good applications from their products, and not any gloomy side-effects. So it would never have occurred to them to attach warning labels onto their inventions, informing consumers that a degree of quality family time may become squandered away, however inadvertently, every step along the way.

Modern transportation is without doubt a marvel, but it has led to extended families being scattered all around the planet; machinery has showered us with products that perform wonderfully and need less labor, but the upshot of it all has been the unhappy disappearance of lots of family-together projects; high-tech communications provide us with a world of information, but they have also led to a decline in in-depth discussion involving family members; and we all now enjoy spectacular live and electronic entertainment, but all this has cut sharply into opportunities for families to entertain themselves.

Families of a bygone era labored side-by-side because all hands were needed to get a variety of jobs done; they learned together because much of their education related to in-home work projects; and they played together more than do present-day families because they lacked our modern entertainment machines and transportation options. All this resulted in interaction aplenty, featuring an abundance of verbal interplay and a spirit of cooperation.

Nowadays family-together projects are usually confined to special occasions such as moving to a new house or responding to emergencies; and our hit-and-run communication can wind up garbled amid electronic buzzing.

Behavioral scientists and ordinary folks as well are greatly concerned over the widespread malaise noted in our modern-day youngsters, and they never appear to run out of opinions in their attempts to explain it.

Popular Theories on What Ails Today's Youth

❏ Kids these days get more freedom than discipline.
❏ Parents fail to set consistent rules for youthful behavior.
❏ Kids get torn by separation, divorce, and custody battles.
❏ Modern families have rejected traditional moral values.
❏ Peer pressure is too powerful for youngsters to resist.
❏ Our schools don't teach the basics and maintain control.
❏ Sex and gore are glorified in films, T.V., and video games.
❏ Drugs, alcohol, and lethal weapons are easily obtained.
❏ Attention-deficit and hyperactive disorders are epidemic.
❏ Permissive child-rearing has turned parents into mush.

This list contains some favorite theories about what bedevils young people today, and a hundred people selected at random might come up with a hundred additional theories. Now while kernels of wisdom can be found in all these explanations, they for the most part relate to surface factors or symptoms rather than to root sources of the issues. Further, we suspect that there would be no mention at all of any theory pointing to the shortage of quality family time as a culprit. *Yet the quality-time deficit not only belongs on everybody's top-ten list, but its rightful place is at or near the number one spot!* Yes, two loving parents in a modern household may work with great energy and diligence to respond to the needs of every member of the household and of the family as a whole; but in spite of their best efforts, our quality-time-devouring way of life might make it difficult for them to obtain a score as high up on the family-togetherness scale as was achieved by a substantial majority of their ancestors. And remember that these ancestors in many instances made no special efforts to promote family unity.

Infant and non-infant nurturing differ in so many respects, and the former is certainly a lot more concentrated; however, all nurturing is cut from the same cloth. Warming the heart makes us feel good, but it is also essential for the maintenance of life itself. When newborns suffer from insufficient T.L.C., they become withdrawn and lethargic; and if their deficit gets to be severe and prolonged, some even succumb--as is documented in studies related to nursery-confined infants in the pre-Dr. Spock era of clockwork feeding and super-hygiene. Growing children are affected similarly. The worse the shortfall--other factors playing a large role as well--the more they gravitate toward health and life-endangering behavior like reckless driving and other daredevilry, eating disorders, substance abuse, and suicidal thinking.

If we are to reverse the shriveling of quality family time we must first become sufficiently alarmed about the problem. During out-of-town family vacations we delight in sensing how close-knit everybody becomes; then all too soon it's back into the old grind, and that spirit of closeness gradually fades away into the distance. Then we tell ourselves that this cannot be helped. But it need not and should not be that way. The shortage of quality family time is not a necessary evil in today's society, but a complex yet solvable problem. And we are determined first of all to bring this issue into sharper focus, and next to offer you the help needed for locating realistic solutions. Let us now look at how the scarcity of this precious time has impacted our lives.

How the Quality-Time Deficit Has Affected Families

Some traditions disappear.

Youngsters these days would flunk a course in "Family History 101," and their parents might get higher, yet still poor grades. Foreign languages have gotten lost in the shuffle too. Those spoken by parents only rarely get passed down any more to children, whose old-world-born grandparents are seldom living close by in contrast to grandparents of the past. Modern-day parents seldom have enough time or energy to pass down their special career or hobby-related skills to their growing youngsters, who in any case might have little if any interest in learning them. And scenes with the family all sitting down together for dinner are most often found in television reruns and nostalgia-laden movies.

The flow of information becomes slowed.

Family members are seldom well-informed about one another's school and work routines unless problems and crises grab center stage. For certain, oodles of information gets shared with peers, co-workers, and schoolmates, but little of it trickles down to family members. In households blessed with tweeners and teens, the chances are very good that one youngster might never have met several of a sibling's close friends. And when little ones get surveyed about those they most admire, they routinely score cartoon characters and icons of entertainment ahead of family members--who in so many cases capture less of a little one's attention than do the characters on the screen.

Misunderstandings flourish.

Lobbying to be proven right, engaging in put-downs, and playing one-upmanship are par for the course in households with growing children, who hopefully outgrow this phase in the fullness of time. But many needless conflicts are rooted in false assumptions that spring up and spread like wildfire whenever information is jumbled, incomplete, or lost. Such miscommunication is far less of an issue in families that converse comfortably and spend blocks of time in one another's company; but it becomes magnified and gets massively troublesome in households where family members get to voice little more than "hello" and "goodbye" as they meet on their way in and out of the house, or who have their attention riveted on a routine basis on the television receiver, head-set radio, telephone, or computer.

Conflicts may fail to get resolved.

An atmosphere of emotional openness sets the scene for resentments to melt away before your eyes, for misconceptions to get cleared up, for key issues to have light shed on them, and for compromises to be hammered out. But when quality family time is nowhere in sight, solutions such as these might never get off the ground. Dialogue-poor households become spawning grounds for the likes of verbal sniping, histrionic shouting matches, the cold-shoulder treatment, long-festering rancor, and a tendency to look for sympathy from outsiders. Tactics like these make it difficult for all the involved parties to resolve their differences, and are likely to add fuel to the fire.

Positive reinforcement gets squeezed out.

Nurturing behavior in its concentrated form is more likely to take place during quality moments than in the catch as catch-can variety. And it goes without saying that the more quality time families have at their disposal, the more nurturing will emanate into the scene. Thus, as quality time contracts, so do the opportunities for supportive and loving interactions. Small doses of caring such as hugs and pats on the back, an attentive ear, offers of assistance, shows of appreciation, and words of reassurance, take giant steps toward promoting good will in the household; but because tender words and actions are neither mandatory not scheduled ahead of time, they oftentimes get left with nowhere to sit down in the game of household-routine musical chairs.

Non-family influences grow stronger.

Whether loving or contentious, family bonds largely shape our overall outlook on life. But when in-house nurturing time is in short supply, outside influences command a larger role. Affected adults get lots of their social and emotional needs satisfied in the community--in workplace bonding, cultural clubs, helping groups, etc. Non-family influences loom particularly large for children, who pick up values from T.V. shows, movies, advertising, and the peer group. Television shows, films, and commercials for the greatest part promote superficial values and a craving after instant gratification; and peer groups tend to create pressure toward conformity, provide dubious information, and hide personal insecurities behind group-member bravado.

Parental self-confidence flounders.

All four Cornerstones of Confident Parenting are crucial for parental self-esteem, but preserving quality family time is a key to each of the other three. When quality time ends up in limited supply, the other cornerstones simply become nice-sounding theory. The self-confidence of performance and therapy group leaders accrues largely from their having sufficient time for promoting vital communication and cooperation among members; and your leadership of the family group is no different. Even if you are steady at the wheel in your work place, your child-rearing self-confidence is bound to flounder if you and your youngsters spend precious little distraction-free time together.

If by now you have become convinced that a large shortfall in quality family time is a real problem yet also a fixable one, then you might already be thinking about steps to take for remedial action. And because modern-day parents tend to be resourceful and highly adaptable, you will no doubt find a variety of creative, practical solutions. Once family-together time gets cemented into your household routine, you will no longer need to rely on the whims of the scheduling process and on happenstance to provide you with a sense of functioning together as a close-knit group.

A we're-in-this-together feeling arises out of every type of interaction, with activities often serving as a springboard for some extended discussions. The following are a few of the possibilities for family-group activities:

Activity-Focused Family Togetherness

Weekend, vacation, and free-time outings

Family outings are an outstanding source of togetherness, and they offer you a sense of getting away from it all. In addition you get the bonus of physical exercise when your outings include swimming, hiking, bike riding, beach volleyball, or a host of other activities. Cultural stimulation can be found in such as excursions to scenic and historic locations, and to museum and gallery tours. Weekend camping trips are a popular favorite, and they might include picnicking, boating, hunting, fishing, or simply lolling around. Other choices: attending sports events, window shopping, garage sales and flea markets, visits to close by family members and old friends, unplanned journeys off to "wherever the road may direct you," and vacation trips to far-away places. If time does not allow for weekly or even twice-monthly outings, endeavor to make it at least once per month. Another hint: keep your outings varied and cater to everyone's interests and needs, including your own.

Family projects and youngsters' activities

Creative family projects allow you to work closely together towards a productive goal in a highly enjoyable manner. You may decide to brush the cobwebs off old skills and plunge right into a few new ones as well. On the lengthy list of choices are scientific experiments, sewing, model building, carpentry, music, astronomy, coin and stamp collecting, and creative crafts. Should you choose to embrace some of your youngsters' interests, please resist the temptation to take the project over. Constructive participation in children's organized activities is found in volunteering as den parents, coaches, outings leaders, fund raisers, van chauffeurs, food preparers, etc. Even a smallish measure of time spent together in these activities earns you bushels of admiration and gives you and your youngsters much to talk about.

Community-based family oriented programs

Churches and schools can be great places to start searching for such programs. Some churches offer wide-ranging activities and take pride in catering to the family unit. Family-oriented offerings may be difficult to find in certain locations, but new community resources tend to spring up as the need for them dictates. So as you speak out individually and in groups for greater family-together activities, local organizations--business, religious, governmental, and non-profit--are likely to heed the call. In addition, there is always a need for volunteers in good-works projects--cleaning up rivers, visiting the sick and the infirm, etc. It might be especially satisfying if you could devise your own type of volunteer project, possibly breaking new ground on some long-unmet needs in your community. When the entire family gets into the swing of volunteering, everyone comes out a winner.

Home entertainment

No, not through gigantic home theater systems, A.B.C. and X.Y.Z. players, or computer games, but in such participatory experiences as vying over chess, checkers, Scrabble, Trivial Pursuits, charades, bingo, or games of your own creation. Further, you can indulge your nostalgic yearnings by harmonizing and playing musical instruments together, telling tall stories, and camping out and picnicking in the back yard. Who knows, this might even lead to your deciding to place aside one entire evening a week for a turn-back-the-clock-and-the-calendar activity such as those you find in old books and movies. So search out those old movies not just for a dose of nostalgia, but also to get some ideas for a few "innovative" home-together projects. You may even find that some of the activities that got replaced are not missed in the least.

We realize that your time for projects like these might be limited, as so many evening and weekend hours get devoured by various activities. You have business travel and second jobs; solitary hobbies; civic, cultural, self-help, and self-enhancement meetings; sports practices; music and dancing lessons; and other items that wangle their way into your schedules. Simply do your best to save some room for family-group activities, keeping in mind that they not only feel good, but that they also afford you a substantial dose of preventive medicine and pave the way for greater family unity. (See Chapter 15)

In-depth discussions among family members are certainly another form of quality time in the home, and the following are a few ways in which family get to talk with one another.

Discussion-Focused Family Togetherness

Discussions arising from people's needs

When family members explode into a rage or dissolve into tears, the involved parties are not likely to find themselves lost for words. You might also help words to begin flowing when youthful body language--e.g., slumped shoulders, a nervous twitch, lingering moodiness, a furtive demeanor--indicate that things are not all well. Other conversation opportunities come in stress-filled times, such as the passing of a pet or the imminent arrival of a final exam or a competitive event. These confabs, however, are typically the one-on-one variety. What is more, your words may easily get cut in mid-sentence when the relentless clock demands that you haul off to school, the job, football practice, piano lessons, or a garden club meeting. And, sad to say, needs-related discussions are for the most part focused on the negative, since happy events seldom have a sense of urgency about them.

Discussions related to certain times of the day

Many parents seize the moment, often without an agenda, in order to converse with youngsters. Bedtime, supper hour, drive time, and intervals in between scheduled activities are typical examples. These opportunities, however, can prove to be iffy. Family members fresh from the job or school might not feel particularly talkative, traditional family dinners have been for the most part replaced by eating in shifts or on-the-run, bedtime huddles might get cut short by drooping eyelids, and automobile chats can lose their focus when passenger safety takes priority over completing a talking point. You can chat with a mate or little ones about the day's events, issues of concern, or whatever may be on people's minds; but you will seldom have enough time to cover complex, sensitive issues. Also, just as is the case with needs-related conversations, these chats are more likely to be the one-on-one kind rather than ones involving the family group or a segment of it. By the way, we by no means wish to discourage one-on-one talks, but rather we would like to see them complemented by group discussions.

Discussions related to family activities

The more time you and your family spend together pursuing activities, the more you will talk together. Some of the talk will relate to the activity at hand, and the remainder of it will be about anything and everything. As we noted earlier in the chapter, this type of discussion was prevalent in homes of several generations past; but these days there are precious few family group activities that come up on a regular basis, especially involving adolescents. And since so many households have so few group activities going on, they might feel awkward about opening up when such an activity presents itself. So the involved family members might wind up with superficial chatter, silliness, or blocks of silence.

> *My dad read bedtime stories and took me to base-ball games, and we exchanged great thoughts and laughed a lot together. But when he lost his great job and ended up really bitter about life, I felt that I had lost my closest friend. I talk with my kids about everything, and no matter how many struggles I go through--like the divorce from their mother--I'll keep the lines of communication open. I recently volunteered to lend a hand with the boys' scouting, and I'm learning more than I ever wanted to know about surviving in the woods.*
>
> *Father in blended family*

Family-together discussions and projects contribute greatly toward promoting unity in the household; but our away-from-home schedules fill up so rapidly, and the T.V., computer, and other electronic gadgets cast a lengthy shadow over family solidarity. What is more, the inclinations of adults and teens especially to seek out closeness from outside sources can keep the time necessary for these activities in short supply. For all these reasons we see family hour, the once-per-week stalwart in the household, as the most logical solution for this dilemma. You say that your family already spends lots of time in projects and conversing as a group? Great, but we still recommend that you give the family hour experience a try to see whether it may bring you a few additional benefits.

Family meetings can be used for both discussions and activities, and their becoming a fixture on your schedule guarantees that quality time will be available--time during which you need not worry about getting constantly interrupted. What is more, every available family member will be attending, which both provides for more efficient use of time and promotes a spirit of oneness in the home. Now while we are on the subject of saving you time, family meetings might find themselves focusing on topics such as a more selective use of the television set, computer operations, head-set radio, telephone, and other gadgets and gizmos.

The following are just a few of the many benefits you enjoy when you carefully safeguard just one hour per week for household members to spend together.

Family Hour: The All-Purpose Form of Family Togetherness

- ☐ Brings family members up to date on all the latest.
- ☐ Promotes mutual support and nurturing in the home.
- ☐ Serves as a forum for debating issues of import to all.
- ☐ Allows participants to be heard and to speak their minds.
- ☐ Helps to clarify issues and to nip mixups in the bud.
- ☐ Serves as a planning and decision-making forum.

❑ Engenders a sense of solidarity among family members.

❑ Allows people to let off steam in a safe atmosphere.

❑ Gives family members a chance to resolve sticky issues.

❑ Serves as a showcase for young folks' skills and talents.

❑ Lets all family members make educational presentations.

❑ Helps prepare little ones for a self-reliant future.

❑ Provides an atmosphere conducive to youthful creativity.

❑ Builds immunity from obsessive and depressive thinking.

❑ Allows family members to let their hair down and have fun.

❑ Helps enhance leadership skills in all age groups.

In our complex, rush-around world, we over and over again find ourselves at the complete mercy of crammed-full schedules, bill-payment and work deadlines, and pressures coming at us from every direction. Rather than actively managing our time, we feel instead that the clock pushes us around. Sadly then, our goal can easily become simply to keep our heads above water. Yet relief is only just around the corner, and it won't even require the help of a time-management consultant or a positive-affirmations coach. Instead, it comes about merely from turning more of your total time into quality family time. As you readjust your household routine to establish a regular niche for family hour, and as you promote more family-group activities, you are bound to obtain a greater sense of being in charge. Now you will be able to use the clock as an ally in the campaign to look after your own needs as well as those of others in the household.

We had lots of fun on family vacations when I was I was a little shaver. My brother and I especially enjoyed playing "Chevvies and Fords" when we rode together in the back seat on our trips The one who spotted the greatest number of his make of auto in one hour would win the contest. My two girls are great kids, but they don't seem to enjoy nearly the same degree of kinship that my brother and I had. We just started with family hour, and I hope that will be of help. Perhaps I may encourage them to play "Chevvies and Fords" on our next trip. And if that sounds all too old fashioned, then maybe it can be "T-Birds and Corvettes--or Mini-Coopers and -----."

Business owner, father of 2

CHAPTER THREE

THE ULTIMATE HELPING GROUP:
YOUR OWN FAMILY

*We recently had a special in-service training expe-
rience at work; they had us meet once a week for
two hours, and this continued on for a total of eight
weeks. Management and workers were mixed all
together, we called each other by first names, and
we couldn't discuss anything related to our jobs. It
was painfully awkward at the start, but by about the
third session it got to flow much better, and sometimes it got intense. I was amazed to see so many
people talking about their youthful upbringing, and
there were lots of teary eyes. It was also amazing
to see how supportive everybody was, and this included a few who had been blatantly snotty to each
other before the training started. When it was over
I noted an improvement in our communication and
productivity, and certain staff members even talked
about meeting together on their own.*

Office manager, single parent

We are social beings to the core, growing up in one family
and later on settling into other household units. Yet the socializing

instinct takes us way beyond the nuclear family. At a rather early age we start out bonding together with people who share similar backgrounds and interests, and this tends to continue through the years. The need for fellowship with those who lend us a big helping hand is indeed a potent one. Even those proverbial isolates, the prehistoric cave dwellers, most likely attended "underground" meetings along with like-minded hunters and gatherers.

Associations dedicated to a common purpose in an atmosphere of true fellowship remain in demand today. Most folks have been affiliated with youth groups, churches, alumni and veterans organizations, sports teams (as player or booster), cultural circles, neighborhood associations, political parties, professional societies, and hobby groups, to name just a few. These entities are like extended families, offering us a sense of kinship while at the same time espousing interests that benefit the group as a whole.

Helping groups serve a different purpose. Self-enhancement comes in a variety of forms, examples of which are sharpened negotiating talents, recovery from addictive and compulsive behaviors, resolution of at-home and workplace conflicts, and advancement of career ambitions. In contrast to common-purpose associations, self-improvement programs serve people's needs in a more personalized way. Membership in most cases is limited to discussion-group size, goals are kept consistently in view, and the kinship is more of the nuclear family type.

Just several decades ago, self-improvement groups were few and far between. Group therapy was largely old-school psychoanalytic; Alcoholics Anonymous, the only twelve-step program in town, was still in its infancy; and there was not much else from which to choose. Embarrassed group members tended to be secretive about their participation, since searching for help with personal problems at that time was looked upon as an indication of weakness. But then, self-help-group affiliation started to skyrocket both in popularity and in social acceptance, and it is now receiving huge amounts of positive coverage in the media. It is safe to say that reaching out for a helping hand has become rather trendy.

A Sampler of Self-Improvement Groups

☐ Psychoanalytical and other traditional group therapies.
☐ Gestalt, rational-emotive, primal scream, etc.
☐ Inpatient groups for physical and mental handicaps.
☐ Groups in prisons and in substance abuse facilities.
☐ Outpatient groups for newly discharged psych patients.
☐ Probation, parole, and alternative-to-prison sessions.
☐ Court-ordered programs for the predatory and violent.
☐ Voluntary programs teaching anger and impulse control.
☐ Twelve-step groups for alcoholism, drug abuse, etc.
☐ Drying-out-type recovery and rehabilitation programs.
☐ Encounter sessions geared to racial and cultural conflicts.
☐ Support groups for illness, accident, and abuse survivors.
☐ Support groups for those grieving over kinfolk or pets.
☐ Al-Anon and other programs aimed at co-dependency.
☐ Workshops for marriage enrichment, self-esteem, etc.
☐ Fat farms, health and fitness retreats, and the like.
☐ Seminars on earning capacity and on speaking skills.
☐ Meditation, prayer, and psychic phenomena groups.
☐ School-based drug prevention and peer counseling.
☐ Training and problem-solving groups in the workplace.

The above programs are but part of an extensive helping-group menu that offers something for everyone. It is not unusual these days to see some dedicated folks scurrying off to different meetings almost every evening of the week. Attendance at some groups to be sure is mandatory, but more than a few foot-draggers have later become true believers. And since new kinds of groups are cropping up on a regular basis, it would appear, therefore, that the helping group movement is here to stay.

Why Self-Improvement Programs Have Become Popular

Our age of enlightenment

We are now decidedly more tuned in to the nuts and bolts of human behavior than were our grandparents or their ancestors before them. This enlightenment not only shines a lamp onto our innermost workings, but as a corollary it also generates empathy for human frailties. As a result we have become inundated in recent times with books and articles that explore the whole gamut of human distress, and urge sufferers to search after help. And once the A.A. approach proved to be a very popular choice for maintaining sobriety, it was just a matter of time before twelve-step-variety recovery programs would branch out into other problem areas.

Our dysfunctional families

Some may say we are more problem-riddled than were our ancestors, and thus in greater need of intervention. In some respects this might be true, as rates of divorce, latch-key parenting, and homeless living have soared in recent decades. So too have rates of violent crime, drug abuse, eating disorders, and youthful suicide. But then too, child abuse and abandonment, incest, rape, drunken rampages, and other horrors not only existed a century ago, but they often got to be epidemic. However, they were consistently hushed up by the perpetrators and victims alike. What is more, religious-inquisition torture and race-based lynchings were seldom listed in the category of violent crime. So it is safe to say, then, that in those areas in which we are now more dysfunctional, many are indeed searching for help.

Our pocketbooks

The popularity of group therapy came about in a serendipitous way. Mental health, family treatment, and child guidance clinics, concerned over their long waiting lists, started forming groups as a way of getting folks into treatment sooner. Clients responded favorably, this format lowered clinic costs, and treatment thus became more affordable. Then too, a vast array of group treatment programs in hospitals, prisons, and school systems would not now be available without government funding. And for sure the bare-bones budget of twelve-step and supportive programs have made them accessible to everyone regardless of income.

While this glimpse into the big picture sheds light upon the popularity of self-improvement programs, the proof of the pudding lies in the eating. No amount of social acceptance, governmental funding, or trendiness could fuel the movement if participants were not getting their needs met in the short and long runs. And it does seem clear that self-betterment strivers on the whole feel at least reasonably satisfied.

Typical Comments from Helping Group Members

- ☐ I feel close to others in the group. We're like a family.
- ☐ It's comforting to know that we're all in the same boat.
- ☐ When someone has the floor, the others all listen.
- ☐ I can talk about my hang-ups without getting ridiculed.
- ☐ When others confront me, I know it's for my own good.
- ☐ More than anything I enjoy being able to help others.
- ☐ The instructor really gets us motivated to grow and learn.

- ☐ Anger expressed in our group doesn't become hateful.
- ☐ Encouragement and support giving become good habits.
- ☐ The group leader shows us down-to-earth ways to cope.
- ☐ Even natural-enemy members end up helping each other.
- ☐ Hugs and pats on the back feel so much better than pills.
- ☐ Self-pity and blaming have no place in our meetings.
- ☐ Group members are urged to take charge of their lives.
- ☐ Having a regular agenda keeps the discussion on track.
- ☐ The humorous moments seem to happen spontaneously.
- ☐ Everyone's ideas and feelings are considered important.

The above commentary touches on both the learning and nurturing aspects of the group experience, but more so the latter; and this makes complete sense, as learning indeed flourishes in a nurturing atmosphere. In the household, richly-nurtured little ones soak up information like a sponge; the effectiveness of first grade teachers flows more from a giving temperament than from a lofty I.Q.; adolescents, notoriously poor listeners, get their ears perked up when they feel a strong sense of kinship with their parents; and then throughout our lives we tend to accept--at times uncritically-- the information provided to us by those who make us feel positive about ourselves.

Food nourishes our bodies' cells, and this in turn builds up physical strength and the capacity to ward off diseases. But that is not why we eat--we eat because we feel hungry. In a like vein, we realize that attending self-improvement groups can help over-come problems; but once we become acquainted and comfortable with other group members, we simply start hungering for the feel-ing of familyhood we find there. This is what motivates many par-ticipants to stay "in the family" long after they have exorcised their worst demons and achieved greater serenity.

Although nurturing is a cornerstone ingredient in our self-helping groups, the term itself appears in the group setting far less often than it does in the newborn nursery. Yet when you study the relationship aspects of nurturing, infant care has a much in common with therapy and support groups. Infants as well as therapy and support group members are given unconditional acceptance, receive frequent hugs, are told they are lovable, find their needs placed on center stage, and don't get chided for spontaneous expression. No wonder so many helping group participants keep on coming back for more!

As children grow, however, the nurturing picture changes; and as we saw in the previous chapter, modern living modes have drastically reduced the amount and quality of family nurturing that we had in generous supply several generations back. *So now we arrive at the overriding factor that is fueling a dramatic increase in attendance at self-improvement groups--members are searching for a sense of family in all of these groups because they fail to find as much as they need of it in their own households!*

Today's parents cram as much nurturing as they possibly can into the crevices and crannies of their compact schedules, but their households seldom match a therapy or support group in providing an atmosphere of closeness and sharing. When you attend a helping group session, you don't see people running in and out, yelling over background noises in order to be heard, or gazing at the television or computer screen. Also, you don't get interrupted by knocks at the front door or the ringing of telephones. You head to these group meetings with the expectation of sharing strongly-felt opinions and feelings in a caring atmosphere in the company those who genuinely listen and give thoughtful feedback.

Are the participants in these programs more caring by nature? By no means. The difference lies simply in the atmosphere of intimacy you encounter in a group setting. As family members you have the workplace and schools to scurry off to, and meetings and practices to attend; and you surely can't be faulted for slumping into an easy chair near a T.V. set to unwind after a tedious day. But a cohesive family needs at least a small amount of distraction-free quality time to spend interacting together. Almost every self-improvement group, after all, affords their members no more than an hour or two each week.

The good news: this same experience of intimacy is within easy reach of today's heads of household. In your own home you can accomplish every exploit that helping groups do--in less time, at no expense, and with greater long-term benefits. And by now you well know we mean the weekly family meeting, or family hour. Toward this end we urge you to jealously guard a narrow space on your weekly calendars to use for all-important family group time. Now if it sounds strange to imagine your family gathered around in a circle talking about the day's events or issues of concern to all in the home, it doesn't sound nearly as strange as your sitting down in the presence of complete strangers to lay bare your innermost feelings and your outermost failings. Yes, your community-based group gets to be more comfortable after a short while, and so too does your family discussion group.

While therapy and support groups deliver lots of help, the family group surpasses all of them in the potential for personal enrichment. Chapters one and two laid the groundwork for this, and further evidence will be located throughout the book. Suffice it to say here that when young people grow up having family hour as a part of their regular routine, they acquire tools for resolving many issues of daily living and develop an emotional resiliency that enables them to recover rapidly from traumatic experiences. It takes some grown-ups months or even years in therapy and/or recovery programs to develop these skills; and even then, it is unlikely that their emotional scars will get substantially healed.

> *I've been going to Weight Watchers and Overeaters Anonymous groups for a pretty long time, and when I heard about family meetings, my first reaction was that it sounded rather strange. But when I gave it a little more thought, the logic was clear. I will confess, however, that the idea made me nervous. We started out, but the grumbling never seemed to let up, so we packed it in after a few sessions; but then I came to realize that I don't like being a quitter, so we gave it another whirl. It's been two months now, and we're still chugging along, but at times I'm not sure in which direction. It's a major struggle, and it brings up some feelings I don't like, but I trust it will all be worthwhile in the long stretch. I'm thinking of asking my "anonymous" friends for some help.*
>
> *Waitress, mother of 3*

Now if family hour is potentially the most effective and efficient of all helping groups, why then do we not notice more people already having jumped onto the bandwagon? Let's see if we can get a few answers from comparing community-based groups with the home-spun variety.

Why Family Hour is a "Poor Cousin" Helping Group

Group-member motivation

New arrivals at therapy and recovery groups might have found their motivation from feeling internally tormented or terrified over the prospect of losing a spouse or a job. Those joining into empowerment groups typically become driven to soar to greater heights financially, spiritually, or in expanding their influence. And those taken by the scruff of the neck into court-ordered treatment mostly worry about the consequences awaiting them should they fail to show up for the sessions.

Your youngsters, by contrast, are apt to grumble or shrug their shoulders over the mention of family hour; and adults don't always jump for joy either. Slogging through everybody's early-on resistance--particularly your own--and giving household members sufficient time to build up their motivation could become the number one challenge of your whole family hour experience. This is where your taking the long view can be a true life saver.

Commonality of interests

Twelve-step and support group members all check in toting a similar-type monkey on their backs; those entering into therapy groups all crave inner peace, a steadier grip on the wheel of functionality, or more harmonious relationships; and attendees at empowerment programs are all in search of a similar dream.

Your children, by contrast, might need to get glued to the floor at their first meeting. Family members, nevertheless, share the deepest of bonds; but they may not see the great potential of this bonding as they begin their family hour adventure. Considerable patience may be your saving grace.

Professionalism and experience in the leadership role

Leaders of helping programs typically come with degrees, credentials, enthusiasm, and in certain cases a measure of charisma. And while twelve-step and support groups are most often chaired on a rotating basis by regular members, these folks are as a rule seasoned participants.

You, on the other hand, may feel like the greenest of rookies as you undertake family hour leadership. But all group leaders are rookies at the beginning; and the seasoned pros are ones who have gotten assistance along the journey, learned from mistakes, and persevered through the inevitable rough spots.

Uniformity in treatment style

Support and twelve-step recovery groups employ proven formulas that are easily recognizable wherever their sessions are held. And therapy group leaders often spend years learning and fine-tuning their methods.

Your family hour style--subject to change as desired--shall be tailored to your family's interests and needs. And help for your doing this is just one chapter away. Then as you gain experience, the sessions should begin to run more smoothly.

Anonymity vs. familiarity

Except for family therapy sessions, family members don't often go to helping groups together. Sharing your vulnerable side with strangers might be awkward at first, but there is some comfort in knowing you need not go home with them after you experience embarrassing moments or a butting of heads.

In spite of their sharply contrasting personalities and interests, family members have more--many more--than a few things in common. After a nerve-jarring family hour session, however, they might start wishing they lived in separate houses. For this reason we offer a range of techniques for keeping difficult situations under control or nipping them in the bud.

Trendiness

The helping community has evolved trumpeting the clarion message: "If you need help for any type of interpersonal or family issue, go somewhere outside of the home to seek solutions." The message behind this is that your family itself isn't a proper source of providing the much needed help.

Family hour bucks this trend by showing you that the finest help, the largely preventive variety, comes from getting your family members to work with you, and you all turn out to be big winners. Trend-bucking is a tough job, but someone has to do it! And then you have a new trend.

Reliability of scheduling

Being only human, group therapists can feel weary, out of sorts, and aching all over; but it doesn't very often sideline them. Their diligence, however, may be less driven by altruism than it is by practical considerations--e.g., work-performance expectations, potentially lost income, and the difficult task of notifying members of the group at the last moment. This is perhaps even more so the case for empowerment seminar leaders. Support and recovery groups experience their share of rotating-chair no-shows, but here someone else quickly jumps in to take over.

By contrast, when *you* have a small touch of the flu bug or a big touch of the resistance bug, your weekly meetings can slide right off the calendar--permanently even, if family hour has yet to become a securely entrenched feature of your household routine. Here is where a sense of commitment comes in handy. Lots more on this in the next chapter.

Publicity and protected status

Innovative new-age therapies, the very latest in recovery and support groups, and a wide range of empowerment programs are publicized through books, newspaper and magazine articles, on-line features, talk shows, paid advertising, word-of-mouth recommendations, etc. The courts and other governmental agencies, on the other hand, don't need publicity, as their self-improvement groups are built into broader programs.

Now in contrast, the family-circle group is looked upon as a poor relation, and parent leaders have sharpened their pioneering leadership skills in obscurity. Then again, some parenting writers do discuss--albeit in softened tones--about scheduling meetings in your own home. Their focus, however, is consistently narrow, and they seldom devote as much as a single short book chapter to the subject. This situation needs to change if the weekly family meeting is to gain popular status; and by bestowing family hour with top billing, we are making a push in this direction.

Community-located helping groups contribute a great deal to our lives, but the one and only group which is rooted in our own homes--family hour--has to join all the others in order to complete the self-improvement spectrum. As we have just seen, people are flocking to away-from-home groups for a great many reasons, but most of these folks are also hungering for the sense of family that they find too little of under their own roofs. And unfortunately, all too many of these family members are also searching for a sense of belonging in cults, bravado-infused gangs, bad-influence friendships, and hate groups with a racial or ethnic flavor.

If our favorite restaurant closes up its doors, we may feel a twinge or two of sadness; but then we quickly go on to satisfy our palates elsewhere. If, however, our families no longer give us that home-folks sensibility, we make up for some of the shortcoming in community-based groups and in other involvements; yet we still must come to grips with our family relationships. Struggling families simply do not go out of business the way pizzerias do; nor do they disband, as all self-improvement groups do in the fullness of time. Instead, they become dysfunctional or break up into other configurations, or both.

Struggling families can be helped in a huge way by bringing a measure of emotional intimacy back into the household. In Chapter 2 we saw a variety of methods for meeting this challenge, with the weekly family meeting as the centerpiece. Yet while each and every parent has the capacity to assume leadership of family sessions, each one is also capable of self-sabotage.

"Reasons" Why Family Hour Would Never Work

☐ I'm simply not suited for leading those discussions.

☐ Assuming another project would pressure us even more.

☐ Our schedules wouldn't allow for a convenient time.

☐ We couldn't drag the kids away from their T.V. sets.

☐ I would have absolutely no idea as to where to start.

☐ We could never get the kids to feel mutually supportive.

☐ The rest of the family would never appreciate my efforts.

☐ That's all we need--to sit around staring at one another!

☐ I can just see it now--total and complete chaos.

☐ I can just see it now--everybody clamming up tight.

☐ Our kids are too young--they would never sit still.

☐ Our kids are too old--they would never even show up.

☐ We could never get the kids to open about themselves.

☐ The kids would use the sessions to try to get their way.

☐ The kids would think we were trying to get our way.

☐ My husband likely won't show, so why should I bother?

☐ It may start out well, but everyone would soon get bored.

☐ I prefer a group where everyone is really enthusiastic.

☐ My super-sensitive teenager might get her feelings hurt.

☐ It sounds like a really nifty idea--that is, as ideas go.

☐ I'm sure we can all survive very well without family hour.

☐ Why should we? We see too much of each other now.

Comments such as these often arise from fears and mis-conceptions--elements that can steer any parent toward finding a lengthy list of reasons for not giving family hour a reasonable shot. However, you can resolve these and other such questions with a little bit of patience, a willingness to experiment, trust in your family's potential, and confidence in the long-range benefits of family hour. We shall address a great number of these lying-in-wait pit-falls throughout the chapters.

> *I remember when daddy said we were going to sit down all together every Sunday to talk. I figured it was just another way for him to get us to do more chores. He told me it wasn't, but I did not believe him. I guess I didn't trust in him when he promised he'd never get married again after my mommy died. Then in one meeting I got all upset and told him he lied to me about never marrying, and how I did not believe him any more. He was so surprised, and I even saw some tears in his eye. He talked with me about it for a while, and after that meeting I <u>did</u> cry, but not so he could see me. Later I felt a lot better. Now Gloria (stepmother) and I are even friends in a way--but I'm never going to call her "mom."*
>
> *12 year old in blended family*

Among parents who feel skeptical about undertaking family hour, not many will disagree with the concept of people all sitting around in a discussion circle. This is because many of these self-same parents have been participants in outside-the-home helping groups; and even if they have not, they have very likely supported family members or friends in their attendance at twelve-step, support, or other helping groups. So let us now look into successfully run family hour sessions, and make note of how they contain the best elements of groups located in the community.

Infusing Helping-Group Elements into Family Hour

A comfortable, distraction-free setting in which to meet

A relaxed, homey atmosphere aids community-based helping groups flow smoothly. Now comfortable in no sense indicates luxurious--just a few chairs and cushions, a bit of elbow room, and temperature-controlled air in the room or hall. The distraction-free element is more important still. This involves the limiting of access to telephones, radios, T.V. sets, and reading material; then making sure that outside noises don't become an irritant.

As family hour leaders you can create such an atmosphere easily by coming up with a naturally quiet location that lends itself to a relaxed mood; silencing all in-the-vicinity telephones; keeping all television sets, radios, and other electronic devices turned off; making certain family members do not meander in and out of the room; and instructing young folks to talk to their friends about not knocking on the door during family hour time.

Commonality of interests, issues, and purpose

Whether doing battle with same-type compulsive or addictive demons, recovering from a similar form of loss, or sharing like ambitions and goals, community-based group participants bask in the spirit of kinship and derive comfort from knowing they are all in the same boat, and headed hopefully in the same direction.

Members of the household know they are in the same family boat, but some may at times feel like rocking it or even jumping ship altogether. This presents you with possibly your biggest challenge as family hour leaders--to be patient but persistent in helping group members, yourself included, to wade through some foot-dragging stages early on. Your task will be eased by your keeping the first few sessions structured, accented with a light touch, and sprinkled with some practical, productive work.

An expectation of receiving help

People seek out helping groups in order to put their lives back together or enhance their functioning--e.g., by conquering addictions, resolving conflicts, finding their path to inner serenity, or attaining personal power or self-realization.

This is yet another challenge you face right away as family hour leaders. Family members, especially early on, need to gain something positive from the sessions. This could be bits of inter- esting and useful information, the opportunity and encouragement to speak up about sensitive issues, the spotlight placed upon their talents or interests, some input into family business matters, or a few smiles or even guffaws. This is not the least bit difficult to ac- complish. Then as family hour gets more settled, the kind of help everyone obtains will take a variety of forms.

Competent, decisive group leadership

Leaders of psychoanalytical therapy groups have walls full of advanced degrees and training certifications, while empower- ment seminar leaders ooze charm along with every word; but the great majority of helping group leaders are simply ordinary mor- tals. They stay up to date on issues, follow an agenda, keep the discussions moving, and make certain that the interaction doesn't get out of hand; and their task is made easier when new members quickly get in step with the routine--a helping group tradition.

As family hour leaders you need to establish your own rou- tines and behavioral expectations, and some of this may flow out of your own personality traits, strengths, and interests. The good news is that you will have no limits on opportunities to get matters working smoothly. This experience will shore up your leadership skills and your parental self-confidence as well.

Clearly defined goals and steps for reaching them

Some helping groups make bigger productions over setting and keeping track of goals than do others; but experienced group leaders always keep a close eye on everyone's progress, making sure that things are going in the right direction and at a reasonable pace. And they are always ready to shift gears as needed.

Successful family hour leaders likewise learn to keep their eyes and ears focused on the direction or change in direction of the group. This need not be a formal process, but just one of asking family members what they would like to accomplish in the sessions, and then checking periodically to hear everyone's feedback. However, you need to steer clear of the dangerous trap of striving to accommodate everyone at all times.

A listening atmosphere

In therapy groups, those who listen at their convenience or tune others out at their whim are sure to get confronted. Then in recovery and support group meetings, "having the floor" is taken seriously, since drowning others out and interrupting capriciously get hooted down with gusto. Furthermore, everyone is expected to make a real effort to listen with sensitivity and with understanding--basic ingredients all genuine listening. (See Chapter 6.)

Patience and perseverance may be needed for you to establish this sort of system in family sessions, especially if there are little ones in the group or if listening hasn't been a high priority for certain family members. Remember, however, that your effort will be richly rewarded, and before long you will delight in seeing improvements carry over beyond the sessions.

The sharing of helpful information

All reputable helping groups depend on accurate, complete information; and educational groups and seminars obviously need it to be the main course. In support groups it may relate to recent breakthroughs in the medical and other fields; and in twelve-step programs, it flows from the sincerity of personal stories and from the feedback offered by others. In therapy groups it also plays a critical role in one's quest for inner peace, as intrapsychic conflict can easily get fueled by ignorance and twisted thinking.

As family hour leaders you surely have much information to share and can easily access lots more. But there are several traps to avoid. One is the temptation to overload your group with data, especially if you are paying scant attention to their readiness to absorb it. Other traps are a refusal to look at any gray areas of issues, and the need to appear authoritative on subjects beyond your scope of expertise. Your ignorance, after all, can be endearing; then as you seek "the latest" from your young sages, you are sure to learn a few things, and you might even become "cool."

Encouragement for expressing feelings and needs

Educational and empowerment seminars tread lightly into these areas, therapy groups tread heavily, and recovery and support groups usually fall somewhere in between. Yet in every self-improvement group, a participant's thoughts, feelings, and desires are greatly valued, and one's readiness to express them is viewed as a strength rather than as a weakness.

Family hour becomes an enriching experience when members of the household have no fear in voicing their notions and emotions; but it goes on the endangered species list if expression becomes constricted. Family hour leaders have little need for the expertise of trained therapists, yet they must remain ever vigilant about allowing emotional outbursts to escalate into insult-spewing carnivals, fisticuffs, or chaotic spectacles. Your one-person-at-a-time talking rule may be one way to steer away from such danger, and employing a more structured format also helps. But remember, quick action always beats cleaning up a mess.

Loving acceptance of weaknesses and failures

When helping group participants begin to bare their souls, it is a sure signal that they feel safe in an environment of respect and support. This can become a crucial point in getting their lives turned around, and demonstrates that they fully expect to receive much-needed help from others in the group.

Family hour sessions rely on a similar brand of supportive atmosphere. You accomplish this by encouraging spontaneous expression, but by at the same time putting the lid on destructive actions--threats, put-downs, dead-end wrangling, screaming, etc. The more quickly and efficiently you deal with divisive behaviors, the more time you will have at your disposal for supportive, sympathetic responses.

Heavy doses of support, encouragement, and praise

Leaders of educational and problem-focused groups alike realize that making people feel positive about themselves greatly accelerates the process of learning and healing. Then too, wise group facilitators save their praise for real achievements and offer encouragement only for attainable goals.

Positive reinforcement can also be a potent force in family hour, and it needs no instruction manual. You will feel good about passing it on to others, and then even better as it echoes back to you. This self-esteem fundamental is particularly important these days considering how easy it is for expressions of support, praise, and encouragement to fall between the cracks as family members pass by one another like ships in the night.

Constructive feedback and criticism

No matter how on-target it is, we often turn two deaf ears to the feedback of friends who offer us unpleasant commentary "for our own good." Yet feedback gets a better reception in helping programs because the prevailing atmosphere paves the road to unconditional acceptance, unwavering support, and unfaltering encouragement. Also, these confronters don't get away with using pressure tactics or guilt to get others to mend their ways.

Feedback from listeners will inevitably weave its way into family hour sessions, and you no doubt will be on both the giving and receiving ends. Simply keep in mind the helping group model of bathing feedback in an ocean of kindness. In time the process becomes second nature but goes a long way toward bringing vitality and strength to family relationships.

Protection against out-of-control conflict

Educational seminar leaders may get startled by emotional flare-ups, while group therapists tend to look upon these outbursts as grist for the healing-process mill. But in every helping group, a leader must be prepared to keep chaos and free-for-all combat out of the sessions.

Family hour leaders must keep a vigilant eye on any signs that chaos may be lurking close by. This is especially important in the early going. We suggest that you devise strategies in advance and get ready to jump in post haste if the wheels begin coming off. What is more, it might be a very wise move to discuss your strategies with the family from day one. Then no one can complain later about not having been warned.

Encouragement toward self-responsibility

In psychotherapy groups and twelve-step programs, grumblers and blame-shifters may get cut a little slack at first, but they soon get confronted hard and often. This is to encourage them to begin dealing with their alienating and self-defeating behavior and to take control of their lives.

A he-made-me-do-it mind-set is normal for four year-olds, but it is never too soon to begin teaching the lessons of assuming responsibility. You do this by refusing to accept young ones' portrayals of themselves as victims of fate or of the cunning of others;

and by offering encouragement and help, but not rescuing, as they inch themselves toward solutions.

Abundant mutual help

In therapy, recovery, support, and even education-focused programs, participants start taking on the helping-hand role rather quickly. And it is not simply a matter of mimicking everybody else. Group participants, once they experience genuine kindness from other folks, tend to want to return the favor. This might be called a contagion of good works.

A help-and-be-helped instinct is deeply ingrained in human nature, which means that mutual cooperation is sure to amble into your family hour sessions--perhaps not as quickly as in a support group, but quickly enough. You encourage this by reaching out to others without any expectation of having the favor reciprocated. It will be especially gratifying when you see mortal-foe siblings slide into the helping-hand habit.

Powerful emotional bonding

As helping group members let loose their emotions, begin to express unmet needs, stay the course in combating compulsive urges, and move steadily toward their goals, their sense of kinship blossoms. Group-member bonding obviously gets bolstered in the exchange of encouraging words and magnanimous deeds; but it also gets nurtured in routine discussions, confrontations, and simply by being witness to others who are struggling with their failings and are striving toward self-healing.

This is one area in which family hour leaders hold a distinct advantage over their community-centered counterparts. Helping group numbers rise and fall, and performance contingent membership also fluctuates over time; but the kinship among all family members begins at birth and continues on over a lifetime. These bonds might become strained due to conflict or to long-time geographical distance, but the sparking of familyhood always appears ready to get rekindled at a moment's notice. Even in congruous households with growing children, the bonding process can lose some luster as everyone goes off in different directions; but family hour can add a luminous glow to the picture. So while some families feel grateful for merely keeping their heads above water, family hour folks take pride in keeping their heads held high.

Everybody goes on about the generation gap as if it were completely normal, but it never really materialized in our family. Our brood are all teenagers now, and they have their issues like everybody else, but we all discuss our gripes pretty freely, and it doesn't get ugly often. I know this has a lot to do with the regular discussions we have always had after Sunday dinner. It all started naturally when Tom and I vowed to keep the Sunday meal as at least the one time we would always have just for the family. I've felt so gratified upon seeing the kids turning down a few tempting invitations because they were conflicting with our time for "dinner and discussion."

YWCA coordinator and
mother of 3 teenagers

SECTION II

FAMILY HOUR

LEADERSHIP

CHAPTER FOUR

PREPARING THE

FAMILY HOUR SCENE

We had several different ideas about where to hold our family meetings, and then one of the kids suggested the hot tub. Anthony and I thought that was funny, but the other kids all wanted to do it, so we all jumped in for our first session! After two or three times and a good deal of splashing, we called a halt to it. It was nothing against the hot tub itself, but it just gave us too many distractions Then we put it to a majority vote (the hot tub was now off the list), and now the den is our regular venue. Anthony is a real character, and he started our first den session by singing the old favorite "How dry I am."

Freelance writer, mother of 4

Gestalt therapy meetings in Brooklyn, New York have a sound distinctly unlike those in Brooklyn, Minnesota, as the difference in geography brings with it differently accented speech; but the participants in both locations talk to an empty chair with quite the same catharsis-producing purpose in mind. And Overeaters Anonymous programs in Portland, Oregon may have more of a new-age flavor to their activities than their sister programs in Portland, Maine; but group participants on both coasts rush lovingly to the assistance of those who have fallen from the diet wagon, and right onto the dessert table.

Rehab centers, twelve-step programs, supportive groups, special-needs therapies, and popular self-realization seminars all possess tried-and-true formulas that function in more or less the same fashion all over the country and beyond. Such uniformity in programming enables new groups to become established quickly and successfully in just about any locale. It also works out well for prospective group members, who have many issues in common, since they will know exactly what to expect. What is more, if you become dissatisfied with the atmosphere or leadership in a certain program, you will most likely find a different one nearby that better suits your needs.

By big contrast, your family hour operation, with relation to style and content, will not likely resemble one across the country, let alone the one next door. Every family has similar goals on the horizon--oodles of love and emotional support, robust communication, the spirit of cooperation, a smooth-running household routine, and the tools for resolving troublesome issues, to name just a few. But our families all have dramatically different modes of interacting, sharply contrasting interests and values, and desires for self-improvement that stand out uniquely as their own. So if you would hardly expect a compulsive gambler to blend into a cancer survivors group, why then would you ask every family to conduct family hour sessions in essentially the same fashion?

Writers advocating family get-togethers have consistently chartered a narrow path, giving families step-by-step formulas for arriving at household business decisions and resolving issues of everyday living. Yet certain parents would surely fare better using steps other than the ones offered, and others don't take very well at all to any how-to-do system. These writers to be sure don't tell parents *not* to do things their own way, but they certainly don't encourage it either. So what about the family group that would thrive on the spontaneous sharing of information about recent goings-on among family members, or one that would delight in engaging in wit-sharpening debates or in creative and fun projects? And what about a legion of other family-together purposes?

What you will not obtain from us, therefore, is a family hour format of our choosing along with a set of instructions for carrying it out. Instead we will offer you a roster of possible choices for the style and content for family hour, along with our strong urging that you consider putting together a menu of choices that cater to the interests and needs of everyone in the household. Take into account your family's "personality" and areas that both concern and delight family members, mixing and matching as it pleases you. If there are burning issues, you may look for a problem-solving format; and if your family is heavily into music and the arts, you might want to reserve some sessions to showcase talents and to further career-enhancing goals. Thus we encourage you to design, with input from everybody in the household, a family hour format that feels most comfortable and works best for you. Then you can experiment further down the line as your family's needs and interests change. Flexibility is the key.

My family thrives on structure, so we set up a family council along the lines of a club. We elected the officers, started up a treasury to be used for outings, kept minutes, and posted our agenda on the refrigerator door before each meeting. Some of the kids even wanted to name the club and make uniforms, but that was voted down--thank heavens! One of the kids decided to give us a name anyway, and it is cute to see how the name has stuck.

CPA, mother of 4 adoptees

My mother-in-law is an independent sort of person, and she lives in a separate wing our house. When we started up family hour it never occurred to us to include her, but before too long she expressed curiosity, so we invited her in. She attends lots of the meetings now, and has toned down her bossy side. She has also passed on some stories my husband had no idea about.

Mother of 2 teenagers

While there are many pathways that guide you toward family hour success, there are also pitfalls lurking in the shadows at every turn. Some can give you a really bumpy ride or cause momentary detours, while others may hurtle you straight into a giant pothole. Yet for every pit you might stumble into, there are many ways, including the trial and error method, for extricating yourself quickly. We want your family hour adventure to be as enjoyable and trouble-free as possible, so we offer you down-to-earth suggestions in the chapters ahead and the Help section. This advice is rooted in our many combined years of practice as family therapists, in the experience of families we have helped to prepare for family hour, and in our having organized and established a family hour project in our own homes.

At our third meeting Sarah invited her best pal, another fifteen-year-old, to join in with us; and they sat together whispering and giggling for the entire time. Afterwards I told Sarah not to invite her friend back, as they separated themselves from the rest of the group. She got very sullen for some time after that, but eventually she spoke up about how she felt she didn't get enough attention from her dad or myself. That really got us thinking about things.

Mother of 3 teens

Let us now probe into the nuts and bolts of family hour--the who, what, why, when, where, and how or organizing and running the weekly sessions.

Motives for Undertaking Family Hour

Some questionable thinking upon getting started

- ☐ We really need to work on our marital problems.
- ☐ I'm going to talk to the kids about cooperation.
- ☐ We want to know who's at fault when the kids fight.
- ☐ This will teach our whirling dervishes to sit still.
- ☐ If the kids plan to take over, I've got news for them.
- ☐ I'm going to demand some appreciation for all my work.
- ☐ I hope this makes my wife happy; I'll keep my arms folded.
- ☐ I'm an organized soul, so it's all planned in advance.
- ☐ Our little ones will learn some respect for their elders.
- ☐ We've got a long list of questions that need answering.
- ☐ I'm getting nervous about the kids arguing all the time.
- ☐ I bet my hubby will start running the show--big surprise!
- ☐ If I hear bad language, there will be consequences.
- ☐ I'm shaking in my boots. I hope the kids don't notice.
- ☐ I doubt if this will be as pleasant as my support group.
- ☐ This had better be fun. I don't want to see sour faces.

Many of the sentiments conveyed in these statements are reasonable sounding enough, but the companion wording hints at trouble lurking a little way down the road--from pressuring, lecturing, unrealistic expectations, a gloomy-gus outlook, insecurity, or manipulation going in both directions. Also, these sentiments may indicate that these parents lack trust in the power of freely-flowing communication, the lifeblood of family hour.

Some reasonable ideas about holding family meetings

- ☐ We could surely develop better communication skills.
- ☐ I really want us to become a more close-knit family.
- ☐ There must be a better way to work out differences.
- ☐ We don't spend lots of time together, so this should help.
- ☐ I want to see the kids become confident speakers.
- ☐ We could spend some time talking about budgeting.
- ☐ It would be great for us to do family projects together.
- ☐ We have young comedians, so maybe I'll get amused.
- ☐ I'll give information and opinion-sharing a high priority.
- ☐ This may help the children in following their own path.
- ☐ I'm not sure why, but I think this will be important for us.
- ☐ Sure, we expect resistance; but hey--time is on our side.
- ☐ There goes some hobby time, so this can be a new one.
- ☐ I think we should call ourselves "talkaholics unanimous."
- ☐ You know, I can't think of a single reason <u>not</u> to do it.
- ☐ I went to the workshops, so now I have no excuse.

The above comments sound open-minded and optimistic, and come from parents who appear both reasonable and realistic. Families like these have every chance of getting off to an excellent start. But whether the early going is delightful or dreadful, it is always O.K. to experiment and shift over into new directions. Then again, you may hammer out goals from the start, but then see an evolutionary process taking over. Go with the flow.

Family Hour's Form and Function

Thus far we have referred exclusively to the regular weekly meeting; but family hour has yet another format, one that lets you respond to participants' needs that call out for more immediate attention. The following is a summary of what both types of household meetings accomplish.

The regular weekly meeting

Family members who gather together regularly tend to become closely bonded, a priceless benefit in this era of on-the-run family activities. Then the longer they continue with the sessions, the stronger these bonds grow. This experience helps individual family members, and little ones in particular, to grow in sophistication and creativity, learn to hone problem-resolving skills, and gain resiliency in dealing with personal setbacks.

The on-the-spot meeting

Some issues simply can't wait until the appointed meeting time arrives. Family members, as many as happen to be on the scene, can gather together whenever someone feels the need for immediate discussion or action. These on-the-spot sessions are the perfect complement to regularly scheduled ones, not a substitute. The one exception we note is for families who have been in family hour for quite some time, and then transition to on-the-spot sessions. Since participants tend to feel emotionally volatile "at the moment," certain issues might get resolved more quickly, and thus conflicts can be nipped in the but or at least kept from worsening. These impromptu sessions also promote family solidarity, since family members who are not involved in the issues at hand often become a big part of the solution.

Family Hour's Major Components

Every family's adventure into family hour finds its own signature, but a few central elements become indispensable ingredients for success in each household. These elements are present in smooth-running meetings of all stripes--group therapy, support and recovery groups, job training sessions, corporate board meetings, fund-raiser strategy groups, etc.

Atmosphere of togetherness

Attaining a sense of family togetherness might appear to take forever, so your patience is a sine-qua-non ingredient. Then again, you cannot get everybody to talk--nor should you even try--during weekly sessions. But you pave the way toward a sense of unity by attending to several relatively routine chores. Have everyone gather in a circle or around a table so that no one is hidden from view; ban reading, head-set radio usage, T.V. watching, and getting into any dozing-off position; keep whispering or rib-poking pairs separated; and quickly put a halt to all disruptions other than true emergencies--which should be as rare as they are in therapy and support groups.

Non-competing status

As is the case with therapy and recovery group sessions, family hour should not have to compete with other activities. Post mealtime may be a worthy time to meet, but the mealtime itself is best reserved for eating and casual chit-chat. While automobile trips present the advantage of a captive audience, the importance of keeping attention on the driving can seriously compromise your focus on family-member interactions. Mealtime and car trips may nevertheless produce spirited discussions, but success in settings such as these is generally a hit-or-miss proposition.

Use of a fixed timeframe

A one hour time span seems to work best for most therapy sessions, business meetings, and other small discussion groups; and family hour is no exception. However, this timeframe should serve as a guide, not a stern taskmaster. Family discussion and activities may run beyond the scheduled hour whenever the interaction is especially fruitful or when a burning issue needs to get to closure; and sessions may get shortened up when things begin to drag, when toddlers are part of the group, or when time pressures arise suddenly. The timeframe for on-the-spot meetings requires more flexibility. One hot-potato issue might get resolved in five or ten minutes, while another may hold your family group's attention for an hour or more.

Clearly delineated leadership

While single parents automatically slide into the family hour leadership role, things can get complicated in two-parent homes. Whenever co-leadership generates friction, you might go in other directions. This could involve your alternating as agenda minders, clearly defining and adhering to your separate duties, or agreeing that one person shall hold onto the reins--most probably the prime mover of your family hour project. If there are other grown-ups in the home, they also may emerge into the leadership picture; and older children in veteran family hour households should get to take on some management chores, which is excellent training for leadership in the future.

Planned agenda and guided interaction

Depending on your family hour style(s), you might prefer to keep your agenda loose or fashion it with elaborate detail; but be careful to steer clear of a structure so rigid that it muzzles spontaneity and muffles dialogue. If your family decides to stick with free and open discussions, then *that* is your plan; and if the interaction seems to flourish easily week after week, then it obviously doesn't need much active guidance. But it is advisable to keep a watchful eye on the interaction, and to consider employing a more business oriented format and more tightly structured activities if you notice signs of chaos, boredom, speech making, or round-in-circles conflict creeping onto the scene.

When to Schedule Family Meetings

Regular meetings

Once a week is our sure-fire choice. Two weeks between sessions could noticeably weaken group continuity, twice a week would be too demanding for most families, and resorting to five or ten day intervals could bring chaos into the scheduling. Every effort should be made to stick to the same day and hour each week, but you can tinker with the scheduling as often as you may please. Haphazard planning is akin to playing Russian Roulette with your family hour experience; and your failure to reschedule right away after a canceled session is also like playing Russian Roulette, but now with the added danger of having two or three bullets placed in the chamber.

On-the-spot meetings

Obviously, your on-the-spot meetings should take place as soon as is convenient after a compelling issue pops up, but sometimes waiting an hour or longer will weed out the false alarms. It is advisable to convene these sessions when family members seem genuinely upset or when a significant event has just taken place or looms on the immediate horizon. But it is not wise to let your little ones buffalo you into "emergency" sessions in order to hound you with demands or to get you to take sides in sibling disputes. Then again, the sessions are also not meant for you to do the hounding. To be on the safe side, however, you can always call for a session even when you have questions about the validity of an emergency, and then cancel it quickly if your doubts get confirmed.

Where to Hold Family Meetings

Among favorite family meeting spots are living room, family room, or dining table--especially for after-supper sessions. Other possibilities include nearby outdoor areas, such as porch or patio. It would be unusual for families to hold their regular sessions in an off-site location. In deciding on where to gather, the following factors call out for consideration:

Comfort and convenience

Sitting on chairs, particularly around a full-size table, lends an aura of formality; the use of sofas and/or easy chairs in the living or family room is less formal; while scattering cushions around the floor signals a casual atmosphere. But any location, temperature controlled if possible, is really great so long as it allows family members to feel comfortable and relaxed.

Freedom from interruptions

Repeated interruptions create major trouble with the focus of your family hour sessions. Precautions include keeping nearby telephones silenced, letting answering machines take messages, asking non-members who happen to be in the vicinity to disappear from view, urging extended family or friends to refrain from calling up at meeting time, and conveying similar messages to children's pals who might come knocking at the door.

Freedom from distractions

Distractions can spring up in a flash. Find a naturally tranquil locale, and be sure to avoid the following: open windows that face out onto the street or other noisy locale, thin walls conveying anything clearly audible from the other side, and a turned-on T.V. set that is either visible or audible. Having meditation-type music playing softly in the background could possibly enhance people's mood. You might even want to hold a vote about the background music, but it must meet the requirement of being soothing.

Who Should Attend Family Meetings

This might sound like a really simple one--the whole family, of course! And yet there are valid questions about who should or should not be included in your weekly sessions. Making judicious decisions about the make-up of the group could spare you from a lot of grief. Let's look at the following categories:

Immediate and live-in extended family

Parents and their growing-up youngsters usually constitute family hour's core, although live-in partners would usually be considered as immediate family. Also, non-custodial parents and their children spending weekends, vacation time, and other quality time together are obviously a family group as well. Grandparents and other kinfolk residing in the home and solidly integrated into family life should be family meeting invitees; and for relatives residing in separate on-premises quarters or near by, the appropriateness of their attendance is in proportion to the degree of their involvement in the family's affairs.

Households of unrelated adults

For people sharing a house or apartment, family hour can be a big help in addressing particulars like assuming responsibility for household decisions and chores; dividing up the rent payment and other expenses; assigning living and sleeping space; hashing out disagreements; and determining and enforcing standards for neatness, cleanliness, privacy, and quiet. The sharing of personal information can assist in bringing "roomies" closer together.

Non-member attendance

It is generally unwise to let outsiders join in family meetings until your group has gotten to be a cohesive unit--usually a period of three months or possibly more. When preteens and teens bring close friends to beginning sessions, innocent sounding on its face, this can lead to sub-grouping and disruptiveness. In more veteran family hour households, family members might choose to bring in a curious friend or a serious romantic interest, and the reasons for doing this should be made clear to everyone. Also, when relatives or friends stay at the house, you might want to consider including them rather than allowing their presence to knock your session off the calendar--possibly a dangerous precedent.

Voluntary vs. mandatory attendance

Calmly leading a foot-stomping six-year-old by the hand to your initial meeting may be a wise idea, but threatening a no-show sixteen-year-old is a serious no-no. Youngsters should never get punished for failure to show up, nor for their in-session behaviors. Then again, consistent and unrepentant disruptiveness merits exclusion from the session. This is can be a complex and controversial issue. More in Chapter 8 and in the Help section.

Deciding on Family Hour Style

When it comes to choosing a family hour style, don't simply copy-cat what your close friends are doing. Instead, choose one or several formats which seem comfortable and workable for your family. Feel free to try them on for size, as if you were purchasing a hat. The following are several of the more recognizable models for family hour style. The format(s) you wind up with may be taken straight out of our examples, may combine some elements of one or more of them, or may be a hat of a totally different color.

Corporate boardroom style

Group members usually all sit around a table, officers are assigned or elected to carry out duties and head up committees, a secretary takes notes, a formal agenda is followed, certain family business decisions are voted upon, and the chairperson keeps a close watch on the interaction. Just the thing for households that include several Capricorns.

Public forum style

The moderator guides the discussion through a predetermined agenda, possibly involving some controversial issues. One person at a time has the floor, and presenters as well as onlookers must stay glued onto the subject. The moderator keeps close tabs on the tenor and direction of the discussion. A wonderful chance to hone oratorical and debating skills. Parent-moderators need to keep a cool head while nipping shouting contests in the bud.

Workshop style

This offers a vehicle for expanding knowledge and talents. Reading, audio-visual aids, or crafts materials might be part of the program; and the leader may lecture, facilitate the discussion, or supervise activities. In such a learning environment a spirit of co-operation tends to spring up, and creative energies of both adults and youngsters are likely to get stimulated. Family hour children are encouraged to grow into the role of workshop leaders.

Newscast style

Group members take turns talking about the latest goings-on in their daily routines, and taciturn ones may defer any time to others. The agenda might include news of the day on the job or at school, reports and editorials on community or world happenings, or musings about anything else of interest. Discussion might follow, so look for verbal fireworks. Newscasters have opportunities for practicing diction, pronunciation, voice projection, etc.; and the feedback they receive will test their willingness to listen and to use the experience for personal growth.

Think tank style

This format highlights intellectually challenging interaction, including brainstorming--voicing the first thing that comes to mind. This atmosphere gives great opportunities for wit sharpening and practical-issue resolution. Everybody's thoughts and opinions are respected, even while disagreements may be flaring; and intuitive thinking is greatly esteemed. Such an experience can give youthful self-confidence a big boost.

Support group style

An all-in-the-same-boat feeling permeates these sessions. The accentuate-the-positive interaction features acceptance, support, practical help, cooperation, encouragement, praise, constructive feedback, and pats on the back. Group members are invited to express their feelings, but ugly encounters are discouraged. A mighty challenge for you is to get family members to become cohesive around core issues (and every family has a number of potential core issues), but the rewards for achieving this household solidarity can make the effort well worthwhile.

Troubleshooting style

Family members search for help with problems, and others work as a group to find a resolution. They might supply pertinent information, speculate about underlying issues, and offer practical advice. This approach teaches youngsters to look in lots of directions for answers, and then delights them when they contribute to resolving older sibling or parental issues.

Talent show style

This is a great vehicle for humorous skits, formal debates, art showings, musical recitals, dramatic performances, etc.; and those not affiliated with the production may serve as audience participation. This can be lots of fun as a showcase for both youthful and adult creativity.

Encounter group style

Gripes and clashes of ideas are aired out, and the participants speak their minds freely. No limits are placed on any show of emotion or on the decibel level; but intimidation and insults get silenced immediately, and physical violence is never tolerated. A one-at-a-time talking rule is advised unless group members show self-restraint. When the interaction remains civil, this experience can prove truly therapeutic. Only for parents who are prepared to intervene quickly and calmly to maintain decorum.

Teamwork style

This is a wonderful format for every family, as cooperative projects have become lost in the shuffle in so many modern-day households. There are lots of board games featuring teamwork, including those where teammates work as a group to solve problems. What is more, you might also introduce practical work projects in which everyone pitches in to help.

Quaker meeting style

There is no prepared agenda and no expectation regarding whether or when group members speak. This relaxed atmosphere is a natural one for households in which folks tend to be generally laid-back, as participants for the most part avoid serious conflicts. If the atmosphere turns ugly or gets boring, however, we suggest that you think about other styles.

Spiritual journey style

An appealing format for devoutly religious households and those with leanings towards the esoteric. Expressions of thanksgiving, inspirational readings, meditations, and exploration of psychic phenomena are a few of the many possibilities. But be sure to put the lid on extended discourses and lecturing, as this might stifle free-flowing communication. These sessions can serve as a springboard for community-based good works.

Choosing Content for Family Meetings

Once you've made your decision as to the style or styles for family hour, the range of possibilities for selecting content gets narrowed down considerably. And this is a good thing, as the list of choices is a long one. We will therefore give you mostly broad categories instead of specific items. But before we delve into our ideas about suitable content, we will take a stroll over to the dark side--items that have no rightful place in any family hour session. Some of the items on this list, however, can easily creep or rocket right into your sessions, and they should be expunged quickly and without any fanfare. In most cases these troublemakers will do no long-term damage unless they pervade the atmosphere and continue on unabated over some time.

Content inappropriate for family meetings

- Intentionally hurtful remarks and tactics of intimidation.
- Threats of punishment for in-session bad behavior.

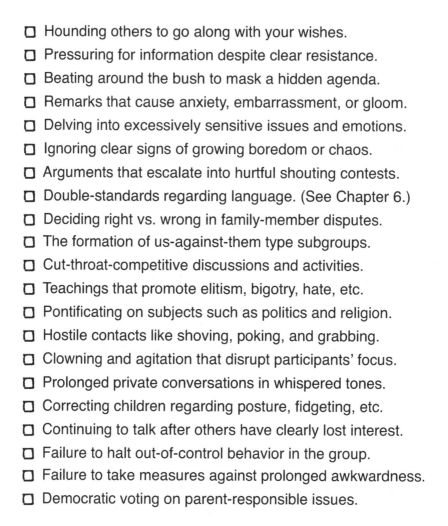

☐ Hounding others to go along with your wishes.

☐ Pressuring for information despite clear resistance.

☐ Beating around the bush to mask a hidden agenda.

☐ Remarks that cause anxiety, embarrassment, or gloom.

☐ Delving into excessively sensitive issues and emotions.

☐ Ignoring clear signs of growing boredom or chaos.

☐ Arguments that escalate into hurtful shouting contests.

☐ Double-standards regarding language. (See Chapter 6.)

☐ Deciding right vs. wrong in family-member disputes.

☐ The formation of us-against-them type subgroups.

☐ Cut-throat-competitive discussions and activities.

☐ Teachings that promote elitism, bigotry, hate, etc.

☐ Pontificating on subjects such as politics and religion.

☐ Hostile contacts like shoving, poking, and grabbing.

☐ Clowning and agitation that disrupt participants' focus.

☐ Prolonged private conversations in whispered tones.

☐ Correcting children regarding posture, fidgeting, etc.

☐ Continuing to talk after others have clearly lost interest.

☐ Failure to halt out-of-control behavior in the group.

☐ Failure to take measures against prolonged awkwardness.

☐ Democratic voting on parent-responsible issues.

The sort of content you choose for your sessions will to a large degree reflect your family's interests and values. One family might thrive on playful exchanges, while another would look upon that as a waste of time. Also, one set of parents might view their child's emotional outburst as highly therapeutic, while their neighbors down the block would consider it to be a blatant show of disrespect. Yet there are some items that transcend personal tastes and value systems, and they should help make family hour a joyful and productive experience for your whole gang.

Content appropriate for family meetings

- ☐ Expressions of kindness, encouragement, and support.
- ☐ Information that proves interesting and useful to others.
- ☐ Programs that encourage independent thinking.
- ☐ Helpfulness that is tuned in to others' wants and needs.
- ☐ Smile-producing discussions and program material.
- ☐ Discussions that help clear up misunderstandings.
- ☐ Discussions that help air out simmering resentments.
- ☐ Fruitful planning and decisions in family business matters.
- ☐ Activities that stimulate and showcase creative talents.
- ☐ Expressing emotional needs in an non-demanding way.
- ☐ Program planning that enhances leadership skills.
- ☐ Projects that encourage the use of problem-solving tools.
- ☐ Interactions promoting self-reliance and responsibility.
- ☐ Activities that make people feel better about themselves.
- ☐ Heartfelt complaints expressed in a reasonable manner.
- ☐ Constructive feedback aimed at improving the sessions.
- ☐ Emotional unburdening that improves one's mood.
- ☐ Intellectually and spiritually uplifting presentations.
- ☐ Programs that engender heart-warming interactions.
- ☐ Any constructive activity that promotes family unity.

IN FAMILY HOUR'S EARLY STAGES, MUCH ENERGY GOES TOWARD HELPING FORM GROUP COHESION. SO WE ASK YOU TO WAIT FIVE SESSIONS OR LONGER BEFORE YOU BEGIN EXPERIMENTING WITH CONTENT. DURING THIS TIME WE RECOMMEND THAT YOU DO THREE THINGS IN EVERY SESSION: SHARE PERSONAL EXPERIENCES, DISCUSS AND SETTLE ONE FAMILY BUSINESS MATTER, AND DO SOMETHING THAT IS LIKELY TO BRING SMILES TO EVERYONE'S FACE. WE ALSO URGE YOU NOT TO LET ANY SORT OF DISSENSION BECOME HEATED OR PROLONGED.

How Long to Continue with Family Hour

This is an easy one. How long should family hour continue on? Until the hour is up, of course! Seriously now, the question of *when* your family ultimately discontinues holding weekly sessions is closely tied into *why* you are calling it a day. First let's check out a few comments that sound typical for parents who make an early exit from their family hour adventure.

Questionable reasons for discontinuing family hour

- ☐ It was fun at first, but the novelty seems to have worn off.
- ☐ Dragging the kids to the sessions has been a big hassle.
- ☐ It soon became clear that no one was going to cooperate.
- ☐ All the kids did was argue and out-shout each other.
- ☐ After four sessions, nobody showed signs of opening up.
- ☐ We thought the children's behavior would improve. Hah!
- ☐ I got stuck with all the work, and I got zero appreciation.
- ☐ All hell broke loose once; I won't go through that again.
- ☐ My teenagers became icier than ever after we started.
- ☐ My hubby went AWOL, even after I pleaded and begged.
- ☐ The kids got resentful over missing favorite T.V. shows.
- ☐ We began getting into a rut. I even nodded off once.
- ☐ I started seeing a side of myself that I don't like at all.
- ☐ We had to cancel a meeting; then we forgot all about it.
- ☐ Our schedules are full now. Should we meet at 2 AM?
- ☐ Roy's dog died, and he wouldn't talk. That was it for us.
- ☐ We returned from vacation and got busy with other things.
- ☐ Our marital woes burst open. The kids don't need that.
- ☐ Our kids are young, and we couldn't get them to sit still.
- ☐ The first meeting felt awkward; I think that was a sign.
- ☐ I tried discussing family unity; then they started to laugh.

All family hour leaders in due time fold up their tents (that is, if they have been holding meetings in the back yard) and come to a (hopefully) fond farewell. For some, it may happen when the nest empties out, and others may wind things down after watching communication sharply improve and noticing an upsurge in family unity. Then they may gather together just for specific reasons; or they may decide not to meet formally at all.

Still other parent leaders may decide to pull the plug after one or two sessions, convincing themselves that family hour just makes things worse, is not worth the bother, or simply isn't meant to be for their families. But in fact, the only folks unsuited for family hour leadership are those not suited for parenthood in the first place--and thus not suited to be even a trifle curious about family hour. Then again, you might be a top-drawer parent, **but you just don't want to do it!** Fine, forget about family hour, and don't feel any regret over it. Then too, you might be undertaking family hour because **you feel like you're supposed to.** That will never work, so see if you can get the "supposed to" over to a "want to." Let's leave this subject with the following idea: if, for whatever reasons, you decide not to go ahead with family hour, that doesn't indicate that you have to close the book and put it away. You still may find it useful in a variety of ways. Read on.

The just listed dubious reasons for discontinuing your family hour sessions contain several examples of three enormous pitfalls facing many family hour leaders: **frustration, avoidance,** and **weakness of commitment.** The first two might get resolved in a variety of ways, such as by lowering your expectations, easing off pressure on yourself, quickly and decisively squashing disruptive behavior, letting certain small dramas play themselves out, and by shifting directions if your chosen family hour style doesn't pan out as you had expected. These issues and other similar ones will be addressed throughout the chapters.

We met for a few weeks, and then we skipped one session because of a family emergency. We failed to reschedule right away, and as we all had lots of projects on our plates, that was the end of it for us. I brought the question up again later, but it seemed like too much trouble to get started all over again. I do have some regrets, because those few meetings were interesting; but I won't deny that there were a few stressful moments as well.

Police officer, father of 3

A one-foot-in-the-door-and-one foot-out spirit of dedication on the part of parent leaders is the biggest threat to the viability of the family hour experience. For this reason, we urge you to carefully consider the following:

The three-month commitment

If your family hour project fizzles after a few weeks, it has hardly been afforded a reasonable trial. This is not unlike quitting law school after a month due to the intensive work and the paucity of ego satisfactions. What keeps law students plodding on, to be sure, is their vision of a rewarding future career. You earn neither degrees nor titles after a year or even more of family hour, but the rewards of improved communication and closeness among family members are greater than anything you might ever get from sitting in a classroom or performing on an athletic field.

It can take up to three months and possibly even more for your group to become a cohesive unit, for the family hour style(s) you have chosen to find smooth functioning, and for enhancement in family interactions to become noticeable. During this time it is crucial for you to keep the long-term benefits in your sights. Also, it will make the going easier if you keep your sessions less tedious and more fun-filled than beginning law school classes.

For the first several sessions we conducted family forums, and this helped us to come together as a group. Furthermore, it got us to open up some fascinating and informative discussion, like the effect of advertising on youthful psyches, theories about the afterlife, and the merits of one chocolate candy over another. We still use this format, but we now do lots of other things too. Oh, and we never let it get too deadly serious.

School psychologist, mother
of 3 multi-cultural adoptees

CHAPTER FIVE

PREPARING YOURSELF FOR

THE LEADERSHIP ROLE

We all sat down for our first meeting, and I started to explain as well as I could as to the purpose for doing this. I had prepared pretty well, or at least I thought so. Then I noticed that everybody looked really bored, so I made comments about it. Not a single person responded. More awkwardness followed, after which we agreed to adjourn early; and as you might imagine, I was not in the mood to re-schedule. How can I exercise leadership if no one has any interest in following?

Librarian, single mother of 4

We appear to have a huge love affair--actually more of an obsession--with high achievers who imprint themselves on our society. We gobble up the most insignificant details of their lives and careers from magazine write-ups, books, movies, and television documentaries; we idolize them with larger-than-life statues; and we name our schools, boulevards, and offspring after them. Then again, our adulation isn't inspired merely by people who have led exemplary lives, since we seem equally fascinated over the biographies of ruthless crime lords and bloodthirsty tyrants.

Powerful leaders and innovators come in every shape and size, and the following list attempts to outline very briefly some of the more important categories.

A Sampler of Society's High-Profile Leaders

☐ Explorers--fashioning new frontiers out of the wilderness.
☐ Military heroes--brave of heart and brilliant of strategies.
☐ Political revolutionaries--rallying people against tyranny.
☐ Religious leaders--preaching about the righteous path.
☐ Philosophers and poets--wise words on life and love.
☐ Royalty--attended by fawning servants in splendid castles.
☐ Mentors, tutors, and coaches--advocates of excellence.
☐ Corporate executives--ruling over big-money empires.
☐ Stars of entertainment--basking in starry-eyed adulation.
☐ Therapists and gurus--exorcising demons of self-defeat.
☐ Political bigwigs--masters of governmental chess games.
☐ Martyrs--self-sacrificing in service to the oppressed.
☐ Underworld and gang leaders--cunning and intimidating.
☐ Inventors and scientists--crafting comfort and efficiency.
☐ Cult leaders--pied pipers inspiring over-the-cliff loyalty.
☐ Motivational experts--orchestrating symphonies of success.

This list covers a broad spectrum of movers and shakers. Which type of leader, then, is the most influential of them all? As a matter of fact, the pinnacle leadership position will not be found in this listing. Further, should a panel of experts be asked to choose their one hundred most significant categories of leadership, it may not get mentioned on that list either. The most powerful among all leaders are those who appear to get the least glory of all--women and men who are entrusted with the nurturing and the guidance of children throughout their formative years. And no, our elevation of the parenting role to the peak of importance has nothing to do with the sheer number of parents compared to other leaders. Each individual parent has more inherent power over others' lives than all other leaders in the world, no matter how famous.

In this chapter and all through the book we refer to those who nurture and guide young children as "parents;" and it is true that our primary focus dwells on parents and youngsters who live under the same roof. But nurturing and guidance is by no means the exclusive province of the parents themselves. Foster parents must of course be considered in the parental capacity; and child care workers and teachers, especially those in the lower grades, do a great amount of the nurturing and guidance of young ones in our present-day society.

So if you household executive officers are the most powerful among all leaders, how come you don't receive more acclaim? And why does a parent's work get in the spotlight for the most part only when problems abound or heinous acts get committed?

Why Parents Get Little Recognition as Leaders

- ☐ Producing offspring requires no out-of-the-ordinary skills.
- ☐ The raising of children is routinely done by most adults.
- ☐ One need not "rise to the top" in order to qualify as parent.
- ☐ Parenthood doesn't require titles, oratory, or salesmanship.
- ☐ Large numbers of parents get started purely by accident.
- ☐ Parents have at most a few "followers" under their wing.
- ☐ For many, parenting "happens" while they do other things.
- ☐ Women--undervalued as leaders--are chief child-raisers.
- ☐ No formal standards measure parenting excellence.
- ☐ Bartenders,hairdressers, etc, are parenting "experts."
- ☐ Even the best parents at times confess to feeling clueless.

☐ Genes, fate, etc, often get the credit for parents' work.

☐ Foster parents and child-care workers live at poverty level.

☐ Kindergarten teachers are paid far less than professors.

☐ Parenting classes are mandated "after the horse is stolen."

☐ Highly successful parents are often said to be "really lucky."

☐ There are no awards for meritorious service in child-rearing.

☐ Stay-at-home moms are "homemakers," not "child-raisers."

☐ Even top-notch parents get bad-mouthed by their offspring.

☐ Prolonged custody disputes stain the parenting image.

☐ Parents get headlines mostly for their unconscionable acts.

☐ "What do you do?" seldom gets the response "I'm a parent"

☐ Parents' "grads" seldom say "thank you" until years later.

Let us now look at reasons why parents qualify as the most potent of society's leaders--even more powerful than the conquerors, pioneers, and political revolutionaries who helped in shaping the evolution of our civilization.

PARENT: The Acme Among Leadership Positions

Leadership in academic and real-world achievements

Those who achieve greatness in the classroom and in the "outside world" quite often get spurred into action by key notables in their lives--e.g., inspirational teachers and tutors, parent-figure mentors, high-octane spouses, or slave-driving coaches. Furthermore, many give credit for their success to folks they have never met, like spellbinding public speakers and compelling writers. But then again, super-sized achievers have all had parental imprinting that in all sorts of ways paved the way for subsequent influences. Indeed, even an unhappy childhood experience can be a motivator toward future success.

Academic achievement and status notwithstanding, child-raisers are hands down the most powerful teachers of all, giving us basic language instruction and an encyclopedia of information about the world around. But some parents go far, far beyond the basics as they mold their little ones from the earliest age into becoming math whizzes, musical prodigies, and budding stars in the worlds of sports and entertainment. Then again, a good many of these potential talents do get tutored by experts in their chosen field, but it is almost always their parents who supply the motivation and the guidance toward excellence in the first place.

The role of leadership in shaping character and values

Laboring under adverse conditions, hard-driven indigenous workers can turn long-time delinquents into caring individuals who go on to help others in a similar fashion. And revivalist preachers, calling forth the power of The Almighty, can in one instant become instruments for changing con artists and profligates into pillars of society. The reverse, unfortunately, also seems to be the case, as anti-social gang leaders can seduce even apparently level-headed youngsters far away from the straight-and-narrow.

The well-intentioned, alarmed over modern young people's being so self-absorbed and rebellious, urge parents to "teach children right from wrong." This is all too simplistic. Discussing moral issues with children is fine, but their character is molded mainly by their parents' own rectitude (or lack of it) and by the strength and functionality of family relationships. Parents may have personality quirks and they might goof up quite a bit, but if their kindly nature and sincere efforts over the years engender close, loving familial bonds, their little ones will most likely become solid citizens. Then again, we all hear stories of children from "wonderful" homes who fall under the spell of ne'er-do-well gang leaders. Yet a closer look might reveal some hidden character flaws in their parents or might uncover parent-youth relationships contaminated by intimidation, turbulence, overprotectiveness, or emotional distance.

Duration of the leadership role

The impact created by certain high-profile types tends to be fleeting--rock stars, latest-fad hucksters, and action heroes on the screen serving as witness to this. The influence of cult leaders and heads of state can remain for quite a time, but the exploits of frontier-expanding pioneers and political revolutionaries extend a lot farther. They can leave a profound imprint on an entire society for generations or even centuries.

It may seem at an initial glance that parental influences are short-lived in comparison with those of history-changing explorers and scientific whizzes. After all, parents and children--while child-rearing is actually in progress--live together under the same roof for only twenty years or so. Yet parents cast a really long shadow over their grown children, for better or for worse, even after having shed their mortal coil. What is more, the parental influence shows up in grandchildren and great-grandchildren. And your children's influence over their own offspring likewise goes way down the line. Then moving back the other way, we are all strongly influenced by great-grandparents we most likely have never even heard of. And those great-grandparents were strongly influenced by those coming before them. So parental imprints are not just long lasting, but are in a certain sense unending.

Breadth of the leadership role

Mohammed, Jesus, Galileo, Curie, Edison, Mandela, Joan of Arc, the Dalai Lama--the list of world-famous leaders is lengthy indeed. Their scientific breakthroughs, inspirational shepherding, and insights into the human condition have influenced the lives of countless peoples. Then too, that publicity-shy shaper of the first wheel surely helped in shaping the course of human history. Yes indeed, all of society's headliners and innovators combined have had an astounding impact on every aspect of our lives.

We have now seen how parental influences get passed on down through the generations in an unending cycle. But they also spread outward--way, way outward. Your stamp appears not only in your offspring's dealings with their own children, but also in your offspring's dealings with their spouses, friends, students, etc. Also take into account that every human on the face of the planet, all of society's movers and shakers included, have been deeply imprinted by parental influences. This includes genetic makeup, amount and quality of nurturing, molding of character, and offering a foundation for beliefs systems, values, and interests. There is in truth precious little in early childhood that sees no parental imprint on it. Yes, society's megastars have had gigantic influences on our day-to-day existence, yet the rippling-out effect of parents' influence--individually and en masse--is a lot greater by comparison.

Yes parents--especially those of you who never create any headlines--are the most powerfully influential of all leaders. But in addition to your power, you all exercise a leadership which is truly unique in its complexity. Indeed, parent-children relationships, so routinely taken for granted and so often made to appear trivial, still puzzle experts despite all their studies.

PARENT: The Most Complex Leadership Position

Onset and early stages of leader-follower relationships

Followers of venerated gurus and political revolutionaries, most of whom have no direct link-ups with the top-dogs, join these movements voluntarily and remain on board as long as their zeal continues to burn on. Working under corporate executives, on the other hand, usually involves one's search after a piece of the action; and those in training under high-intensity coaches and tutors are seeking, through the sweat and struggle, headlines that tout their stellar performances. Then again, whenever these disciples or trainees get over-stressed, suffer disillusionment, or fall victim to the axe, they as a rule head for the exits without any delay; and the brightly-shining leader-follower involvement soon goes on to fade gradually from memory.

The parent-offspring relationship is unique insofar as the "followers" start out totally dependent, their very survival hinging on the nurturing and protection they receive in the earliest stages. And the first year of one's life, as the experts all concur, is *by far* the most important one in everybody's existence--adult happiness being heavily influenced by one's experiences in the parents' arms or under their watchful care. Toddlers mimic your every word and mannerism, and soak up information and opinions from you much more readily than do seriously brain-washed cult members in the presence of their charismatic leaders. So with no need for extraordinary creativity or talents, you as devoted parents provide the most intense early-life relationship on the planet. No other influence later on can ever come close.

Long-term course of leader-follower relationships

Some remain faithful to leaders for the length of their employment or training, as in the case with professional athletes and art students. Political constituents and church members remain in the flock until they start hearing dissonant messages; and twelve-steppers stay in step with the program until they no long feel they are getting the help they need. So people follow leaders for lots of reasons--e.g., to bask in the glow of stardom, to get psychological healing, to reach nirvana, to climb up the ladder of success, to feel beloved and appreciated, or to get out from under the pressure of having to make their own decisions.

The parent-child relationship in some sense resembles the tutorial bond. Just as the expertly tutored advance in competence as they prepare for doing battle in their chosen fields, young ones mature through the years in their preparation for a satisfying, self-reliant life. But tutors wait for students to show up and teach in a narrow field of specialization; whereas *you* start your work even before a newborn exits from the womb, and then you remain as overseer of youthful development in every area--physical, psychological, social, spiritual, and academic. One crucial aspect of your parental role is the gradual diminution of control over the years, as youngsters attain ever-greater self-determination as time passes. Another important key: you shoulder legal and financial liability for your young charges all through the years of growing up; whereas tutors, therapists, spiritual gurus, and military commanders carry few if any of these burdens.

Later stages and termination of leader-follower relationships

People begin breaking away from a mentor, common-purpose group, or organization for a variety of reasons. They might come to the end of their period of training or apprenticeship, grow bored and move on to another venue, watch their guru fall off the pedestal, relocate or find their leader doing likewise, feel pleased over having obtained what they needed, feel resentment over not having gotten their needs met, or see their once powerful organization crumbling into little pieces. So once the leader-follower relationship wraps up, in most cases it sooner or later becomes just a distant memory.

Like their counterparts in society, young folks break away from their parents' jurisdiction for reasons both sound and shaky. The positive circumstances might involve marriage, university, the military, a religious order, beginning a career, or moving out into an apartment. In contrast, others run off in order to escape abusive or contentious family situations, or to naively seek a "nirvana." Yet whatever the circumstance, adolescents all seem to have it in their minds to establish themselves as self-sufficient young adults. The breaking-off process, as we all know, can be a messy one. Some repeatedly threaten to leave, finally depart, and then come back-- in some cases repeatedly. Others make a clean beak, but later on return in the wake of a failed relationship, money problems, or an emotional crisis. Still others go and stay gone; but some time later get to spend more quality time with their parents, in phone chats and visits, than they did while growing up.

The post-leadership period

When long-timers say good-bye to a sizable organization, like a huge spiritual center or a corporation, their departure only rarely brings tears to the eyes of those running the show. This is because the bigwigs in most cases were not even aware of their presence in the first place. And wherever the leader-follower relationship has been a personalized one, as in the case of a mentor or coach, sporadic social contacts or even a warm friendship may keep them feeling bonded. However, in most cases the wrapping up of the mentorship period results in everybody's going their own separate ways.

On the household front, the termination of the apprenticeship period simply indicates that the relationship between you and your offspring takes different directions. Some young adults never completely let loose of their dependent status, some parents find a variety of subtle or blatant methods of continuing to supervise, the relationship for others evolves primarily into a strong friendship, it becomes for others a no-cease-fire-allowed battleground, and in a number of homes the roles eventually reverse when infirm parents get taken care of by their caring adult offspring. But whatever the circumstances might be in each family, the fact is that the parent-child bond is the only leader-follower relationship that starts off at the very beginning and continues on for a lifetime.

Indeed, parents have both the most powerful and complex leadership position in the world, whether or not they recognize it consciously. Now if their leadership role is such a lofty one, why then do so many modern-day parents conclude that the only leading going on in their households is their youngsters' leading *them*--on a wild goose chase?

A review of the three opening chapters will uncover some clues to this puzzle. A century or more ago parents felt more like leaders because they took the lead in many family-together activities, like planting and harvesting crops; tending to meat-providing and working animals; storing canned and dried goods and preparing meals; spinning, weaving, knitting, and sewing; and operating a family-run trade. Then in their spare hours, families often played together in recreational adventures led by parents or perhaps the older children. In addition, parents were as a rule in the forefront of conversations taking place at the supper table, by the fireplace, and on the front porch.

In our modern-day urban and suburban lives, much family-together activity is long-gone, and in its wake are interactions offering few chances for close parent-child sharing. Among parents' household roles today you might find: cook and server for on-the-move meals, scheduling coordinator, chore taskmaster, chauffeur, homework hounder, clock-watcher and gatekeeper for youngsters' out-of-house activities, physical and emotional first-aid attendant, guardian of the purse-strings, referee in disputes, and warden for those "serving time" in house arrest. This gives parents a largely scatter-gun type of leadership rather than the genuinely satisfying kind that emerges as a result of toiling and recreating together in a more substantive way.

You can get your law school degree, but if you devote little time to your practice, it will be difficult for you to get that "attorney feeling" in your bones. Raising children is no different. You might pour through lots of books and attend classes on child rearing, but your sense of running the show at home could flounder if you and your young charges suffer from a shortage of quality time together. Mentors, coaches, and tutors hone their leadership skills by working intensively with their proteges; and it is the same for parenting leadership, although your family interaction needn't be so intense. In Chapter 2 we saw a variety of projects families can do together on weekends, holidays, and in their spare time; but our chief focus in the book has been and shall continue to be on the weekly family meeting, or family hour.

> *I'm the team leader at work, so taking charge of our family hour group seemed natural. But working to keep everybody on the same page was a big challenge. Then when Reynard started showing me my missteps, I got sarcastic and asked him if he could do better. He's pretty laid back, so I was surprised to see how successful he became. I tried to be his assistant, but that didn't work out well, so we finally agreed to alternate the weeks of leadership. I must admit that when his turn comes, I do get a chance to sit back and relax--and relaxing is good for me. Now if I can only find more time to relax at work.*
>
> *Customer relations in a public utility*

Family Hour: The Ultimate Leadership Experience

Family hour helps in solving the modern-day parent leadership dilemma for two reasons. First, spending high-quality time together enhances parents' leadership position no matter how that time is used; and what is more, organizing and running the weekly sessions is a can't-be-beat exercise in leadership. Leadership in family hour calls for no advanced degrees and no charisma; you simply make ordinary, practical decisions, many of which may be by trial-and-error. Make a few mistakes, and then learn a thing or two from it. Now for you parents feeling antsy about being hosts of the family hour show, stay relaxed and keep in mind that it's all part of an exciting learning experience. So go and get yourself in the swim. You might learn a few new strokes along the way; and who knows, you might even turn into a fish!

The following rank highly among family hour's major leadership chores. Some of them should call for scant or no attention from you as you run your sessions, while others that are not even mentioned below will undoubtedly crop up at one time or another. Don't try to memorize all of these items before you start, but rather keep this list handy to serve as a reference guide when challenging situations arise.

Leadership Tasks for Family Hour Leaders

- ☐ Explain family hour to participants and answer questions.
- ☐ Work out physical arrangements for weekly meetings.
- ☐ Broker compromises regarding a time and place to meet.
- ☐ Be firm but uncoercive in dealing with reluctant attendees.
- ☐ Get group help relating to family hour style and content.
- ☐ Be flexible but decisive as to starting and ending times.
- ☐ Be *very prompt* about rescheduling canceled sessions.
- ☐ Get periodic feedback about reactions to the sessions.
- ☐ Keep the talk from wandering or getting dead-ended.
- ☐ Put a quick stop to private, whispered conversations.
- ☐ Keep hostile or impish pairs separated to avoid trouble.

❏ Don't let early-stages resistance get you discouraged.

❏ Quickly shift gears to nip boredom or chaos in the bud.

❏ Spontaneous expression is O.K.; harassment is not.

❏ Give liberal doses of praise, encouragement, and support.

❏ Get reactions from participants who seem visibly upset.

❏ Get group help re: your own upset feelings or gloominess.

❏ Practice relaxing when others are holding the reins.

❏ Delegate certain chores, especially if you feel overloaded.

❏ Encourage maturing youngsters to begin taking leadership.

❏ Get derailed discussion moving again. (See next chapter.)

❏ Learn to wear two hats comfortably. (See next paragraph.)

Wearing Two Hats as Family Hour Leaders

Wearing two hats in a group setting means both operating the agenda and, whenever feasible, also being a regular member of the group. Trained psychotherapists in almost every case wear only the leadership hat because they are designated as the givers and not the receivers of the help--and this permits them to keep a steady eye on group interactions. Seminar and training program leaders are one-hatters because they teach and train from start to finish. Facilitators of twelve-step and support groups, on the other hand, are more apt to take on both roles, especially when they are regular members who get rotated into chairing meetings.

As family hour parents you will put on both leadership and group-member hats. You are, after all, household members; and the sessions are neither group therapy nor exclusively vehicles for teaching and training. So while you need to juggle two roles, you assume less of a burden than do therapists and seminar leaders. And yes, you wear both hats outside of family hour as well. One minute you might be wrestling with a small one or getting schooled by a teen at your computer; then in a flash you might find yourself grappling with a sibling battle-royal or hounding a young scholar to prepare for the scholastic experience.

Going back and forth between leader and non-leader roles, then, is something you do each day. In your family hour group you simply remain "one of the gang" until a need for leadership arises. Then when your directorial duties are over with, you revert back to being a regular. But be cautioned--if you try to be all things to all people, the pressure on you will mount, and your effectiveness will surely diminish. So just relax and slide into the flow of the interaction as much as the circumstances allow.

While we are on the subject of making things easier, let us look into some methods for easing your load during the sessions. This calls for your steering clear of certain chores that others may expect you to do, or that you think you ought to latch onto. Such "shirking" will save you lots of grief, and will free you up for being helpful in truly constructive ways.

Tasks To Be Shunned by Family Hour Leaders

Prodding group members into talking or participating

You might find yourself applying pressure on little ones to attend to begin with; but once the session gets underway, all pressuring should stop. Encouragement is great; but if you fail to back away soon, especially when the tight-lipped ones have their heels dug in, you will in most cases find the resistance escalating. So it is not your job to get others to speak up, but it is your job to figure out when to back off.

Judging as to a group member's guilt or innocence

Your "victimized" little ones so often scurry to you seeking sympathy and justice. Then comes your nearly impossible task of determining who *really* threw the first elbow or epithet. This quandary, to be sure, has no legitimate place in family hour, as assigning blame tends to complicate relationship issues far more than to resolve them. Refusing to play the blame game enables you and the others to engage in more constructive and enjoyable pursuits. What is more, your youngsters will make further and further gains in self-confidence and self-responsibility when they receive an attentive ear and some constructive feedback from others, and not when they are delivered "justice." This form of justice never truly resolves issues between family members, but only leads to more rounds of contentious behavior.

Solving other participants' problems

Some sessions might contain a problem-solving focus, but even when such help is sought out by pre-schoolers, you and their older siblings should limit yourselves, with rare exceptions, to the role of problem-solving assistants. Helpfulness in the group can assume many formats, like giving feedback, advice, support, and encouragement; but little ones always feel delighted about figuring out solutions for themselves, even when they endure a few small frustrations along the way. Self-reliance gets fine-tuned all during adolescence, but it cranks up well before youngsters even realize what the term means.

Coaxing dejected group members into feeling better

"There, there, don't cry" is in every case spoken with noble intentions; but this, unfortunately, is not really helpful. Observing youngsters or even a spouse get all weepy-eyed might feel unsettling, especially when you suspect you might have contributed to the problem. Talking with tearful ones about the issues may help the eyes dry up more quickly, and this is a more natural way for it to take shape. Weepy folks, even if they are slow to get started, in most cases wish to talk about their issues; and when they do this, they are apt to get straight to the point. On the other hand, those who sit somberly with crossed arms and pouty faces may prefer to suffer in silence; and if encouragement fails to break through their armor, prodding will leave them even more stubbornly entrenched in their self-pity. Ignoring them is the best approach.

Persuading others to agree with you or follow your wishes

Working your persuasive charms on other group members could well take up the entire hour each week--that is, for the relatively short duration that your family hour experience would go on! So if you feel a burning desire to engage in salesmanship, please do so outside of family hour. Your exercise of restraint during the meetings will in due time generate an abundant harvest of freely shared information and cooperative efforts from participants in the group--youngsters in particular. Keep in mind that everything you say in a thoughtful, well-intended manner is profoundly influential on young, impressionable minds.

Teaching youngsters "some things they ought to know"

If you are a professional workshop presenter or a training group leader, offering information and opinions is what you do the livelong day, and those in attendance need and expect it from you. But if you approach family hour this same way, your audience will likely react with groans, yawning, or even snores. You should instead strive to elicit everyone's input--tossing in your own as well-- on a variety of issues of mutual interest, as this will promote much needed give-and-take among group members.

Keeping everyone entertained so as to avoid dead spots

They say that professional stand-up comics learn from an early age to amuse those around them in order to overcome their own melancholy. Therefore, some might be tempted to develop a comedy routine as a means of averting "group depression." However, this takes buckets of energy (Ask any stand-up comic.), and leaves the group at risk in case you run out of material. The right answer for dead spots is to keep on experimenting with styles and content until you and others in the family troupe happen upon the winning formula; and to inquire into what is really on the minds of stony-faced participants. Jokes are optional.

Handing out consequences for misbehavior in the group

Punishment might be indicated on occasion for little ones, but there is no proper place for it in weekly family sessions. When disruptive behavior continues, and talking about it goes nowhere, exclusion from the session may be indicated. Is that just what the child wants, you inquire? Well, on the next occasion a family project arises that was planned in the meetings, that young offender may also get excluded--and the next time a big favor is requested, you may think twice about granting it. These measures might give a good lesson in cooperation. Once the punishment card is taken out of your deck, you will notice solutions over disruptive behavior emerging in other forms. (See later on in this chapter, in Chapters 6 and 8, and in the Help section.)

> *Our family meetings really got off to a shaky start. My wife spent most of her time fussing around trying to keep all the kids happy, and then I found myself worrying about her. The result was that we got precious little accomplished, and our sessions were more of a burden than a benefit to us. So we gave up the ghost. Some time later, however, we heard about classes they were giving, and that helped us quite a lot. Jeannie still has guilty feelings at times about sitting around doing nothing when one of our*

> *kids gets bent out of shape, but she settles down*
> *once I remind her of the need for the kids to work*
> *out their own feelings. I notice that she also seems*
> *a bit more relaxed around the house as well. Now*
> *we're working on getting our oldest girl to stop fret-*
> *ting in the sessions about the younger ones.*
>
>   *Property manager, dad of 5*

Earlier in the chapter we discussed personal qualities and talents that are not needed for success in family hour leadership--academic brilliance, a charismatic charm, organizational wizardry, and persuasive magnetism. Now let us look at how your outlook and approach to these sessions can help you get the most out of your leadership experience. And if you feel you are not naturally gifted in certain of these areas, any efforts you make towards improvement will help a great deal.

Qualities and Skills That Enhance Family Hour Leadership

A realistic outlook as to how family hour works

Everyone wants family hour to succeed, and your realistic attitude can help make it a reality. Youthful battlers will almost certainly see the group as an exciting new combat zone, family hour won't convert a still-waters spouse into a babbling brook, and marriage and parent-teen conflicts might prove stubbornly resistant to the group interaction. But family members' issues aside, excellent results are likely to emerge when sessions remain enjoyable and productive. So throw your energy into getting the communication flowing, and then prepare to be pleasantly surprised.

Keeping the agenda moving smoothly and efficiently

Any agenda can become discombobulated very quickly, as is the case with long-winded speeches, games of one-upmanship, wandering off the subject, persistent interruptions, etc. So as the discussion shepherd, you must keep vigilant. For example, when the first two news sharers take twenty minutes each instead of the allotted five, some won't get to share at all. It may help to explain and discuss your no-nonsense ground rules beforehand, and bear in mind that keeping your agenda running efficiently is in no way a sign of bossiness.

Keeping the talking and listening in reasonable balance

Public speaking courses arm you with the self-confidence needed for impressing and convincing your audience; and listener training shows you how to keep both your ears tuned in and to use questions and comments to get others to express themselves. As family hour head honchos, you should situate yourself somewhere in the middle. So while you cannot turn others into good listeners, you can keep them from dominating the discussion. Likewise, you cannot make others speak up and express their feelings, but you can nudge them in that direction by fashioning an atmosphere that is comfortable and conducive to openness.

Patience with the progress made by members of the group

Patience will serve you nicely throughout your family hour adventure, but nowhere more so than at the outset. Family members may resent having to forego a favorite activity, grumble over the strange feeling of a family-together scene, and quail over what the sessions might bring. But do not lapse into a semi-comatose state. While you will not want to cut short "pregnant" pauses that afford others' comments time to sink in, do not hesitate to replace awkward silences with a spark of structure. Also, resist squelching discord too quickly, as it can often lead to clearing the air; but plunge in the moment chaos rears its gruesome head. And catch yourself if you start wondering how much time this or that will take, as this is a sure sign that impatience is nipping at your heels. Of course the most insidious impatience of all is the kind you direct at yourself. So sit back, relax, kick off those heels, and let the world go on by--at least for a few precious moments.

Perseverance through the doldrums and rough spots

Many an exercise program gets scrapped after the first leg cramps or sore muscles; and family hour is vulnerable in precisely the same way. There are bound to be bad-news days, bad-scheduling days, and sessions where nothing seems to go right. This is an excellent time to check on how sturdy your commitment is for this project. Off-days also offer you an opportunity to think about loosening up or tightening the atmosphere, depending on your circumstances. It may also be a good time to review Chapter 4 and Help section material relevant to your situation. And please keep in mind that you are not expected to endure unending misery, but only to put up with a few trouble spots on the way to greater family harmony and unity--indeed a small price to pay.

Willingness to abandon failing tactics and to experiment

When people cling interminably to stress-riddled jobs and contentious marriages, they always have their reasons, however masochistic they might appear to be. But as family hour leaders you will never get yourselves into such a dilemma, because once trouble enters in and continues to hang on, your leadership days are surely numbered. This is most unfortunate, as there are endless possible formats for family hour, and the one most suitable for you might be just around the corner--if you persevere long enough to reach the corner. Then again, you needn't be at your wit's end in order to begin experimenting. You might want to try this at the first sign of trouble, or just because you want some variety.

Ability to see the humor--even if the joke's on you

Lots of situations don't seem so funny at the time, but then a year or so later we look back and get a few chuckles over them. Why should punch lines have to wait so long to be delivered? You can delight in family hour's foul-ups and laughable misunderstandings as they happen; appreciate your little rascals' silliness as long as it doesn't drown out the agenda; indulge yourself with harmless teasing of others in the group, and then be truly gracious when the laughs come at your expense. Then too, the agenda itself may be laced with outrageousness designed for tickling the funny bone in the form of joke fests, parodies, and the like.

Decisiveness and toughness while keeping a cool head

When youngsters are hurling insults back and forth, your gently telling them to stop it won't likely get the job done. Instead, you may need to stand right between them and keep interrupting until they finally get the picture. There are other ways of asserting your authority without coming unglued or threatening the offenders with dire consequences, and we cover this topic in Chapter 8 and in the Help section. What we need to emphasize at this juncture, however, is that the survival of your project might depend on your appropriate application of police powers as the situation demands. And if you are consistently firm as well as fair, you may even come to be known as "Officer Family-Friendly."

Our sessions started getting awfully routine, and I guess you would say we were in a rut. Our twelve-year-old kept on griping about feeling bored, so I asked if she wanted to lead the next session. She was hesitant at first, but then she agreed to do it. So we all ended up reading a chapter from a fairy tale book, and we had a discussion about it the fol-

lowing week. I felt a little silly, but it turned out O.K. That led us to deciding to have a book review once a month, and we took turns making the selections. And oh yes, our nine-year-old even got us to read a super-hero comic book. (The good guys win in the end.) What's really interesting is that our non-book-review sessions livened up noticeably as well.   .

Homemaker, mother of 3

We had been doing family hour time for about four months when Larry (7) and Laura (8) spoke up at the end of one session and told us that they wanted to do a project next time, and that it would be a big surprise. When the time arrived, they came into the room with some cans of soda, and said they would be conducting a burping contest. The other kids got all amused, but George and I respectfully declined to enter the contest. In truth, we were considering nixing the project altogether; but then we didn't see any harm in it, and it did seem like a way to channel their initiative. So the kids all had a big laugh, and the two ringleaders assured us that they well knew that this experience didn't give them license to go burping all over the house--or all over the neighbor-hood--whenever they pleased.

Mother of five

CHAPTER SIX

GUIDING AND MAINTAINING

THE FLOW OF DIALOGUE

My daughter and I communicate a good bit. Actually, though, I'm the one who does almost all of the communicating. I try really hard to get her to open up, but she mostly responds to me with one-word answers, and I realize she is not always telling me the truth. It seems like it was just yesterday that I could not get her to keep quiet. I wish I could turn back the clock, but as that is not possible, I wish I at least knew what happened between us. I hope we might get back some day to our former sense of closeness--even if it is after she goes away on her own. I hate crying myself to sleep.

Single mother of only child

Dialogue is straightforward, all-directions communication. What could be simpler? Yet in our everyday lives we see so many examples of this "simple" process going haywire. In politics and in the law, many cut-and-dried matters get tortured beyond recognition; and the more adept folks become at muddying up the waters, the more quickly they ascend on up the ladder. T.V. commercial writers are skilled at sincerity-dripping manipulation; bureaucrats interpret their regulations in fluent wordspeak; and academicians and scientists, who seldom entertain ulterior motives, tend to think and talk in a techno-jargon that a lot of us struggle to understand. Thus it is extremely important that our homes be fortresses of un-varnished, down-to-earth family-member communication.

We like the term "dialogue" as a single-word definition for free-flowing communication. This points to an honest exchange of words, whereas "talk," "conversation," "discussion," and "commu-nication" are large-umbrella terms that could well apply to a verbal mugging or a host of other language-oriented activities. There are a number of phrases that are an equivalent to "dialogue," such as "collaborative verbal interaction" and "spontaneous conversation;" but they become cumbersome when repeated over and over. And let us mention that spoken, electronically composed, and sign lan-guage all adhere to the same criteria in qualifying as dialogue.

As noted earlier in the book, the term "dialogue" shows up frequently in news about political summitry, labor negotiations; and other high-level dealings; but it is a stranger to the world of family relations, friendships, and workplace communications. Instead of describing a dialogue with a good friend, you are likely to mention talking openly and honestly, hashing out mutual concerns, or arriv-ing at the underlying issues. But why must ordinary folks use so many words to make the same point that wheeler-dealers do with the succinct term "dialogue?" So we have decided to simplify mat-ters. While phrases such as "free-flowing communication" are to be found throughout the chapters, the word "dialogue" gets the top billing from us because it is more concise.

The term "effective communication," now riding the crest of popularity regarding interaction in personal and business relation-ships, appears regularly in books, magazine articles, and self-bet-terment workshops. This dialogue-equivalent phrase, however, is a no-show in parent education circles. Yes, there are communication "scripts" being presented to parents nowadays for dealing with their youngsters over nitty-gritty issues. But prepared scripts tend to put a damper on spontaneity; and little ones, who are provided with no scripts of their own, tend to be adept at ad-lib speaking.

> *One time when we visited my brother's family, my five-year old asked his little cousin how come his mother was so ugly. This of course got back to my sister-in-law, and she got bent out of shape over it. My brother wouldn't discuss it, and his family has been cooler with us ever since. I often wish we had all been able to talk it through. Also, I feel bad that my boy might be blaming himself over the incident. He was simply being honest about how he felt, but since then he appears to have become more tactful. I've never said anything to Jordan about it, but I must agree that his aunt is no great beauty.*
>
> *Race track official, 4 kids*

Despite being left out of an "effective communication" line-up, parents and children these days manage to engage in a good deal of dialogue, as it is a natural way of relating. Yet few families begin to tap into dialogue's large potential. The scarcity of quality time available to modern families gets part of the blame; but there is lots more to this situation, as family counselors know very well. Whatever the issues for a family's seeking help, one factor often appears to head up this list--seriously dysfunctional communication. Again and again, family therapists keep steering household members toward discussing issues in a more plainspoken fashion. So wouldn't life be a great deal more pleasant if parents mastered the "talking cure" before outside intervention might get called upon to pull troubled families back from the brink?

You may choose to prepare questions and commentary in advance in order to prime the pump for family hour discussions, but you will discover that your sessions, even in tightly structured formats, will feature a great deal of spontaneous interaction. Then as you move forward you will discover that dialogue in no way at all threatens parental authority, as some people dread, but in truth strengthens it. For sure, you might have to on occasion exercise your authority as family hour leaders to keep the sessions running smoothly; but as dialogue builds up a head of steam, your need to use this authority will sharply decrease. It's amazing to note how agreeable youngsters can become when they feel comfortable in expressing themselves.

Yes, dialogue sounds almost too good to be true; but you well know it is true, and you already engage in it--lots of it. Your big task is to learn how to steer it successfully all through deeper waters. We shall examine dialogue from lots of angles, and the initial item on our agenda is to determine which elements go into its makeup, and which ones don't.

Basic Components of Dialogue

Reversibility of speaker and listener roles

This sounds simple enough--in a two-person dialogue, you take turns speaking and listening, right? No, not necessarily. Dialogue in some scenarios has one party holding forth and the other remaining silent all the while (except for a few perfunctory words here and there). The key here is the *potential* for reversing roles at a moment's notice. As a listener, you should feel free to speak out whenever you get the urge; and as a speaker, you should be prepared to put your tongue on hold if the other person opens up. So there is little potential for dialogue when talkers are determined to hog the podium by drowning others out or by interrupting them a lot. And dialogue is also a gone goose when listeners keep their lips tightly sealed, or when they feel too embarrassed, intimidated, or resentful to speak out freely.

Mutual respect among the discussants

In your estimation, your dialoguing partners may fall a few points short of a quorum on the I.Q. scale, and may suffer from a deficiency in psychological maturity, emotional stability, and ethical standards; but you must accept that they possess the exact same rights as you do for expressing themselves; and you must remain open to the possibility of learning something from the interaction. When people open a discussion with mutual respect, they are not likely to throw insults around or to engage in browbeating. Tactics such as these are designed to obtain a competitive advantage or to inflict verbal wounds. Nevertheless, some high-decibel, salty-language arguments might qualify as dialogue so long as people speak honestly, stick with the issues on the table, and refrain from subtle or blatant manipulation.

Listener-aware speaking

When at the podium in a jam-packed auditorium, you may notice only the most obvious listener reactions, such as laughter, coughing, or the sight of people racing for the exits. But with an audience of at most a few, you can make note of subtle reactions such as smiles, head nodding, restlessness, or glazed-eye looks. If it is to be a dialogue, you must be aware of listener reactions-- an occasional studious glance doing the job nicely. But if you go chattering on and on in the face of blank stares or other signs of boredom, you may as well be talking to the mirror. At least in that case you would be looking at someone who has some interest in the material. Our recommendation is that when your listeners dis-

play an obvious lack of interest, you might inquire about their reactions, or you might simply stop talking altogether.

Reflective listening

Paying careful attention to the words of others and identifying with their cause or plight can contribute greatly to the listening
process. Yet good listening also involves a reflective element, one
in which you ponder the meaning of what you hear. Then again, if
you are well acquainted with the other person, your task is made a
bit easier. You may not like a speaker's verbal inflection or choice
of words, but a general understanding of their meaning is crucial.
And if it's all Greek to you, the next step is to pose as many questions as needed until you see the light--that is, if you still care. But
should you feign understanding or employ your own biases or past
experiences to fill in the blanks, you will nip any reflective listening
in the bud. And with little or no reflective listening, dialogue is on
the skids before the rubber hits the road.

Flexibility of goals

When starting up a conversation, you may have a specific
goal in mind, like getting others to see your point of view, become
sympathetic, do your bidding, or stop annoying you. In the latter
scenario, you can simply insist that they cease--end of story. Yet
in many situations a discussion ensues, and in order for it to be a
dialogue, your goals must have some flexibility. When you listen
reflectively and remain listener-aware as you speak, your original
goal or position might remain exactly the same, but your approach
to it might soften up, and this might elevate your outlook and your
mood. Then too, an open exchange may uncover information that
works through misunderstandings; or it might help you in getting to
know your speaking partner better, and thus help forge a stronger

working relationship. In summary, if a dialogue leads to changes in your goals, they will without a doubt be changes for the better. How many times have you voluntarily changed certain goals--and then felt good about it--since leaving the parental nest? Another time or a few couldn't possibly hurt.

Above-board presentation

Being above board goes beyond merely telling the literal truth. Your agenda must also exclude misleading statements, hidden motives, and the purposeful withholding of crucial information. How, then, can anybody survive this way in the world of politics? Well, while our purview does not extend into the political arena, we hope that folks in every profession abide by this formula amongst family and friends. Giving voice to your thoughts openly and honestly, however, doesn't guarantee that those around you will follow suit. If others cannot or will not play fair, you might consider walking away or changing the subject. And if they keep on bending the rules, you might look around to find dialogue-minded folks. Being above board can at times make it harder for you to win a case, but it will bring you respect and trust. And having credibility is a much more satisfying experience than having word-game victories.

A minimum of distractions, especially in larger groups

Though stereotypically one-on-one, a dialogue can involve groups of almost any size, in which case all but one are listeners at any given moment. Yes, groups may have several discussions going on simultaneously, but each one constitutes a separate dialogue; and the more sizable the group, the less it is able to tolerate outside distractions. Dialogue in informal groups like those in school corridors and shopping malls must compete intensely with noises and interruptions from everywhere, and thus it tends to be more superficial. By contrast, dialogue tends to move into deeper waters wherever distractions are held down to a minimum, such as in formally structured groups like committee meetings, twelve-step groups, and family hour units.

Freedom from coercion

Persistent prying and pressuring are obviously dialogue squelchers, but the ultimate test of coerciveness rests in one's re-action to other people's tactics. So if sensitive types merely *feel* poked or prodded, then the action takers, regardless of their inten-tion, should quickly back away. When shrinking-violet children in family sessions are allowed space, they almost always open up sooner or later as they begin to feel isolated and to sense that it is safe to speak out. Then again, children themselves can be coer-cive with non-stop hounding; and it is imperative to deal with this quickly and quietly, so as to help dialogue get going again. Tight schedules can also be coercive in a way, so don't get too deeply into dialogue when the clock is ticking.

Freedom from fear of consequences

The fear of being penalized for what they say or don't say motivates children to choose their words carefully and to say what they believe others want to hear; so some family hour leaders will face a substantial challenge. At issue here are "crimes" of raised voices, sass, glaring looks, taboo language, etc.; and the punish-ments: getting yelled at; slaps to the face; and the loss of freedom, possessions, or privileges. Parents have a right to set down tough standards; but bear in mind that when youthful speech gets highly censored, dialogue in family sessions will stay on the shallow end of the pool. We recommend adopting the same standards for both children *and* adults regarding choice of words and loudness of the voice, and also for all aspects of body language. And remember, freedom of speech for young ones does *not* mean freedom to run roughshod over parental authority. (See just ahead.)

Freedom to exit the discussion at any time

It is indeed frustrating to watch your discussion compadre suddenly clam up or storm out of the room just as you were arriving at the crux of an issue. Now it is natural for you to plead for a resumption of your talk, but it is unwise to resort to hounding. Just as all dialogue starts voluntarily, it must end that way too. Keep in mind that discussions suddenly cut short at the pinnacle of emotion may oftentimes get resumed later when cooler heads prevail. However, this will not likely be the case for those suffering from old yet still tender emotional wounds. In such a situation, the wisest course for you might be to steer your conversation away from the minefield and into a less sensitive area.

These concepts cover much of the heart and soul of dialogue, but there is yet one more element that holds special importance. We refer to it as:

The Golden Rule of Dialogue

"SPEAK UNTO OTHERS AS YOU WOULD HAVE THEM SPEAK UNTO YOU"

The much quoted "Do Unto Others" calls upon you to practice kindness, patience, understanding, generosity, tolerance, forgiveness, and other such virtues; and not to wait for people to "do unto you" first. However, while "Do Unto Others" involves words and acts, the Golden Rule of Dialogue refers to verbal exchanges only. Accordingly, if you are convinced you merit an attentive ear for your verbal outpourings as well as tolerance for your unavoidable cranky moods, then you should treat others the same way--fully aware that they might not return the favor. The main idea is that talking to people in a kindly manner is not only a proper thing to do, but should also be seen as its own reward.

"Do Unto Others" is mostly concerned with the adult-adult arena, but the "Speak Unto Others" formula aims at how all family members interact. However, since you maintain responsibility for and authority over youngsters, doesn't that give you the need and right to a more lofty standing regarding expression? First consider this. As you enforce household law, shouldn't you be as kindly as possible? Now children may sometimes get you frustrated, thus raising your voice is natural. But your children get frustrated with you too, regardless of who is right or wrong; so it is just natural for them to raise their voices as well. In fact, if they start smothering their feelings regularly from the toddler stage, they become prime candidates later on for problems such as depression, destructiveness, risky behavior, and substance abuse.

Since nobody is born with the Golden Rule of Dialogue imprinted in the genes, doesn't that give an enormous disadvantage to "Speak Unto Others" parents? Well, starting out life powerless, the first tools we find for getting our way are pressure and manipulation. Your challenge as parents is to sift through all the tactics to determine what you are able and willing to deliver. And if you do this in a fair-minded way, you will be richly rewarded. Remember that youthful character is largely molded by an adult example. So young ones raised with the Golden Rule of Dialogue will very likely follow in the parents' footsteps. If you want your children to show you respect--and true respect cannot be demanded--be respectful to them consistently. Results may not arrive immediately, but they will show up according to each youngster's internal "schedule" for maturation. The same formula holds true for expecting little ones to be straight-arrow honest, kindly, willing to listen, open for compromising, and of sound character in other respects.

Rest assured that the Golden Rule of Dialogue poses no threat whatsoever to your parental authority. From our respective counseling practices we have witnessed youngsters insulting and defying parents, and doing as they pleased; but parental kindness has never been a factor in the problem. While such scenarios are complex in nature (See chapters 7, 8, and 9), they invariably get to a resolution when the parents learn to exercise true leadership, and when communication undergoes dramatic improvement. Indeed, we know of many families in which the parents observe the Golden Rule of Dialogue and find their authority enhanced rather than compromised.

Let us emphasize here that the Golden Rule of Dialogue is intended to be a guiding tenet, not a straightjacket for parents. So do your level best and don't worry over goof-ups. Just learn from them. And don't let "Speak Unto Others" get in the way of the exercise of your authority. For example, when you interrupt youthful haranguing and devious manipulation, you are in no way infringing on anybody's freedom of expression.

"Do Unto Others" has endured all through the ages, and its value lies in how we apply it to ourselves. But far too many folks use these words of wisdom to scold others about *their* behavior; and as they do so, they are in truth violating the rule themselves, as they undoubtedly would resent others lecturing them in a similar fashion. So we trust that you will give yourself a good pinch if you start admonishing youngsters over tarnishing the "Speak Unto Others" guideline with their chattering little tongues.

Parents who wholeheartedly embrace this Golden Rule of Dialogue out of choice, and not as a result of their feeling insecure or defensive, may seem to be hard to emulate. Yet to be a Golden

Rule parent, you need not apply for sainthood or enlightened master-hood. This rule leaves scads of room for personal foibles, silly mistakes, and grousing moods; and it asks only that you try to be understanding and tolerant with your youngsters when they show these same human shortcomings. Parents who pepper their little ones with harshness and impatience will eventually get the same thing in return, or possibly something even worse; and those who practice the Golden Rule of Dialogue will become rewarded both as parents and grandparents.

> *My dad is a wonderful person and he works really hard, but I just find it very hard to discuss anything with him. Every time we start getting into any subject, I have to get ready for his speech about how I should do this and that. My mom is totally the opposite, and I can open up to her. We don't always agree, and sometimes we even get mad with each other, but that's not a big problem. The main thing is that she listens to what I have to say, and cares about what I am thinking and feeling. When I get married I want to be just like her, but I would also like my husband to be at least a teensy bit more willing to listen. Is that asking for too much?*
>
> *16 year old in family of 6*

Dialogue comes in many shapes and sizes, and folks can slide into and out of it in a flash. All dialogue is productive in some way, whether in getting work accomplished, fostering understanding, bringing people closer together, or simply engaging in mutual pleasantries. Also keep in mind that you can always re-establish dialogue, again and again if need be, after it has become derailed. The following categories contain examples of how dialogue takes its place in daily life. And don't worry about which grouping a particular discussion might fall into--it very well could be several.

Forms of Dialogue

Small-talk dialogue

We all engage in superficial banter on occasion, such as with the neighbor we barely know, at cocktail parties, and during the check-out of groceries at the supermarket. To be sure small talk usually remains on safe ground with weather-related chatter, humorous observations, and the like. While such chit-chat might not seem worthy of being called "dialogue," it usually meets all of the criteria. Furthermore, it gives otherwise incompatible or unacquainted people something comfortable to discuss, and creates a pleasant atmosphere in situations that would otherwise feel awkward or boring during silences. Another term for such small talk would be "dialogue-lite."

Low-risk dialogue

While superficial banter is an obvious example of low-risk discussion, other forms of dialogue follow along a safe path--e.g., kindred-spirit political discussions, pep talks, teenage telephone gabfests, reminiscing about the way-back-when days, swapping yarns, and exchanges of encouragement and support. Compatibility seems to be a huge factor when people pair off together, and their presentations are likely to get sprinkled with agreeable terminology. Then again, congenial exchanges can turn sour if someone is in an ugly mood, misconstrues a statement, or touches an emotionally raw nerve. That's when dialogue has a warning sign--danger, that of entering into high-risk territory.

High-risk dialogue

As is the case with congenial interactions, the possibilities for contentious verbal exchanges are countless. We observe this in religious debates with true believers, discussions where a nasty mood or the spirit of one-upmanship prevails, the reopening of old emotional wounds, or any discussion with folks who love to press your buttons. Sure enough, dialogue hurtles over the track again and again in these situations. So the wisdom is that if frustrations begin to take over as you struggle to find any common ground for discussion, you might want to go take a walk instead--unless you simply delight in verbal chaos.

Marginal-quality dialogue

Dialogue can become shredded when you are half asleep, suffering a migraine, not especially in the mood for talking, in the company of a really tedious person, etc. However, second-class dialogue is not necessarily a bad thing. Sometimes it helps combat loneliness, and it can also give your brain a much-needed rest. Then again, certain folks possess only marginal listening skills and sensitivity, and seem unable to follow the parameters of dialogue for more than a few moments; and thus, marginal-quality dialogue, unfortunately, is the best they will ever experience.

High-quality dialogue

To qualify as premium quality, dialogue need not be highly productive; it need only contain all the key elements of a dialogue and follow all the rules. Then again, some talks accomplish a lot and therefore qualify as being of high caliber--even if they should suffer frequent dialogue mishaps along the way. We observe this in parent-child shouting matches in which a responsive chord gets struck at long last, and then core issues open up, perhaps accompanied by floods of tears. In fact, the very highest quality dialogue is achieved more often by your venturing out onto thin ice than by cautiously staying on shore. This is demonstrated in therapy and sensitivity groups, where foaming-at-the-mouth verbal combatants often become expertly guided toward making dramatic emotional breakthroughs. Then again, professional guidance is not always required for these breakthroughs, as we noted in the parent-child example earlier in the paragraph.

Low-distraction dialogue

Listener-aware speaking, flexible goals, and other central core factors contribute to dialogue's having high quality, but also of importance is its not having to compete with blaring television programs, people's scurrying around and about, and rush hour traffic. This works well in committee meetings, helping groups, and family hour sessions. But in non-family-hour houses, unfortunately, low distraction discussions are mostly the one-on-one variety, and are often on the unpleasant side--heated arguments, chore-oriented beefs, disciplinary dealings, emotional crises, health emergencies, etc. The pleasant discussions, often of the "How was your day?" variety, in many cases tend to be superficially chatty.

High-distraction dialogue

Dialogue can survive many kinds of distractions, but it may suffer some serious wounds in the process. And the bigger the interference, the more dialogue sputters. Obstacles strewn onto the path of serious conversations may be seen in automobiles driven in rush hour congestion, in crowded shopping malls, in school corridors, and in chats with folks who have shaky attention spans; but our abodes hold some of the biggest dialogue busters of all. T.V. sets, computers, plug-in and head-set radios, wired and cell telephones, other electronic devices, knocks at the front door, and the search by folks for refuge in newspapers, magazines, and books-- all of these work incessantly to garble or sidetrack dialogue.

Pseudo-dialogue

Some communications may sound like dialogue, but they in fact have bogus credentials. Spontaneous-sounding conversations between actors on stage--a different brand of dialogue--are carefully rehearsed; and ditto for some "off-the-cuff" banter during comedy routines. Con men practice all the proper things to say to soften someone up before they move in for the kill; and the victims might feel like they were dialoguing all the time, but later they find that they were merely puppets on the string. Still another example of pseudo dialogue is the back-and-forth between Mr. or Ms. Big-shot and the boot-lapping subordinate, the outcome of which is all too predictable.

Esoteric dialogue

Talking with critters large and small falls into this "strange" grouping. Figuring out the communication protocols can get complicated, but studies have yielded some fascinating results, such as that chimps--surprise, surprise--are much more straightforward and honest than most humans. And then there is communication with "the other side." Some folks to be sure feel that dialogue with spirit entities is so much hocus-pocus, but a good many swear by their contacts with intermediaries and beloved ones in the beyond, which is usually facilitated by sensitive mediums.

Dialogue is, as we have well noted, an entirely natural skill requiring no tutoring. Simply observe any playground where four and five-year-olds gab about anything and everything. Toddlers in truth, though unversed in great works of literature and in political dealings, are lots more comfortable with dialogue than are adults who regularly impose their will through manipulation or who build walls around themselves to avoid closeness. We have made reference here and there to dialogue roadblocks, and we will now dig deeper into the subject. Let us begin then with some of the most popular tactics that play a major role in disrupting, damaging, and destroying dialogue.

Some Serious Roadblocks to Dialogue

Intimidation

Tactics of intimidation include sneering, derisive laughter, finger-pointing or poking, eyeball-to-eyeball glowering, demeaning comments, sarcastic sniping, heavily-loaded questions, impatient demands for immediate responses, and veiled threats. Intimidating queries and comments are designed to put others in a trembly position, thus weakening their footing in the interaction. Without a doubt, dialogue gets obliterated in this process.

Pulling rank

"Because I'm your mother" is simpler to say than going into detail regarding opinions and decisions, and "Don't you dare talk to me like that" resorts to rank-pulling in order to squelch anger. In truth, all reminders to youngsters about parental status constitute rank-pulling, as little ones are well aware of who makes the decisions and pays the bills. Authority, higher status, and more extensive experience are some obvious justifications for pulling rank, a skill mastered by many a clever older sibling. The business-like exercise of authority by parents is no threat to dialogue, whereas frequent rank-pulling puts others on their guard--and puts spontaneous interaction on the ropes.

Interrogation

Grilling by the police under the proper circumstances is a universally accepted practice; and so is a grilling by parents, such as when delinquency enters the scene or when a child's physical or emotional well-being stands at risk. But gendarmes don't have to reside under the very same roof as their interrogated suspects, whereas parents do--and therein lies a serious danger. Frequent interrogations by parents, no matter how compelling might be the justification, leave young people evasive, and all this undermines mutual trust; thus the result is that these parents procure far less pertinent information about their charges than do family hour parents, whose effective information-gathering tool is a harmonious parent-child relationship.

Harassment

This is something of a catch-all category covering a multitude of sins; and prominent among the parents' "sins" are caustic nagging, outlandish although idle threats, the icy silent treatment, targeting emotional sore spots, predictions of failure, and chronic sarcasm. Worrisome and frustrated parents are among the worst culprits, and they seldom reflect on the damage such harassment might cause, especially when it takes place regularly. Whether or not a valid message is voiced, harried children tend to hear only the verbal onslaught. Then again, some children are also adept at harassment, but their sting is softer because their parents are not struggling through the formative years.

Sermonizing

Advice giving becomes sermonizing as soon as the person holding forth wanders away from listener-aware talking--that is, if it was ever in the picture to begin with. With glazed-over eyes in the audience, sermonizers find their words reduced to blather. Regular sermonizing by parents, although it generates less resentment than does intimidation and grilling, is nevertheless a waste of time as well as a monkey wrench thrown into the family communication machinery.

Non-stop talking

You can spot this when less than a nanosecond passes by between sentences, even when the speaker changes the subject. While viewed as cute in little ones, non-stop talking by grown-ups can be seriously off-putting. In family hour homes where someone has even a modest case of logorrhea, you might want to reach for a life preserver with the one-person-talks-at-a-time rule, with strict time limits imposed for each one's turn "at the podium."

The game of one-upmanship

Friendly competition can add some spice to the discussion, but when it goes to extremes, dialogue vaults into the trash heap. "Listening" now becomes almost exclusively a way of getting more ammunition for the following salvo of one-upmanship, and the only goal is to win, win, win--oodles of strategy and no sincerity. Verbal jousting might provide you a momentary flash of "victory," whereas dialogue lets everyone feel like a true winner.

Deceptive tactics

Some debaters present questionable facts, conceal crucial information, couch language so as to mislead listeners, hide true motives, portray themselves as victims, and go on the offensive or change the subject when placed on the hot seat--and all this spurs them on to victory! Political campaigners garner votes from tactics like these, but when people conduct themselves in this manner in the company of friends and family, they bring in a harvest of soap-opera confusion and mistrust, which gets passed right on down to the next generation.

Name calling and other insults

Even among the prim and proper, the urge to spew forth a vile epithet or two can on some occasions become irresistible; and no matter how smoothly dialogue is moving along, a sudden insult barrage can bring it to a screeching halt. Yelling out "moron!" is so easy, but it explains little and entices more epithets back into your face. On the other hand, spelling out to people exactly what they did to offend you (decibel level optional) requires effort as well as emotional restraint; but it brings you nice benefits, especially if the "culprit" is someone you care for and/or dwell with under the same roof. Among the benefits are respect from others and an opportunity to resolve issues of daily life. You can save your vitriol for the windbags and lowlifes you watch on the T.V. screen.

The game of accuse-and-defend

This is a favorite with all age groups. Like one-upmanship, accuse-and-defend can turn cut-throat competitive; but instead of aiming to prove themselves smarter, more powerful, or better connected, these jousters battle over right vs. wrong or guilt vs. innocence. And with no jury to determine a verdict, the object is to put opponents on the defensive, opposing-attorney fashion. However, since the listening is strategic rather than reflective, dialogue gets banished from the "courtroom."

Bailing out

While deceptive maneuvering helps you to avoid sensitive issues, bailing out actually guarantees your escape from the hot seat. Zipping up the lip is a favorite tactic used by small fry, while storming off the scene in dramatic style is a popular tactic among teens and adults. People bail out in order to get off the defensive, flee from emotional wounding, or obtain the upper hand by leaving others frustrated. Fortunately, those who bail out sometimes allow themselves to be coaxed into resuming a dialogue later on. Some degree of bailing out is also found in tactics such as turning everything into a joke and feigning ignorance.

Intellectual snobbery

Intellectual snobbery may involve rattling off facts and figures with self-assurance, which serves to dazzle others and also to fend off critical examination. Special-field experts dip into snobbery when they address lay persons in techno-jargon phrases and concepts, and bureaucrats do likewise in spewing out streams of word-speak. It goes with saying that professional experts should use down-to-earth language in their weekly family meetings.

Attention-getting clowning

Class clowns make weird faces and sounds, jump around, and mock the mannerisms of others; while their adult counterparts reel off jokes and snappy comebacks. When comedy flows naturally, it can enliven the group, whereas continuous goofing around gets to be disruptive, especially if the cut-ups get big laughs. Skillful clowns not only attract lots of attention, but they also get off the hook from anxiety-producing inquiry.

The need to please

Dyed-in-the-wool placaters can be even more disruptive of dialogue than rank pullers, intimidators, and name callers. These genial types censor their thoughts and feelings before they speak, and then replace them with words intended to charm or appease. Then when confronted, they tend to get defensive, which pushes them deeper into a need-to-please mode. Those with a mild case of "placate-itis" are more amenable to dialogue.

Helplessness

Helplessness is conveyed in many ways, such as through stammering, confusion, being lost for words, protestations of ignorance, and self-deprecatory comments. The chronically helpless typically have little potential for engaging in quality dialogue since they are poor listeners. Then again, those who act helpless only in sticky situations--and little ones are experts at this--can usually be coaxed out of the shadows when they gain consistent support and encouragement. And it is a distinct pleasure to watch children go from a helpless mode to a helpful one.

The above roadblocks to dialogue cover a good deal of the trouble-making spectrum; but unfortunately, there are many others around, some of which are most likely to put in an appearance at your weekly meetings. Combating them will surely require effort; but as is the case with everything else, your coming-to-the-rescue skills will improve as you gain more experience.

> *We emphasized at the outset that no unbecoming language would be tolerated in the sessions; and that was probably a mistake, as it appears to have put this idea into the children's heads. So pretty soon they started seeing how close they could get without committing a violation; and after some debate, we agreed that no "resembling" words were to be used. A favorite new concoction was "zoogley," and one of the children even lifted words from his action comic book. At times they giggle when they speak "new-cuss," and I'm afraid they might even get their schoolmates involved in it. In truth, however,it has been kind of fun, and it makes me realize how silly a lot of this good-word bad-word business can be.*
>
> *Personal trainer, mom to 5*

How Family Hour Leaders Nurture Dialogue

They guide the agenda

Your family hour leadership becomes enhanced when the agenda flows smoothly and continues to feature fascinating material; and this is made easier from your adopting a style in keeping with your family's comfort level. So no matter what gets onto your docket, you should be businesslike in guiding it through. This involves keeping the discussions on track, dealing firmly with disruptions, managing the time efficiently, giving everybody a chance to speak up, and being ready to shift gears when a project falls apart or when family members get restless and show signs of wanting to branch out into other directions.

They get the discussion started or restarted

You might need to jump-start the discussion as some sessions begin, particularly in family hour's earliest stages; but awkward silences can crop up at any time. You can get the ball rolling with questions, commentary, opinions, and requests for feedback; but if silences persist, you may very well need to switch to a style that depends less on free-flowing discussions. This could involve giving the taciturn one(s) chores to carry out or scheduling some fun activities. However, if the silences appear deafeningly sullen in nature, this can be a signal to begin looking into what might be the source of the problem; and if *everybody* looks sullen, a good guess might be that you need to make drastic changes--with help and feedback from others thrown in.

They rescue floundering dialogue

Round-in-circles arguing, high-flying accusations, and resounding epithets may wind down after gentle but firm reminders;

and if that produces no good result, decorum may return after you introduce anti-disruptive exercises like one-at-a-time talking, having a five second hiatus between speakers, and putting the kibosh on repetition and verbal wandering. You can find still further ideas in the Help section. In certain cases, however, you might want to let verbal combatants duke it out, especially if it looks like it might clear out the air. There may also be times when all rescue efforts fall flat. But don't worry, and don't allow yourself to get frustrated. A most important leadership quality is recognizing when a ship is starting to sink and must be abandoned.

They blow the whistle and start over

Successful business leaders are quick to toss out unworkable plans; and so are successful family hour leaders, who start all over when the agenda fails or the interaction keeps on going haywire. Agenda problems respond to continuous experimenting until you hit pay dirt. Be as creative as you wish. However, if behavior such as fighting, clowning, or chaos is an issue, you must get lots tougher and/or more structured--the one-at-a-time talking rule being a possible solution. You can use it strategically when dialogue cries out for rescuing, or you can use it across the board when the rescue efforts succeed only for a short while.

Family hour offers something for everybody; and the more you all keep on growing and changing individually and as a group, the more wonderful your adventures will become. So happy journeying and happy dialogue.

SECTION III

FAMILY HOUR TODAY
KEEPS DISASTER AWAY

CHAPTER SEVEN

THE PERILOUS PLOYS:
PRYING, PRESSURING, PREACHING,
AND POOR-ME-ISM

When I was growing up my mother was no kind of active disciplinarian, but she ruled us through her downtrodden persona. I clearly remember the routine she invariably went through when we let her down in some way--the sad expression; deep sighing; tapping the fingers; and on special occasions, a tear or two rolling down her face. It took several years of therapy for me to understand how her self-pity made me feel thoroughly guilty about anything and everything. Believe me, I often wish that she had taken us to the woodshed instead; that would have made things so much simpler. Recently we started family hour, and--aware that I occasionally lay guilt trips on them--I encouraged the kids to call me on it if they see it coming. Sometimes they get a bit over-zealous, and this can lead to a few arguments; but at least we are all talking. The only time I want to hear "poor mama" is with a big grin.

*Mother in family with both
natural and foster children*

In previous chapters we noted how dialogue is a perfectly natural means of communicating, but also how it lies vulnerable to an assortment of booby traps that suddenly jump out the moment we begin conversing. First we will look at various pitfalls that not only create havoc for parent-child dialogue, but also diminish parents' effectiveness as heads of the household. Then we will show how the nurturing, healing energy of dialogue helps members of a family wend their way safely around and through these pitfalls.

Prying, pressuring, and preaching by parents are forms of maneuvering that aim to influence youthful behavior; and they are as a rule carried out with the very best of intentions--i.e., to nudge children toward making choices deemed beneficial for them, and to steer them away from troublesome ones. These tactics in most cases are employed when the exercise of authority isn't appropriate, doesn't feel natural, or isn't successful. Poor-me-ism, on the other hand, is an indirect means of influencing youngsters' behavior for parents who, usually without any conscious design, portray themselves as real or potential victims with respect to youthful decision making. Let us now explore each of these perilous ploys in painstaking detail.

PRYING

Yes, I rummage through my 16 year old's personal things from time to time, and I believe that parents who really care about their kids should also do this. It isn't a problem, because he has no idea about my checking up. I would not do it, though, if he would speak to me more; but then again, I guess it's fairly normal for teenagers to keep their own council. Of course my mother didn't have to nose around after me because we lived in a small town, and life was a lot simpler then too. "Yes ma'am" and "no sir" were just about the first things I learned how to say, and I

never even tried to instill good manners in my two.
They would have seen it as a big joke. They'll learn
about the joys of raising children in a few years.

Single mother of 2

Prying's sole goal is to search for information of all types, and in our modern-day society this has become a huge business. Snooping by another name is, among other things, referred to as intelligence gathering, electronic surveillance, and undercover operations. And computer technology has transformed snooping into a fine art. Parental prying involves the quest for juicy details either through surreptitious or direct means, and without children's knowledge or without their having any real say in the matter. Conscientious parents do much surveillance with their toddlers, checking on them for their own safety and security, the protection of property, etc. This cannot be called prying, as little ones feel both loved and protected when parents are watching over them.

Forms of parental prying

Parental prying gets carried out either face-to-face or from behind the scenes. The face-to-face kind can be done manipulatively or in the form of interrogation. Behind-the-scenes prying is as a rule done by the parents themselves, although they also may get others to do the dirty work. And some up-front parents even let youngsters know about their conducting surveillance, although for obvious reasons, specific times and locations for the snooping don't get revealed. Here are some typical examples:

- ☐ Asking piercing questions in the face of clear resistance.
- ☐ Pumping siblings or friends for carefully guarded secrets.
- ☐ Using therapists to aid in ferreting out "the truth."
- ☐ Requiring youngsters to wear beepers.

❏ Making youngsters submit to drug or lie detector testing.

❏ Probing for information subtly, using disguised questions.

❏ Searching clothing, dressers, computers, trash cans, etc.

❏ Listening in on the phone, from behind closed doors, etc.

❏ Electronically bugging rooms or tapping telephones.

❏ Doing surveillance through stakeouts and/or tailing.

❏ Setting traps, like leaving money in temptation's way.

❏ Hiring private detectives to investigate or surveil.

Purposes of parental prying

Parents get motivated to seek out information for all kinds of reasons. They might get concerned when they see worrisome signs like moodiness, erratic behavior, growing secretiveness, unexplained absences, stealing, fibbing, or sudden academic failure. What is more, certain parents become fearful over what *could* go wrong, especially regarding youngsters who are handicapped, rebellious, naive, over-trusting, or who have a long history of making unwise choices. Then there are the parents who feel tempted to rummage around out of curiosity over what their uncommunicative young ones are up to "out there." Among parental concerns about youngsters are the following:

❏ Abuse of alcohol, nicotine, cocaine, heroin, meth, glue, etc.

❏ Membership in antisocial gangs or in secretive cults.

❏ Suicidal thinking or other self-destructive inclinations.

❏ Romances across racial, religious, ethnic, or class lines.

❏ Risky behavior, like driving recklessly or while impaired.

❏ Forbidden and/or unprotected sexual activity.

❏ School misbehavior, truancy, academic failure etc.

❏ Undue influence on the part of friends or romantic partners.

❏ Theft of money or property, or destructiveness of any kind.

❏ Attitudes or behaviors parents want to know more about.

❏ Activities youngsters are deemed too immature to handle.

Results of parental prying

Parents who are clever and thorough at probing can reap a bonanza of information, especially if youngsters are unsuspecting. But once parents get their data, how do they put it to constructive use? Occasional prying in response to a situation of serious concern may even turn out to be a life saver, but if it becomes regular, everybody loses. Ongoing detective work points to an already untrusting relationship, and then the prying by itself undermines trust even further. These parents might extract an "I'll mend my ways" promise, which is sure to be an empty one; and they might further cajole the waywards into treatment programs, but success rates in these cases are notoriously poor. These youngsters get so caught up in the power struggle with their parents that they lose the focus of what lies in their own best interest.

Morale and work production understandably take a big hit when office staff notice surveillance cameras glaring at them, and when they suspect a fellow worker of being a management mole; and government's "big brother" surveillance is detested by all. Yet regularly spied-upon youngsters find themselves in the same spot. When parents spy ad snoop as a routine, little ones become more and more secretive, which in turn engenders an ongoing cycle of stepped-up prying and ever-higher walls of self-protection.

Once parents become deeply absorbed in detective work, they may find it difficult to pull out, even after coming to realize the futility of it all. For one thing, the cat-and-mouse game can actually become habit-forming, lending satisfaction to whichever side has the upper hand at the moment. What is more, switching from communicating strategically to relating in an honest, open-ended manner is hard, since it requires one to be committed to breaking old habits and regaining mutual trust--a complex and often painful process. Then saddest of all, some parents fear that if they abandon their snooping, a large gulf will form between them and their offspring, making it appear to the world around them that they are not caregivers, but uncaring-givers.

But then again....

Detective work by parents is sometimes both justified and necessary. When there is very strong suspicion about delinquent behavior, an old-fashioned grilling might be in order; and when the evidence of substance abuse crops up, spying and stakeouts by normally non-snoopy parents might open up the way for a rescue operation. Then too, when teens borrow the family car or ride with friends, an occasional surveillance will confirm or ease fears about risky behavior. The privilege of teenage automobile use, after all, is based on an expectation of safe driving. Also, you may want to make an occasional phone call (land line) to check up on whether young people are in truth where they said they would be. What is more, it might be a good idea to present them with advance notice about planned checking-up--but not with your detailed schedule.

Dialogue vs. parental prying

There is no place for prying in family hour sessions; thus if detective work has gotten any foothold in your family's routine, the weekly meetings can become a corrective experience. This holds true even if your discussions hardly ever get into deep water. So if there is even a small communication gulf in your family, it will most surely shrivel up or disappear altogether after you decide to leave the detective work to the espionage professionals.

When dialogue pervades your home atmosphere, the urge to pry and spy may never grab you, as oodles of information about youthful activities will be served up to you on a platter. Spy-happy parents, by contrast, work hard to uncover data, but in the process discover little as to feelings, needs, and motives. Now family hour youngsters do hold onto their secrets, but then don't we all? Their hush-hush activities, however, will not likely result in big problems, as robust family communication offers to youngsters layers of protection against anti-social and self-harmful behavior such as rage, cruel streaks, gloominess, isolation, or any tendency to blindly follow charismatic outsiders. But should crises occur, these young folks usually look to their parents first in the effort to avert disaster. Then when a rare disaster does hit home, the outlook for youthful recovery tends to be on the optimistic side.

PRESSURING

We thought we were an ideal family, but then one day Kristin's best friend called up very concerned, informing us that Kristin had recently started talking vaguely about how dying sounded really peaceful, and stuff like that. First of all, I'm so happy that my daughter has such a terrific friend, and then I began to realize that we have been putting quite a load of pressure on her about her grades and her gymnastics training. Jake and I had even talked to her over the possibilities of her getting to the Olympic trials. We recently started family hour, and we've made a big effort to emphasize fun things and to get all the kids just to express themselves. Kristin has clearly brightened up, and she even talked recently as to how great it would be to get to the Olympic games. I was quite proud of myself for telling her that that sounded swell, but that she would have to consider all the pressure that goes with it.

*Woman way up the corporate ladder
but way down the parenting ladder.*

Youngsters need to be leaned on at times, but pressuring becomes a problem only when it continues on long after youthful resistance has gotten entrenched; when children fail to adopt their parents' views even after they buckle under to pressure; or when pressuring becomes a regular feature of parent-child interactions. Parental pressuring may be forceful, gentle, or subtle; and it has more nuances to it than little ones' pressuring, which for the most part consists of persistent pleading and hounding.

Forms of parental pressuring

Pressuring is commonly associated with short-term goals-- coaxing little ones into complying with rules, getting them ready for school or for bedtime, cajoling them into try new foods, nagging them about elbows on the table, etc. With this form of pressuring, the parents' expectations are usually very clear. The following tactics are among parents' favorites:

- ☐ Persistent nagging and reminding.
- ☐ Using incentives or rewards to melt dogged resistance.
- ☐ Making (usually) idle threats about the use of authority.
- ☐ Using authoritative tones in to gain youthful compliance.
- ☐ Shaming or embarrassing youngsters into giving in.
- ☐ Gaining compliance by making children feel guilty.
- ☐ Using scare tactics on little ones, such as the bogey man.

When parents lobby for down-the-road youthful choices or ones that have long-range implications, their tactics often tend to be subdued and at times even disguised. Typically, these parent-endorsed agendas relate to young people's choice of companions, romantic partners, career path, locality in which to live, etc. These parents typically resort to tactics such as:

❏ Glowing references to behavior they wish to encourage.

❏ Pessimistic talk about behavior they wish to discourage.

❏ Silence regarding choices they wish to discourage.

❏ Reacting with anger or hurt over disapproved behavior.

❏ Discussing future events as if they were already decided.

❏ Hints about how desired behavior will be rewarded.

Purposes of parental pressuring

While unscrupulous sorts might enjoy watching as others squirm and then succumb to intimidation, parents almost always engage in pressuring with high hopes that little ones will see the light after getting prodded and poked. Pressure tactics typically begin after parents' pleas for cooperation fall onto deaf ears, and might continue on long after youthful foot-dragging becomes habitual. Pressuring may enter the scene when a situation doesn't call for laying down of the law, yet parents nevertheless feel very strongly about it. Parents who get caught up in continuing cycles of hounding and prodding may have an inordinate desire for control, unrealistic goals for youngsters, or a great discomfort in the direct exercise of authority. Pressure-susceptible areas of youthful behavior include:

❏ Toilet training, awareness of danger, and impulse-control.

❏ Personal hygiene, clothing choices, hair styles, etc.

❏ Cleanliness of bedroom and other personal space.

❏ Bedtime rules, food choices, and other household routine.

❏ General comportment both within and outside of the home.

❏ Observance of rules like getting home at a reasonable hour.

❏ Achieving grades that conform to parents' expectations.

❏ Out-of-school interests such as music, dance, sports, etc.

❑ Choice of friends, dating partners, and free-time activities.

❑ Spending of allowance money and personal earnings.

❑ Religious affiliation and attendance at house of worship.

❑ Time split between parents after separation or divorce.

❑ Decisions relating to higher education and career choices.

❑ Young adult plans for moving away from the area.

❑ Time devoted to parents by independent-adult offspring.

Results of parental pressuring

Parents slink into murky waters when they thrust forcefully against entrenched resistance or keep hounding youngsters long after it is apparent that they are not going to budge. Now the grim tug-of-war itself becomes more significant than the original issue, and everyone involved pays a price for it, such as a loss of mutual trust and the waste of time and energy. Some parents continue to hound long after prospects for success have faded, and they end up feeling trapped in a lose-lose situation. If they keep on with the pressure, they get increasingly frustrated, as they still don't reach their goals; and if they just throw in the towel, they feel defeated-- and they may even begin to label themselves as uncaring parents. Youngsters who tire of the struggle and keep buckling under could grow up to become brow-beaten mates; while those who remain grim contestants in the struggles for power typically turn out to be disgruntled adults unwilling to lend an ear to others' criticism and advice, no matter how well-intended and constructive it may be.

Long-range parental pressuring related to important issues like choice of careers or marital partners can function like a slow-acting poison. Here the hounding itself might be only occasional, and yet the parental wishes hover overhead like a big gray cloud, especially if the youngsters' own desires clash severely with those of their parents. Youngsters who defy their parents' plans for them may end up paying a huge price, such as becoming a black sheep in the family and/or developing self-destructive tendencies. Then again, children who cave in to parents' "happily ever after" scenarios might go on to trudge through their lives drearily, feeling weak of will and vaguely hollow inside.

But then again....

In order to qualify as constructive, pressuring needs to be infrequent, largely successful, and in pursuit of worthy causes, like getting little ones to pick up toys. That rules out any kind of pressuring that is regular or mostly unsuccessful, regardless of how it turns out. Dubious causes cannot be considered as "favorable," even when the tactics succeed; and the same holds true for cases in which youthful feelings and needs are ignored. Some "dubious" situations are clear-cut, like courting young people's partisanship in marital skirmishes and impelling them toward pre-chosen career lines. The good news is that if the pressuring is infrequent, scant harm can be done, though the window of opportunity for "positive" pressure is narrow. Parents in the constructive-results group pick their spots wisely, are realistic with their goals, and know when to back off. And parents who refuse to back off due to viewing their cause as truly urgent might consider making their aims mandatory. (See the upcoming chapter.)

If parents got rid of all pressuring in their dealings with little ones, their daily routines could become chaotic and perhaps even dangerous. Consider that uncoaxed young ones might never use seat belts, eat vegetables, swallow medicine, arrive anywhere on schedule, and overcome the tiniest obstacle in learning to read or to swim. Even in self-adopted activities like ballet lessons, team sports, and school honors programs, youngsters maintaining lofty goals for themselves can easily get frustrated and filled with self-doubting. This is where wise parents apply some "caring" muscle power, refusing to let their youthful strivers give up without a fight. Many of these youngsters look back later on with great admiration for their parents' perseverance.

Now we arrive at a gray area. This involves parents who mold little ones, usually from a very early age, into becoming superstars in academics, athletics, and entertainment. These young folks get tons of direct or subtle pressure from ambitious, persistent parents, and many of them show gratitude for it later on; but others rebel or go around wallowing in misery for a lifetime. The secret of parents whose offspring come to be successful and well-adjusted is that they crack the whip in an atmosphere of nurturing and support, keep their own ambitions from grabbing the limelight, and know when to let go. They enjoy their small ones' successes, but don't own them. Furthermore, they watch for signals that the younger set just isn't getting with the program; and in these cases, they realize when to throw in the towel. Young ones raised in an atmosphere of support are likely to embrace and enjoy the activities chosen by their parents at an earlier time.

Dialogue vs. parental pressuring

Before they begin toddling around, tiny tots need oodles of attention, but the need to apply pressure is nonexistent. You put them into bed as you choose, take dangerous objects away from them, etc. Then when they howl over not getting what they want, you can offer them substitutes, let them cry it out, or create a distraction. When they start crawling and walking, the temptation to pressure begins in earnest. Firmness and insistence are greatly needed now, as tots do not yet have conformity on their agendas, nor do they possess much capacity for understanding why certain things are required or forbidden. But even before young ones get immersed into language skill development, you can begin to ease dialogue into the picture.

Pressuring of toddlers should be a simple process--gentle, infrequent, and brief in duration. Actually, this can become a good model for pressuring children of any age. You can start explaining behavioral matters--and anything else under the sun as well--long before they fully grasp the meaning of your words; and the more you talk to them in a kindly way, the better and better will become their language skills. And even if they comprehend very little, your caring attempt to explain will likely have a calming effect and lead to rapid compliance. Then as their language skills grow, your little ones will partner with you more and more in discussions. This is in sharp contrast to parents who pressure or reprimand small ones in a stern manner. These children learn fewer language skills, but they do learn more about being afraid. In our clinical practice, we have noted that explained-to young children grow very rapidly in comprehension and eloquence.

Applying pressure to little ones in order to keep them from the frustration of making mistakes and suffering disappointments is in all cases a questionable undertaking. So if you feel tempted to go this route, let us remind you that the trial-and-error method is a tried-and-true learning tool and also a huge confidence builder. Please be assured further that dialoguing regularly with little ones bestows upon you *enormous* influence over them before any word is uttered on any subject. What is more, you might feel pleased to know that veteran family hour youngsters, teens included, discuss openly and seek their parents' help for many issues that trouble or challenge them.

Some parents groom their offspring from a very early age for living out their own unfulfilled dreams for career success, and others maneuver youngsters slowly but surely toward a reversal of roles as their full-time companions or dutiful nursemaids. Should you suspect that you harbor any such inclinations, be mindful that celebrating *with* youngsters about their freely chosen exploits rises way above living vicariously through ones foisted upon them; that even modest prestige related to one's own self-image is far more valuable than any amount tied into the family name; and that care given voluntarily and lovingly to parents by their adult offspring is infinitely more precious than that given as a means of avoiding the dreaded pull of guilt.

PREACHING

> *When we got our family meetings organized, Victor was really eager to get started, and then I realized why. He used these sessions to spout off opinions about religion, politics, and anything else of interest to him. When I noticed that the children and I were all getting restless, I asked him to kindly tone down the rhetoric a bit. That didn't work, so I got louder and louder with my objections. Then one night he didn't show up, and after that he began making up excuses about being too busy. I realize he got his feelings hurt, but he wouldn't admit it. The kids and I struggle at times in the sessions, but at least we're talking. I have a feeling that Victor will be coming back soon to join us; but if he does, he had better get ready to change his tune.*
>
> *Temp worker, mother of 3*

Pulpit preaching and parental preaching differ greatly. One has a willing audience, and the other has a captive one. Children become a captive audience as soon as "When I was your age. . ." complete with finger wagging, comes their way. Parents typically view their sermonizing as an attempt to teach; and indeed preaching (the at-home variety) and teaching might be identical as to the speaker's words and intent, but the distinguishing factor is listener receptivity. One's mind opens up to teaching, while it closes when preaching fills the air--and wise parents well know the difference. The most effective teaching is interactive, and the household provides an ideal setting for it; but the didactic, or lecture hall variety, also works well in its own milieu. Parental preaching, on the other hand, is by definition didactic; and typical among the responses to it are groans, grimaces, and glassy-eyed looks.

Lectures on specific behavior might appear to be a form of pressure. Pressurers, however, strive toward bringing about some hoped for result, while preaching parents usually take to the morally or intellectually high ground. Preaching, therefore, surely can be referred to as pressuring without any teeth in it. For example, in the aftermath of a youthful blunder, a pressurer might say "You had better get it right next time, and I'll keep an eye on you," while a preaching parent would instead give a "If you had only listened to me" line. Furthermore, pressurers usually keep tabs on listener responses, whereas preachers tend to get all wrapped up in their own concepts and words.

Forms of parental preaching

Parental preaching falls into two main categories--the hot-air and the confrontational types. The former finds parents telling stories or rattling on about their opinions; and it becomes preachy when parents talk over their little ones' heads, expound on matters of little or no interest to them, or go on ad-infinitum. These unreceptive youngsters see their parents as being windbags. Hot-air parental preaching may feature:

- ☐ Know-it-all analyses of current events, T.V. shows, etc.
- ☐ Discourses displaying intellectual and/or moral superiority.
- ☐ Arguments "proving" the speaker's cause or beliefs.
- ☐ Repetitive story telling, often out of personal experience.
- ☐ Diatribes against religious, social-class, or ethnic groups.

- Long-winded stories about the "good old days."
- Whining about aches and pains, lousy job, lot in life, etc.
- Detailed talks on subjects of little interest to children.
- Going on and on about sports, religion, politics, etc.
- Lectures filled with technical lingo foreign to children.

Confrontational parental preaching focuses on specific behavior or it might touch broadly on a controversial subject; and it may be meant as a preventive measure or delivered after the fact. When chatting among friends, these youngsters may refer to their parents as "old cranks." Among other things, this form of parental preaching may involve:

- Rants to youngsters about the folly of their behavior.
- Warnings about the consequences of youthful actions.
- "I told you so" speeches about failed youthful efforts.
- Frequent reminders about way-in-the-past behavior.
- Diatribes about the evils of sex, drinking, drugs, etc.
- Comparing behavior or school grades to that of siblings.
- Tongue lashings to those too young to understand.
- Scapegoating youngsters because they are easy targets.
- Belittling youthful attitudes, beliefs values, behavior, etc.
- Remarks that convey scant confidence in youthful efforts.

Purposes of parental preaching

Parental teaching is invariably undertaken with good intentions, such as to expand children's fund of information, to instruct them about specific skills, to point them toward steps for achieving success in life, and to warn them about dangers lurking all around. Yet even the highest-minded teaching can get preachy--e.g., little ones may be too young or immature to grasp the ideas presented, or they may simply have no interest. What is more, a parent's talk may be dull, overlong, repetitive, pedantic, or moralistic.

Other parental preaching is obviously self-involved. These parents may be showing off their knowledge or skills, seeking justification or approval for their behavior, or simply wanting someone to listen to their pent-up feelings and needs. Many are lonesome or feel unappreciated, and some of these become full of gab after a few drinks. Little ones are easy targets because they are as yet unskilled in the art of politely excusing themselves.

Punitive parental preaching is calculated to embarrass or to humiliate, even though it may be delivered with a "for your own good" label. Extreme versions devolve into verbally abusive heat-of-the-moment insult orgies; or into carefully reasoned-out, calmly delivered vitriol directed squarely at the jugular. Punitive parents may possess a nasty streak, suffer from chronic misery or physical pain, harbor a dislike for a particular child, or find themselves truly bummed over the utter failure of their pressure tactics or the ineffectiveness of their punishment strategies.

Results of parental preaching

Small doses of instructional-type parental preaching rarely do much damage, and in fact are rather normal; but in wholesale lots, such pseudo-instruction is not only without value as a teaching tool, but it also turns otherwise fine little ones into second-rate listeners. These children typically become super-sensitive, easily distractible, and prone to have struggles with step-by-step formulas. Then later on they get to be prime candidates for sabotaging their own efforts toward career and relationship goals.

The self-involved variety of sermonizing might also be instructional in a sense, but the case for it looks weaker. Now once again, it is normal for most parents to lapse into it once in a while. For those wallowing in self-absorbed blather, however, the effects on their offspring might be devastating. These young people pay precious little attention to the words themselves, but instead focus in on their parents' depression, loneliness, frustration, misery, etc. Then when they mature, they may become self-denying care givers and/or cultivate a powerful instinct to steer clear of emotional intimacy. These young adults may keep flitting from one relationship to another, and they tend to struggle mightily in dealing with emotionally complex issues.

Almost all parents erupt with frustration on occasion, which proves them to be merely human. But youngsters growing up with regular self-absorbed accusatory rantings by parents tend to have difficulty internalizing a healthy self-image, and they often harbor chronic resentment. Some blame themselves for everything that goes wrong, while others blame everyone else. Some spring into screaming matches that never move toward resolving contentious issues, while others go to extremes to avoid angry confrontations. But they all learn to tune out volumes of infformation that would be helpful to them if they just listened.

But then again....

As is also true with prying and pressuring, parental preaching has its relevant place in parental dealings when it is used sparingly and judiciously. Some occasions call for the issuing of stern warnings to children or clearly spelling out the consequences from their impending actions. These might be consequences imposed by parents or by society, or ones that flow from the flawed nature of their plan--and you need not concern yourself as to whether or not they enjoy hearing your message. Furthermore, you may see it as being instructive to offer your opinions about some ill-thought-out choices your young ones may have made. The good news in all this is that you may find out later on that they were listening to your "sermons" a lot more than was evident at the time.

Dialogue vs. parental preaching

Why do some parents keep on with their preaching over all the years, even though their growing children have never shown a smidgen of interest in listening? Because it has become a habit or because they feel stuck, and see no feasible alternative. Begging and maneuvering have not succeeded, and punishing only seems to make matters worse. Also, they fear that should they stop their speechifying, the silence in the household could become deafening. These parents complain that they have tried talking with their youngsters, but to no avail. Of course the reason their little ones don't open up is that they are too busy tuning the parents out, and they dread that whatever they say might become fodder for future sermons. In many of these families there had been scads of free-flowing communication when their youngsters were small; but as issue after issue cropped up and failed to find a proper resolution, the communication began slowly drying up.

It is never too late for getting dialogue started up and moving along, nor is a serious communication snafu ever beyond the reach of a competent professional. And communication cannot be snarled up to the point of putting the kibosh on family hour. Help in unsnarling family miscommunication is sprinkled throughout the book--most especially in Chapters 6 and 14 and also in our Help section. But then again, life can be so much easier when parents and children keep dialogue alive and well all throughout the child-raising years. Babbling, spouting off, and venting steam might be momentary tension easers for parents and young ones alike, but they hardly satisfy as does solid dialogue among family members. This tends to diminish or even eliminate the strong urge to erupt in the first place. Family hour, however, cannot prevent parents from sermonizing altogether; and when they do slide into a long-winded speech, they are apt to hear a chorus of voices saying "O.K., ma, your time is up, so you can stop now."

POOR-ME-ISM

Sean is our baby, and I mean that in every way. He spent more time in the hospital by age 5 than most people do in a whole lifetime, but his health is just fine now. His frailness no doubt contributed to the tantrums and the whining, but I also came to realize recently that he reminds me a good deal of myself when I was growing up. I don't throw tantrums any more to be sure, but I do tend to get pouty for some while when I don't get my way. We've taken Sean to see a therapist, and she recommended that we sit down together for family discussions. The older two have always tended to cater to Sean, but I'm encouraging them now to back off and let him take responsibility for his own behavior. He has gotten worse for now, but the therapist says he should improve as long as we remain firm. My own years in therapy are helping me get through all this, and our weekly family talks seem to be helping as well.

Homemaker, mother of 3

Parents slathered up into a poor-me syndrome convey the message, through their speech and body language, that they feel physically vulnerable, emotionally weak, stymied in the struggle to keep going, or crushed by the cruelty or indifference on the part of others. This poor-me face might be an "honest" one or a mask put on and taken off by parents; but in most cases it is conveyed in an indirect, disguised way. In their pressuring efforts, certain parents find poor-me-ism to be a very valuable tool.

Forms of parental poor-me-ism

Poor-me-ism appears in manipulative tactics convoluted by parents in order to obtain a psychological edge over their children.

Some poor-me parents have loads of inner strength, while others are distinctly on the fragile side, but in all cases their poor-me demeanor uses the specter of guilt feelings to keep little ones in line and/or to punish them for their "hurtful" behavior. And for the more resourceful among these parents, the poor-me tactics are merely one piercing arrow in their behavior-management weapons stockpile. A few examples:

- ☐ Frequent whining over physical, emotional, or money ills.
- ☐ Reminding youngsters of the sacrifices made for them.
- ☐ Sudden headaches or other "bad news" symptoms.
- ☐ Saying "Don't worry, my opinion doesn't matter anyway."
- ☐ Saying "We're counting on you. Don't let us down."
- ☐ Reminding children of the starving babies in Bangladesh.
- ☐ Saying "I would leave him if I didn't have you kids to raise."
- ☐ Moaning "I know you'll be happy when I'm dead and gone."
- ☐ Making children feel responsible for younger siblings.
- ☐ Icy silences or groans when taboo subjects get mentioned.
- ☐ Hinting that children are to blame for marital battling.
- ☐ Telling children that they are driving you crazy.

Other poor-me-ism is an ingrained feature which is in most cases not purposely meant as manipulation, but rather just seems to happen as a matter of course. Then again, some of these parents also use poor-me-ism as a manipulative tool in certain cases. In situations where other parents roll up their sleeves and get to work on a problem, these woe-is-me types react instead in a manner that reflects their self-image of being helpless and hapless underdogs. These parents are typically burdened with a woebegone self-image ever since they can remember. The following snippets are examples of their reactions and behavior:

- ☐ Getting confused or defensive over child behavior issues.
- ☐ Letting children or mates get the upper hand in arguments.
- ☐ Suddenly dissolving into tears during stressful interactions.
- ☐ Catering regularly to youthful whims, but rarely to their own.
- ☐ Becoming hysterical upon hearing of youthful misconduct.
- ☐ Conveying weariness in relating to other family members.
- ☐ Adopting a slow, halting gait and slumped-over posture.
- ☐ Getting cheated often, being mired in money woes, etc.
- ☐ Getting incapacitated from chronic physical or mental ills.
- ☐ Escaping from the house when pressures feel too great.
- ☐ Struggling to understand the feelings and needs of others.

Purposes of parental poor-me-ism

All parents feel somewhat poor-me-ish upon occasion, but relatively few give in to the urge to bludgeon little ones with it. And when poor-me-ism slides into high gear, it can be a devastatingly effective weapon, as guilt-ridden young adults well realize. Even though it might sometimes fall short of achieving specific goals, it is fairly guaranteed to straight-jacket little ones over the long haul, as they get burdened with increasing loads of guilt. Though poor-me parents always end up losers in the long range in the sense of having healthy, mutually satisfying family relationships, they do get to enjoy some dubious pleasures--controlling youngsters manipulatively, wallowing in self-pity, and (usually) warding off a potential confrontation about their devious tactics.

For parents whose poor-me-ism rises out of a woebegone state of existence, managing youthful behavior is something they tend to give little thought to, as it doesn't befit their image to be in charge of much of anything. The rebellious children in these families tend toward self-destructiveness, and the compliant ones toward self-sacrifice. The primary goal for these parents, albeit one

driven by the subconscious, is the avoidance of personal responsibility for whatever might go wrong. Thus little ones and spouses
alike become prime-time candidates for scapegoating. One of the
many "benefits" of poor-me sad-sacks is that they can totally get
away with failing to tune in to others' feelings and needs.

Results of parental poor-me-ism

Guilt is a favorite topic among stand-up comics because
humor affords them momentary relief for this "incurable disease."
Young adults who expended energy in the formative years dodg-
ing poor-me tactics find themselves in a bind. They experience
guilt in areas targeted by their parents, but they also feel resentful
for having been browbeaten--which in turn generates further misery, as their anger toward their "poor, suffering" parents tends to
morph quickly into even greater guilt. Manipulative poor-me-ism
in big doses can be so potent that young adult victims might get
paralyzed not only in areas their parents focused upon, but also
over anything else they imagine *might possibly* have incurred parental disapproval.

Guilt feelings generated by woebegone-type poor-me parents can become equally devastating or even worse. Grown-up
offspring of poorly adjusted invalids, the emotionally fractured, and
the otherwise unfortunate might easily go through life placing the
welfare of others light-years ahead of their own. Not only are they
terrified of their own angry feelings, but they also tend to feel awkward over asserting themselves. The guilt feelings young people
harbor for not living up to the expectations of pressuring parents
tends to be narrow in focus and intense, and at times can lead into
suicidal thinking; whereas the guilt generated by manipulative or
woebegone-type parents tends to be a lot more pervasive and difficult to overcome.

But then again....

There is <u>no</u> "then again" when it comes to poor-me-ism. It is never a good thing under any circumstances for children to be made to feel guilty, despite the glib comments of some that youngsters actually need a dose of guilt as a character builder. In truth outstanding character is engendered by parents who themselves score high on the character scale and help prepare little ones for becoming responsible, self-reliant young adults. These children develop a naturally strong moral code, and the guilt which results from their violating it compels them to think twice before "sinning" again. This guilt is normal in that it serves a useful role, whereas poor-me-inspired guilt makes young people feel bad in situations where their behavior might be totally above reproach.

Dialogue vs. parental poor-me-ism

Poor-me parents look upon dialogue as if it were a contagious disease, and they tend to turn tail or muddy up the waters when straight talk happens upon the scene. The last thing they all want is for the sun to shine on their tactics, and they are as a rule too heavily invested in their misery to get into honest, constructive verbal exchanges. Furthermore, poor-me parents would find it too painful to look at their love affair with self-pity and at the paralyzing effect it might be having on their small ones. This is most unfortunate for all concerned, as raising youngsters in an atmosphere of dialogue not only provides loads of satisfactions at the time, but it also allows everyone to engage in healthy, happy relationships all throughout the post-parenting years. (See the final chapter.)

When your family engages in regular dialogue, everyone is given an opportunity to express opinions, feelings, needs, wishes, and frustrations. This won't always bring them universal approval or even understanding, but it will very likely open up the doors for heart-felt empathy, the kind that nourishes but does not stifle. And

dialogue also opens the door to getting genuine help from others--
the aiding rather than the bailing-out variety. All this works to keep
self-pity out of the picture. Without any doubt it is only natural for
small children to want their parents to feel sorry for them at times;
but in caring, dialogue-rich homes, they easily outgrow this phase
with the passage of time.

Chronic woe-is-me parents, and those heavily invested into
prying, pressuring, and preaching as well, hope for loving, peaceful relationships just as much as everyone else. Yet theirs is an
ethereal wish rather than any kind of a solid goal, and wishing is
what we tend to do regarding things beyond our reach. Perilous-
ploy parents may gain strategic advantages from their tactics, but
when everything doesn't end happily ever after, they look to blame
children for being uncooperative, society for being too uncaring, or
just plain bad luck. Where they are least likely to place the blame,
to be sure, is on their huge arsenal of tactics, which are relentless
troublemakers at work to stifle the selfsame object of their fondest
wishes--loving, cooperative family relationships. So if they in truth
want harmony, they must first recognize their strategies as self-defeating, and then resolve to begin backing away from them.

It is always hard to give up unproductive habits if we don't
have better ones waiting in the wings to be replacements. And no,
we aren't hinting about more effective strategies, but rather about
the straight talking of dialogue. It is never too late to learn how to
generate and maintain communication that flows freely, and a key
part of it is a willingness to play by the rules, as we saw in the last
chapter. To be sure this is serious work, but the results--no matter
how long it takes--are worth it a thousand times over. And bear in
mind that dialogue makes life so much easer and more satisfying
in the long run. Yes, folks formerly immersed in the perilous ploys
obtain enormous relief from not having to steer discussions along

according to their strategies, and from knowing that their who-can-tell-where-they-will-end-up discussions will invariably mosey along toward sensible, satisfying conclusions.

For those of you who lapse into the perilous ploys once in a while--and this includes you and me and the whole family tree--your family hour sessions will allow you and your children together to catch the enemies of dialogue in the act and weed them all out. Then if they pop up again, you do the process over again as often as is needed. Nothing takes the energy out of tactics of manipulation more quickly than their being exposed to the light of day.

CHAPTER EIGHT

REGULATION ROULETTE: REWARDS, REVOCATIONS, THE ROD, AND RESTRICTIVENESS

I got into the habit of making threats whenever the kids broke my rules. Of course they didn't take me at all seriously because I was all talk and no action. Then to make things worse I felt guilty about saying such terrible things to them. Soon they were going wild, and I knew I had truly lost control. Then when I got depressed, my best friend encouraged me-- no, she had to strong-arm me--to go for counseling. The first experience didn't seem to help, but I tried again and slowly got back on the right track. Then we got into doing family hour, and this has been a help as well. When I stopped yelling, they started accusing me of not caring, and I thought that was really funny. The older ones are on their own now, and the two teenagers are still in the house. I don't order them around, but I don't bail them out of their messes either. They have learned some things the hard way, and we usually talk it over later. They'll be OK, because they know they can always come to me when things get rough.

Older but wiser mother of 4

When parents lay down their law, two factors merit serious consideration. The first and obvious question: do their tactics succeed? And next we come to the mystery question: do their tactics help enhance emotional growth in their youngsters, or at least do nothing to interfere with it? Unfortunately, far too many writers and educators, bent on rescuing beleaguered parents, put the blinders on and assume that if the strategy succeeds, everything else will somehow fall neatly into place. Well, the grim reality is that tightly-structured programs of behavior management have proven disastrous for legions of parents; and loads of "success" stories have generated far more problems than they have solved. This chapter starts by examining two such systems.

So many parents nowadays find themselves punishing and then punishing again; and others, preferring the euphemistic term, hand out "consequences" left and right. Is this because modern-day children are so badly behaved? Actually it speaks more to the expectations that parents have of themselves to move into action as soon as trouble starts brewing. This is sad, as many behavior issues can get resolved simply by talking things out. Worse still, action strategies have mostly turned into a game of regulation roulette that tends to stir up family strife, waste everybody's time and energy, and lurk around as a quiet factor in the dreaded disablers we will get acquainted with in the next chapter. Let us now delve into structured systems of behavior control, and also those based on raw power and overprotection. We saw in the last chapter how perilous-ploy parents may fall into two or more categories, and we will see that same situation here.

BEHAVIOR MANAGEMENT BASED ON REWARDS

My sister and I were raised by the numbers--charts,
points, and stars for every occasion. This led into

continual arguments, and the scene got pretty ugly sometimes. On one occasion I was just one point short of getting to go on a fishing trip with my favorite uncle. I cried a lot, and I know my mom was all torn up over it, but she still wouldn't give in. I had problems with drugs in my teen years, and when rehab came along, I breezed right through the program, because I had learned all the angles from an early age. My mom is a truly good person, but she has always been a detail freak. My wife and I have two little children now, and the only charts they are ever going to have to worry about are the ones for getting their eyes tested.

Sales rep and father of 2

How the system works--in theory

Children must behave well and perform up to expectations in order to gain freedom, privileges, and possessions; and the bigger the reward in store, the greater the effort they will exert toward attaining it. Stars, points, and tokens are given or taken away according to how little ones behave; and detailed charts are used to monitor progress toward goals. Extreme reward based programs find children starting out virtually under house arrest and beyond reach of possessions, and then needing to climb their way toward all items commonplace or frivolous. On the easy end, by contrast, another group of children are given basic freedom, privileges, and possessions, but are then required to labor their way toward anything seen as a luxury.

Incentive-reward systems aim at helping parents manage children's behavior in a businesslike way, thus keeping them from getting sucked into haggling over rules and enforcement. What is more, as they get busy with their mandatory detail work, they are less apt to get in a stew over bruising tender young psyches. And in the process, children should pick up good-behavior habits, motivated by rewards promised to them down the line.

How the system works--in real life

Reward-based programs, an "old reliable" for circus trainers, have in recent years gained popularity at inpatient facilities for sex offenders, substance abusers, and psychiatric patients. Thus it was only a matter of time before the carrot-and-stick idea would one day be adapted for child rearing across the board. But now it has become clear that sending growing children into an incentive-laden maze to hopefully wind up as mature, responsible adults is an impossible task, and one that does a lot of damage along the way--damage both to the normal child-development process, and to parent-child relationships in general.

First let us examine the performance aspect. Monkeys are trained for putting on a show; and as long as they are treated with kindness and patience, they tolerate captivity well, just like house pets do. Children who receive tender care can also get trained to perform like circus chimps, at least until adolescence kicks in. But wait, aren't parents supposed to encourage their little ones to think for themselves? Children in inpatient facilities typically learn how to manipulate the incentive-reward system for their own ends; and the same reality--surprise, surprise--tends to hold true for their at-home counterparts.

With regard to motivational tools, circus trainers follow up stunts with food treats; and these beasts get to be pretty hungry by show time. Withholding dinner from little ones in the incentive-reward process is a no-no; but other basic rights, such as a modicum of play time and the freedom to engage in beloved hobbies, are routinely held hostage. In our penal system, all save perhaps solitary-confinement prisoners are assured of all these privileges. And yet children adamantly refusing to jump through hoops could conceivably spend months or even years deprived of hobbies and outside friendships.

Then to add to the pile, incentive-reward systems promote courtroom-type interactions. Parents who keep their weapons on the back shelf to be used only as a last resort discover that household communication and cooperation evolve in a natural manner; but when bureaucratic-style programs dominate the scene, a me-against-you atmosphere starts taking hold. Then when the inevitable complications arise, sounds of arguing and pleading tend to permeate the already heavy air. And sad to say, issues related to the youngsters' growth and development somehow get lost in the shuffle, or at least take a back seat to "the system."

Now for the most important feature of all. In order to get to be mature, self-responsible adults, growing children must be given ever-increasing freedom of action along with the burden of dealing with whatever consequences may ensue. But when freedoms and rights must be earned, conformity-inclined little ones, who tend to become follower-type adults, win the contest; while strong-willed, natural leader types battle fiercely with parents and very often end up seizing their freedom contentiously.

If this system doesn't contain enough inherent flaws, there remain quite a few more regarding how it is executed. In order for parents to find success in incentive-reward work, they must have the "stern stuff" to turn their backs on pleading youngsters, and to remain unquestioningly loyal to the system. In addition, they need to become cozy with all the details of charts, etc. But don't we all want *our* bosses to listen open-mindedly to cogent, management-related arguments? And aren't some highly effective parents only so-so at detail work? Then too, today's enlightenment era is here to stay, the behaviorists' wishes notwithstanding. Thus, thoughtful parents will surely entertain doubts about the system, and many of them will end up becoming more befuddled than ever.

With hard-line reward-based programs now on the decline, a bizarre reversal of this system has gained popularity. Many exasperated parents now shower youngsters with anything from toy cars to real ones in their hopes of motivating them to achieve or to straighten out. Just think, if your salary were doubled as an incentive for you to labor twice as hard, would you do this? No chance, but you *would* think your boss had flipped out. Rewards given beforehand are no incentive; in fact, they help kill incentive.

But in smaller doses....

We endorse reward-based actions that protect basic needs and leave incentives and rewards closely related. An example lies in your withholding any desserts until after the main meal is eaten. And your teenagers eager for a big trip to Europe with classmates might well be expected to earn at least some of the funds needed, even when you possess the financial wherewithal. As a matter of fact, you can place any non-basic item into the incentives process, but you should do so only when this seems likely to lead to a constructive result.

Positive reinforcement, a superb motivational tool, involves handing out compliments and/or rewards following an *unsolicited* and gratifying youthful act, so as to encourage its being repeated. You will never overdo this so long as it is both sincere and spontaneous, but the noblest and most effective bravos of all are those you offer up *for no particular reason.* This gets youngsters to feel pleased with themselves not for what they do, but simply for who they are. Parents find this to be truly a wise investment.

Dialogue vs. behavior management based on rewards

Behavioral advocates noted many "enlightened" parents in agony over tender young psyches and becoming oversolicitous as a result. So how did these behaviorists react? By themselves be- coming oversolicitous--not of children, however, but of their "emo- tionally fragile" parents. This is seen clearly in their efforts to stifle youthful voices. So the pendulum had now swung way over to the other end of the spectrum. The weighty focus on young ones had spawned problems for many parents, so now the weighty focus on parents was supposed to solve these issues? How about a happy medium of focusing on everyone's issues? What family members really need is to become practiced in the skill of dialogue, as this will diminish the likelihood of anyone--large or small--developing a fragile psyche. After all, the family is a *whole* unit.

While herding small children through "performing monkey" training is bad enough, urging parents to squelch debate over be- havior issues makes matters even worse. When discussion flows freely, pent-up feelings find outlets, salient new information might surface, compromises may arise, and parents often learn that dis- ciplinary action is unnecessary. Then as a bonus, parents at times uncover underlying issues. Misbehavior, after all, is symptomatic in most cases of deeper conflicts; and incentive-reward strategies, which unashamedly discourage inquiry into the origins of anything behavioral, guarantee that those underlying issues will continue to stir up mischief from behind the scenes.

Allowing children to express themselves spontaneously, a principal factor in family hour success, poses no threat to parents' authority. Authority gets eroded when parents let go of the reins of leadership or allow youngsters to stomp all over and harass them. So when you run into problem behavior, take youthful arguments into account, but then quickly blow your whistle if this evolves into hounding. And let all your decisions stand firm except when new facts or angles alter the picture. Also, while youthful pleading and sadness may sometimes sway you, they should never get you to ignore your better judgment. The result of all this is that you keep your management chores simplified and therefore have more time to spend together with your youngsters in mutually enjoyable and productive ways.

BEHAVIOR MANAGEMENT BASED ON REVOCATIONS

> *When I was growing up my mother married four or five times, and she was a discipline maniac. By the time she took me to counseling, I was pretty much a "lifer," having accumulated more than one year's worth of detentions. I couldn't display any anger at her as the sentence would get even longer, so I got into the habit of going into my closet and twisting up coat hangers. Some of them became so bent that they broke, and I got quite a few cuts on my fingers. My own two kids are now in grade school, and I am naturally scared about getting tough with them. But I also feel scared they may run amok as teenagers. We started family hour a while back, and I encourage them to express emotions even though I have trouble expressing mine. I get embarrassed when I start crying, but the members of my support group tell me it is OK. My husband is an easy-going guy, and he is super supportive as well. This is all a big struggle, but at least I'm trying real hard to have a happy family and to do right by the kids.*
>
> *Teacher's aid, mother of 2*

How the system works--in theory

This is the reward-based system in reverse; but rather than having to earn their way to freedom, privileges, and possessions, children are given these items at the beginning, and then later on learn about the attached strings. When little ones misbehave and violate house rules--and there is a long list from which to choose--

their freedoms and inventories begin to disappear. What is more, putting up resistance to parents' orders may result in more losses. Then again, when youngsters toe the line as expected, they have nothing at all to worry about. Parents need to keep track of rules, youthful misdemeanors, and the status of leveraged items; and as also is true for incentive-reward systems, they are strongly urged to avoid debates with little ones over how rules are interpreted and enforced, and they are asked to fulfill the letter of the law in a routine, businesslike manner.

Revocation-based programs aim at obtaining youthful compliance, and gaining it quickly and quietly. Thus an eight-year-old refusing to get to bed at the appointed time might not get desserts for one week, and then might go without for an even longer period should new deadlines elapse. This puts an end to parental pleading which could easily escalate into screeching, and this opens the door to unruffled decision making. And once youngsters become convinced that continued stalling is no longer tolerated, they hopefully will begin to fall into line. This system is designed to produce self-assured parents, well-trained and respectful young ones, and a peaceful, orderly household.

How the system works--in real life

While comprehensive reward-oriented programs summon in monitoring of youngsters' behavior from A to Z, those involved with revocations need no intervention at all until trouble settles in. So this may go to explain why these programs have gained a firm foothold in many households, though often in modified forms. After all, they allow children to enjoy freedoms, privileges, and possessions; and they put these items "on the table" only after youthful snubbing of parents' expectations--ones that get clearly spelled out and followed up by appropriate warnings. Doesn't that sound entirely reasonable?

.

On their face, revocations-oriented programs are all about discouraging unacceptable behavior, but in practice they proffer to parents powerful tools for intimidating youngsters into submission and preventing them from defending themselves. Self-confident, fair-minded parents might get rough around the edges when they lay down the law, but they usually move youngsters to cooperate using neither threats nor consequences; and a cooperative spirit tends to become comfortably internalized by young ones. Yet the advocates of revocations urge parents to lie in wait for transgressions and then show them how to pounce on youngsters--no violence, please--to achieve submission.

Now some tykes have an especially obstinate nature, and they could end up losing every plaything they own for refusing to buckle under. Some trainers even urge parents to drag their little ones kicking and screaming to the thrift store to hand over their toys personally! So the program is not just about victory, but it is about--in some cases--maneuvering an entrenched adversary to the point of demoralization. And in these systems, small ones do not gain an internalized spirit of cooperation; rather, their compliance is based on fears of being crushed by the system.

Revocations and incentives-based programs are polar opposites in their manner of operation, but they share many pitfalls and flaws, like leveraging basic rights to give their system muscle; helping spawn a contentious, duelling-attorney household atmosphere; making parents "insensitive" regulators of their program's operation; paying no attention to dialogue's potential for helping resolve parent-child issues; and wreaking havoc with the natural order that finds children turning into self-reliant young adults with the responsible use of freedom of action--freedom that gradually increases (for the most part) according to age, and is not given as a reward for compliant behavior. More later on in the chapter, and loads more in Chapter 12.

Similar to their incentive-reward counterparts, battalions of revocation-system parents lack the obsessive-compulsive nature that leads the way to the program's success. And even obsessive types rather often find themselves unable to continue ignoring the pleadings of their distraught small ones. Furthermore, they shudder over how some penalties keep on piling up, which sometimes sees youngsters scheduled for house arrest for a seeming stretch into the next lifetime. This has led loads of parents to modify their system drastically, and has left many others even more at sea and self-doubting than before they started.

But in smaller doses....

Revocations make complete sense when they are closely related to the offense committed--a case of the punishment fitting the crime. Thus, a toddler wandering off to play with cereal boxes should be made to stick to you like glue in the supermarket; a little one who steals money should have to face the victim and work to pay off the debt; and your tuition-subsidized college youngster majoring in party-going may be given a shape-up-or-ship-out ultimatum. Measures such as these open up the door for young folks to learn lessons from seeing the error of their ways.

Dialogue vs. behavior management based on revocations

Even when we fail to win over the boss in our workplace, we nevertheless cherish the right to voice our questions and complaints; and bosses who refuse to discuss issues with us are suspected of being close-minded and probably insecure as well. Yet that is exactly how hard-line-revocations parents rule their roosts, egged on by behaviorist trainers who equip them with the bureaucratic equivalent of a big stick instead of teaching them to face up to youthful challenges through a combination of firmness, common sense, and that old reliable--free-flowing dialogue.

The architects of revocations-based behavior management programs would not deny grown-ups the right to speak out against elected officials' actions they feel oppressed by, but they consider parents--no matter how skewed may be their judgment--as off limits to questioning by their youngsters. Yet even highly-successful behaviorist parents cannot squelch the inborn urge to protest; and particularly strong-willed youngsters, heaped with escalating penalties, may go past being candidates for reform and into becoming candidates for reform school. Then again, when parents trust in dialogue's power, they keep their ears tuned into any gripes while letting emotions flow; then they lay down the law firmly should action be needed. It will give you enormous satisfaction to know that once your little justice-seekers have had their say and make note of your sincere efforts to be fair--regardless of how they judge the result--they will almost always end up stepping into line.

While behaviorist parents can seldom see beyond the next hurdle in their management-program obstacle course, you--armed with the dialogue you help propagate in the sessions--can delight in observing youngsters grow and develop without your obligating them to jump through hoops. Enriched by discussions within and outside of the sessions; and bolstered by parental support, guidance, *and* limit setting, your youngsters will grow every day in self-discipline, self-sufficiency, and self-confidence.

BEHAVIOR MANAGEMENT BASED ON THE ROD

My ex-husband used to tie the children to a chair to make them eat, and they got smacked in the face for forgetting to say "sir." The list goes on, but that gives you an idea of how the situation was. I tried leaving several times, and when I did make it stick, he made my life a hell on earth. He rarely sees the

> *kids these days, and says that my overprotection is*
> *ruining them. I've been on and off of welfare, but at*
> *least our life is peaceful now. We had family meet-*
> *ings for a while, and I'm thinking of getting back into*
> *it again soon. I don't like feeling like the underdog,*
> *and I don't want the kids to go over into that same*
> *direction. But on the other hand I don't want them*
> *to become bullies either.*
>
> *Part-time maid, mother of 3*

"The rod," according to our definition, is iron-fisted parental control in any form. Among the tools we see corporal punishment (or the threat of it), verbal or non-verbal intimidation, and the just-discussed revocations--ones, however, that are handed out not as features of an organized system, but punitively in the anger of the moment. In comparing the rod to parental pressuring, we see the latter as the equivalent of leaning up against youngsters, and the former as the equivalent of sitting on top of them and then adding a whack or two for good measure. Some parents, as you might imagine, mix and match weapons out of their rod-loaded arsenal. Now while almost every parent becomes blatantly authoritative at one time or another, we refer in this section only to those who do so consistently, with no hesitation, and with no regrets.

How the system works--in theory

The youth-oriented form of iron-fisted control finds parents motivated by dreams of youngsters' achievement or fear that their little ones might fall victim to unhealthy influences in their community or in the peer group. And in the parent-oriented version, small fry are looked at primarily as underlings. These parents demand respect and obedience the same way that sitting judges and army commanders do. Being burdened with the onus of all legal, social, and moral goings-on concerning their potentially unruly little ones, they see it as important to run a tight ship. And iron-fisted parents are well aware that imposing their will over children from an early age gives them a better chance at keeping a firm grip on the reins throughout the growing-up years.

In rod-ruled households, little ones typically obey parents' commands quickly and quietly, and respond to questions without hesitation or evasion. Facial expressions and body language--no room for scowls and snickers--are also vehicles of respect, as are "yes sir" type verbal responses. When children toe the line, every-day routine tends to flow along smoothly, and a sense of stability pervades the scene. However, when they wander away from the trail, the response from parents, at times starting with stern warn-ings, is swift and clear until decorum is restored.

How the system works--in real life

A child-oriented steel-fisted system may or may not permit children to flourish. If parents' ambitions are reasonable, fears of danger well-founded, methods of enforcement totally realistic, and home atmosphere brimming with love and support, the harsh ap-proach may do little if any long-range harm. In fact, it may actually do much good, as oodles of inner-city-surviving and high-perform-ing young adults heap laurels on their parents for having served as stern taskmasters. Dialogue is as a rule rather limited in these households; then again if it were stronger, parents could soften up their controls while keeping youngsters--girded with even greater emotional resiliency--on the same desired track. There are many similarities between this champion-building parenting style and the one covered in the previous chapter under "pressuring."

Things don't turn out so well for youngsters whose parents have unrealistic goals for them and use unreasonable methods for bringing them to reality--and who provide inadequate support and emotional nurturing along the way. These young ones very easily lose sight of the goals sponsored by their parents, and instead put their energies into grappling with the parental harshness. Then as a result, lots of youngsters being protected against bad influences end up strolling right into the danger zone, and many of those getting prodded toward high achievement either drop out of the competition altogether or fulfill their parents' wishes in a dutiful but sad and unsatisfying fashion.

In some parent-oriented authoritarian houses, parents are consistent regarding their expectations for behavior and realistic with relation to rules and their enforcement. A sizable number of these children rebel anyway, but others fall in line with the system and grow up in relative peace and harmony. And as young adults they tend to lead stable lives and to raise their own little ones in a similar fashion. On the other hand, they seldom get to be skilled at learning the nuances in interpersonal relationships and look at interactions with those around them in terms of who has a position of authority or has the higher status.

Serious trouble besets the families in which parents enjoy throwing their weight around, have impossibly high expectations, and/or are erratic about how they set and enforce rules. Many of these youngsters undergo physical and emotional torment, and as young adults a frightening number of them either turn into bullies or chronic victims. And sad to relate, they help to swell the ranks of prison, psychiatric, and substance abuse populations. These most unfortunate folks find it nearly impossible to be straight with their feelings and are inept in handling the give-and-take of everyday human dealings.

But in smaller doses....

Get-tough tactics are crucial in certain situations. If young ones throw a seat-belt tantrum, coercion might be the only way to get them strapped in; and if they start dragging their feet when an immovable deadline nears, they may need to be carried off kicking and screaming. School-age youngsters get much more difficult to restrain, but they're also better able to understand the rationale for their parents' insistence. Yet if they still refuse to comply, a sterner tone on your part, minus fist waving or dire threats, often does the job nicely. Then if that doesn't work, your best option might be to refuse to cooperate with them when they next ask you for a favor. And if you let their pitiful pleadings melt your resolve, you may be making multiple mistakes all at once: overruling your needs over the original incident, paving the way for the problem to recur, and failing to teach a lesson in responsibility.

"We've tried everything else" is so often spoken to explain a spanking. Then again, "everything else" never seems to include dialogue. Corporal punishment is *never, ever* advised, yet an occasional rump thumping may be more effective and far less damaging to little ones' psyches than is their rarely getting to play with a best pal because of earning too few reward-system points, their being forced to donate toys due to their getting into a power struggle with their parents, or their living in dread that the slightest false step might bring swift retribution.

Dialogue vs. behavior management based on the rod

Rod-based parenting and dialogue have trouble coexisting. Small ones in these homes may not live in chronic trepidation, but they at least select their words carefully, hide unpleasant feelings, and dare not contradict. All of this dampens the spontaneity upon which dialogue depends, and thus leaves parents and youngsters readied to converse freely only on surface topics or in emotionally safe areas. Moreover, most authoritarian parents feel reluctant to let their hair down, as this could leave them in a vulnerable state and put a dent in their "commander-in-chief" image.

Iron-fisted parents are powerfully influential over youthful behavior in the immediate sense, but the "supreme commander" approach, in order to function effectively, requires constant reinforcement. Many rod-ruled young folks are sneaky or aggressive outside the home, others go wild once they move out on their own, and still others grow to cast off many of their parents' values. By contrast, dialoguing parents, who dislike seeing youngsters cringe, become influential in a more foundation-building sense. Their role modeling is solid and vibrant, they turn into powerful teachers with receptive students, they provide help and support to young people who trust them, and they have few qualms about letting their own vulnerable side be seen.

Authoritarian parents never express doubt that their tactics help prepare small ones for a young-adult life of responsible self-governance, but they tend to sound vague as to precisely how this takes place. Family hour parents, on the other hand, have 20/20 vision over this process. Their young charges accept house rules willingly because they are relatively few in number, are clearly understood, and in most cases reasonable. These young folks get loads of problem-solving practice through the give-and-take of dialogue, acquire an emotional maturity and stability that grow out of their feeling free to express themselves, and to learn valuable lessons from being allowed the freedom to make choices and then to deal with the consequences.

BEHAVIOR MANAGEMENT BASED ON RESTRICTIVENESS

The first time I showed some anger toward my wife, she stormed off all hysterical. She continued doing this; but one day, instead of running up to her room, she went back to her mother's. After a number of these episodes I went to get help from a counselor, but Annie refused to come along. Then one time with a baby on the way, I cried and begged her not to let this pull us apart. So she finally joined in the sessions, and before long her mother asked to be included--but the counselor said no. That was over a year ago, and now finally we are slowly making progress. Annie can see now that her mother is a large part of the problem, and I've learned to place some controls on my Italian temper. Lynne is great with the baby, but I fear she might become overprotective like her mom. I guess we'll deal with that when the time comes.

Automobile service manager

For their own protection, small children must be monitored routinely and controlled on a regular basis; and as they grow they need to be shown the ropes with relation to surviving and fitting in as civilized and socialized beings. By the time they arrive at their majority, however, they should now be prepared for complete self-regulation; and the only practical way for this to happen is for them to be afforded gradually increasing autonomy along the way. We shall now see how this process gets subverted in an atmosphere of pervasive restrictiveness, one where parents strive consistently to squelch youthful self-reliance rather than to endorse, promote, support, and celebrate it.

How the system works--in theory

Babies come into this world totally helpless, needing protection from perils such as illness, accidents, and exposure to the elements. Later comes the danger of ridiculing and bullying from other children, and physical and sexual abuse from adults. In addition, frustrations stemming from failure to compete successfully can be excruciatingly stressful. The list goes on and on. And for children with physical and mental handicaps, the need for protection is even greater. What is more, since little ones tend to plunge headlong into the unknown, parental reining-in keeps them safe.

The teen years are stressful enough to begin with, but the world outside the family circle is more dangerous than ever these days. The peer group exerts a potent influence over impressionable young minds and tends to embrace questionable moral and social values. Drugs, delinquency, unsafe sex, and risky driving are all now epidemic. Substance abuse and delinquency, though very perilous, can very often be corrected, but not so for the loss of life or limb. For these reasons and many more, parents must be leery about giving free choices to children who are unready to handle them. Then when they get older, there will be lots of time to master self-governance skills.

How the system works--in real life

Hard-core restrictive parents, driven by unhealthy motives, start up their smothering from an early age. Some lack faith in the children's capacity for self-control or for prudent decision making, others have pathological fears about the evil in the world, and still others are narcissistically (and perhaps subconsciously) propelled toward grooming their little ones for permanent companionship for them--and then, if necessary, for nursemaid duties in their old age. Circumstance-driven restrictive parents, on the other hand, are for the most part non-authoritarian types who become more and more protective over time due to disturbing factors like realistic dangers around the neighborhood or in the broader community; or due to their coming to see that their young charges are naive, incautious, secretive, or accident or trouble-prone.

Overprotective parents maintain control through the use of propaganda, arm-twisting, fretting, poor-me-ism, making home life all comfy-cozy, etc. Unlike independence-promoting parents, who make their decisions based on the facts of any case, smothering types look first for reasons to shoot down requests for freedom of action. A dead give-away of their closed-mindedness is the speed with which they come up with a "no" answer. They have a host of reasons for every nay-saying; these, however, do not explain their thinking, but rather simply attempt to put a palatable face on their pre-disposed negativity. Open-minded parents, on the other hand, usually take a while before voicing their well-considered decisions. And children are well aware of the difference.

When the offspring of hard-core restrictive parents reach the teenage years, their overprotection leaves them sorely lacking in the skill of handling the give-and-take of interpersonal dealings; and when conflicts arise, they tend to go looking for safe havens instead of constructive help. Most protective parents, as you may imagine, are more than willing to provide this haven for their adult offspring into their 20's and even beyond. The emotionally seductive type of restrictive parent seldom incurs the wrath of their little ones, but in restrictive households featuring an authoritative parental tone, shouting may often take over center stage. However, because these parents also tend toward indulgence and self-sacrifice, children's anger can easily morph into self-destructiveness, depression, and delinquent behavior.

Circumstance-driven restrictive parents, who as a rule get started later in the game, tend to be less adept at "web weaving" than their hard-core counterparts, but their children are much better off for it. These young folks might rebel over restrictive tactics, but they are less likely to do so if they come to see and accept the reasoning behind their parents' decisions. Relationships in these restrictive-parent homes may be stormy for a time, although in so many cases they are subject to complete repair. Parents in this category are often victims to that modern epidemic, a shortage of quality family time. Such a scarcity leads to diminished communication, which in turn can create all sorts of fears about outside influences over their offspring.

But in smaller doses....

Small children need a lot of supervision and restraint as a precaution against injury, property damage, etc. Childproofing of your house is highly recommended, and in the long term it is a lot simpler than constant vigilance; and you might also try to identify potentially dangerous scenarios that lie in wait beyond childproofing range. That being said, you should always strive to afford little ones optimal freedom to explore their surroundings, and then look to expand this perimeter as they grow and develop greater awareness of perils and a greater capacity for self-control.

Lots of teens function well with few parental restrictions, but there are situations that call for your blowing the whistle. One involves evidence of substance abuse, delinquency, risky behavior, or the like. As we discussed previously, this calls for serious investigation and quick intervention. Also, you may want to put up a stop sign in cases where potential issues arising from youthful freedom could slam you in the wallet and/or leave you having no choice but to clean up the resulting mess.

Dialogue vs. behavior management based on restrictiveness

Hardcore restrictive parents can be great at talking to little ones, but they tend to be less than skilled at talking *with* them. In fact, their potential for dialoguing may be as poor as that of most rod-ruling parents. Their talks tend to be fraught with tales of how outsiders cannot be trusted, how one should never take chances, and how comfortable it is to stick close to the parental nest. Now as you may expect, all this can darken young people's dreams of striding confidently into the world upon reaching young adulthood.

So if parents cannot keep their protective instincts subordinate to the reality that gradually increasing self-determined choices pave the way toward a self-sufficient young-adulthood, they unravel the good accruing from their devotion and run the risk of turning their young ones into emotional cripples. Unfortunately, so many of the hardcore restrictive are highly self-involved, so this warning would in many cases be likely to fall on deaf ears.

A great many circumstance-motivated parents, by contrast, tend to be amenable to dialoguing with little ones, who are seldom shy in expressing an opinion about the restrictions imposed upon them. Shouting matches might take center stage; but even there, issues often surface and get debated, especially if weekly discussions are featured on the family scene. This leaves children more informed and worldly-wise, and thus better able to have a realistic grip on the issues causing their parents to be concerned. What is more, these verbal exchanges help straighten out misconceptions, keep parents tuned in to youthful activities, and increase the likelihood that the parents' assistance will be sought out when youngsters really have need of it.

Some modern-day parents aren't overprotective by nature, don't have trouble-prone children, and reside in relatively peaceful communities; yet even *they* wind up becoming more and more restrictive over time. Fears about delinquency and substance abuse in the peer group is one obvious reason; but a hidden one is that quality time for communication between many teens and parents is in limited supply, leaving parents to suspect the worst when they garner few details about youthful activities and behavior. Dialogue holds the answer for such concerns. When communication flows freely in your household, you become much more influential than any peer group or anti-family guru; and your increasingly self-sufficient youngsters get well prepared for facing up to the challenges of a complicated world on the outside.

BEHAVIOR MANAGEMENT MADE EASY

Among Earth's creatures, we humans appear to be alone in our large capacity for creativity, and this has allowed us to build great empires and to continuously expand the frontiers of science. But along with our capacity to create masterpieces, we also have the capacity for making simple things complex and complex things highly convoluted. Our legal system is one frustratingly confusing maze, bureaucratic red tape chokes government and educational operations; and the raising of children has also fallen victim to this simple-made-complicated model. And the result is that gimmicky formulas for managing behaviors have left already vulnerable parents feeling more and more bewildered.

Let's look at the most important components of parenting--nurturing, protection, and teaching. But hold on, where are all the controls and discipline in this picture? Well, control over offspring, especially newborns and toddlers, falls under the heading of protection; and truly effective discipline relates closely to the misbehavior, thus setting the stage for lessons to be learned. Then too, control and discipline are most effective when kept to a minimum, and also when they gradually and consistently diminish as young people go on their journey toward a self-reliant adult life.

We have much to learn from critters in the wild, who keep parenting simple yet effective. They nurture instinctively, fiercely protect new arrivals against predators and various dangers, teach young by demonstrating their own practical skills, and quickly discipline those wandering off the line; after which everybody moves ahead with the daily routine. The same should hold true, by and large, for humans; but our parenting is far more complex and long-term than it is for most other creatures. The good news, however, is that our capacity for conceptualization and verbal communication also appears to be far more complex than it is for all the other creatures--with the possible exception of the ape family. We also appear to be the only species with the ability to laugh at ourselves. And it's a good thing we can.

Throughout the ages, oodles of mature, emotionally stable young adults have emerged out of families where ideas and feelings flow out freely, while at the same time parents remain steady at the wheel as leaders. Yet in our scientifically enlightened era, this simple idea has gotten lost in the shuffle; and it's not because dialogue is slipping in popularity. Couples communication is now all the rage, and therapy and support groups put great emphasis on emotional openness. But writers in this field, appearing to be protective of "fragile" parents, react to youthful spontaneity as if it were a potentially deadly weapon. We have known a good many insecure parents in our years of clinical practice, but dialogue has never turned up as the culprit. To the contrary, we have observed time and again that once family members feel free to speak from the heart, parental leadership gets quickly revived.

Today's parents are trapped in a bureaucratic maze featuring do-something-right-away tactics in responding to problem behavior, and this maze has no safe exit! Here is where we all might learn from in-the-wild parents. Yes, they lack the language skills needed for talking things out extensively, but a screech or two or a swift whack is far more effective than house arrest or the loss of a beloved hobby. No, we still do not endorse corporal punishment; rather we see it as the lesser of two evils. What we do endorse is talking openly and honestly about issues, as we saw in Chapter 6. Carrying out gimmicky behavioral "consequences" in fact contributes to an ongoing cycle of parent-child turbulence, whereas dialogue is helpful in allowing most issues to get resolved without any need to take action. And by the way, this is not just pleasant theory. We have seen it achieve success on a consistent basis over the years--and so have lots of other therapists.

Dialogue is a major component in couples communication classes, labor negotiation sessions, heart-to-heart talks between friends--and family hour discussions in the home. It's all a similar process, except that in the family, discussions are geared to the ages of the children, and parents are always "boss" in the family. Now if dialogue were only put to greater use in parent education, this would surely decrease the need for teaching communication skills to grown-ups. Then again, professionals do on countless occasions teach parents and children how to improve on dialogue skills, but this is almost always in pursuit of helping them clean up messes that might have been avoided if dialogue had been given a decent chance in the first place.

> *On the whole my mom did a good job of raising us, but she certainly made her share of mistakes. Yet like so many other mothers of that time, she never stopped to question her child-raising philosophy or her methods. When I bring up some incident from the past, she always says something like " Well, I did the best I could," or "That was such a long time ago." I'd like to think I did well as a mother too, but I do recall having lots of doubts about myself along the way. So I'm not sure whether all my worrying was a good or a bad thing. Well, I guess I'll leave it right there. Life is too short. The important thing is that my mom and I really care about each other.*
>
> *Mother of 3 grown children*

SOME BEHAVIOR MANAGEMENT Q AND A

Don't children need protection through the growing years?

Not the undiminished variety. Parents need to back away gradually as they increasingly promote youthful self-governance;

and those who fail to do this run the risk of handicapping children as they look toward the future.

Don't handicapped children need ongoing protection?

The above general rule still applies, but young ones who will require a protected environment as adults clearly need similar sheltering before they come of age. Many handicapped children, however, later prove themselves out to be more self-sufficient than anyone would have predicted.

Don't all youngsters need to be punished at times?

No, and this is not just well-intended theory, but a proven fact. The authors are quite familiar with with a substantial number of never-punished children who have grown to become respectful, responsible adults. In these homes there is usually an abundance of free-flowing communication and a cooperative spirit.

Don't unpunished children tend to become irresponsible?

Youngsters turn out to be irresponsible when their parents are indifferent, overindulgent, scornful of authority, inclined to bail them out of self-created messes, or ready to defend them unquestioningly against accusations from anybody outside the family circle. And yes, children who see their parents acting ill-mannered in public will tend to follow suit.

Don't hard-to-manage children need lots of discipline?

Unruly types need solid, patient, and consistent parenting along with extra attention and watching. What is more, they must be held to account for harming others or damaging property. And should the problem behavior continue, family therapy might be the next step. Dialogue building may take time.

What about the good things punishment accomplishes?

The only benefit we can see is in the "punishment fits the crime" scenario, where important lessons get learned. Examples show youngsters working to pay for damaged property or forfeiting driving privileges for recklessness behind the wheel. Most of the modern-day punishments, like grounding or revocation of favorite activities, are totally unrelated to the misdeeds.

What if the punishment can't match the misdeeds?

This is a sign that the misdeed may be something we don't view as a punishable offense, like failing grades, the expression of anger, and battles with siblings. Talking openly and honestly with one another should always be your first option, and this finds misbehavior much less likely to recur.

Don't many people later thank parents for their tough tactics?

These folks typically talk of having been "bad," which hints at a questionable self-image and a lack of confidence in their ability to master self-control on their own; and at the same time, this takes their parents completely off the hook. Well balanced, non-punished young adults, by contrast, tend to view parent-youngster battles as complex events needing insightful inquiry rather than in terns of the simplistic "bad" behavior.

Isn't punishment a deterrent against future misbehavior?

Yes it is when the punishment intimidates to the extent that children become fearful on a regular basis--a sure-fire formula for adult-life anguish. In our many combined years of family therapy practice we have made note of the fact that the more frequent the punishment, the worse the behavior tends to become.

How should rules for children's behavior be formulated?

They should for the most part be based on those rules you have for yourself, such as taking care of possessions, discharging responsibilities, showing sensitivity and kindness to others, maintaining sound health practices, shunning risky behavior, being fair-minded in business and other dealings, etc.

How should rules be spelled out for school-age children?

The ideal is to have the smallest possible number of formal rules, state them in simple terms, and repeat them only as the occasion demands. We don't respond well to office settings where rules are trumpeted over and over, and young ones don't thrive in a similar-type atmosphere at home.

Doesn't a scarcity of formal rules leave children confused?

No. Little ones generally are given too little credit for their powers of observation. They are ever-watchful for your approval or disapproval, and they quickly learn to imitate what you say and do. Then when they wander over the line, they depend on you to reel them back in.

If not in discipline, then how is youthful character formed?

Good character develops in large measure from identifying with and emulating parents and all other influential grown-ups who themselves lead an upright life. Other components include getting adequate love and support; receiving fair treatment from common-sense parents; being given room to express opinions and feelings spontaneously; and being afforded increasing self-determination, including the onus of dealing with consequences.

CHAPTER NINE

THE DREADED DISABLERS: DRUGS, DELINQUENCY, DEPRESSION, AND DROP-OUT

From the start Del and I talked about how our chil-dren were going to be drug-free. Arlette is now in the fifth grade, and she told us recently about one classmate who sniffs glue, and about several oth-ers who have experimented with cigarettes. She promises she will never do any of these things, but now I am starting to get worried, as she will soon be in middle school, where so many bad things be-gin to happen. We recently started holding family meetings, and I have had to bite my tongue a few times when I felt a lecture itching to come tumbling out. So I'll just keep my fingers crossed, and I'll also put my energy into keeping the lines of com-munication in good working order.

Mother of 3 grade-schoolers

The dreaded disablers create sizable roadblocks along the pathway toward youthful maturity and stability; and their dark shadow can haunt parents even before the firstborn arrives, but most of all when adolescence closes in. Then again, the disablers don't always wait for puberty to hit the scene, since increasing numbers of preteens are now falling victim to them. First we'll take a look at each disabler, and later on in the chapter we'll examine them all in more detail and explore how the steady flow of dialogue offers to youngsters many layers of protection.

DRUGS

The good-drug bad-drug concept is a truly naive one. Any drug is dangerous when it is overused, purposely misused, taken without knowledge of possible ill effects, obtained illegally, used in unknown-result combinations, or likely to cause physical harm or addiction. To be sure, drugs of all types have been consumed in all societies throughout history, and nearly everyone in our culture relies on them at one time or another, often with health-promoting or life-saving results. The misuse of drugs, however, is a growing concern these days, affecting people from all regions around the planet, and our own affluent but substance-craving society stands near or at the very top of the list.

DELINQUENCY

Our definition of delinquency does not stay confined to the police blotter, but rather it encompasses a broad spectrum of destructive behavior, whether brought into play by intention, neglect, or indifference. And yet one person's anti-social behavior may be another person's patriotism, as the actions of the civilly disobedient clearly demonstrate. Some young folks go through rebellious phases, the destructive actions of others may be a sign of an upbringing in a culture of violence, and in the worst-case scenario, a budding personality disorder may be rearing its ugly head.

DEPRESSION

Depression might be the most fearsome of all the dreaded disablers because suicide, the problem with no earthly resolution, can never be fully ruled out as a possibility, especially with suicide rates among young children now moving ominously up the charts. Depressive youngsters tend to keep their gloomy feelings bottled up; and while some are outwardly dour-looking, others mask over their inner turmoil by simply appearing to be shy, by becoming the class clown, or by maintaining an air of smiley-faced congeniality. Yet while young depressives may even fool themselves, they tend to leave clues all around hinting at their sadness and desperation. Parents understandably don't want to see these possibilities, but it is important that they keep their eyes and ears open.

DROP-OUT

Failure to finish school most often comes to mind here, but drop-out also refers to alienation from family and friends, and also to an unwillingness or inability to merge into mainstream society-- and who become emotionally fractured in the process. (This rules out rugged individualists who choose to remain off by themselves, and possess the inner strength to function competently.) Obvious signs of drop-out usually appear in the later teen years or the early twenties, although the seeds are almost invariably sown a lot earlier. Those alienated for extended periods run the risk of suffering from physical, psychological, and/or legal problems; while others, who seem endowed with greater inner strength, may bounce back to become high achievers in their chosen field.

Society's prominent voices often focus on a solitary major issue to explain our present-day plague of the dreaded disablers, suggesting that a war on that front will solve the problem. Among other factors, they single out parental overindulgence, turning our backs on tried-and-true family and religious values, soaring rates of separation and divorce, and excessive sex and violence in the media. Yes, these factors are important, but they tend either to be results rather than causes, or to be found on the fringe as culprits. What is more, focusing on them tends to cut short much needed investigation into influences that may not be obvious but nonetheless are central to the problem. One thing that seems clear is that disabler-afflicted youngsters are typically motivated by an array of factors both obvious and hidden.

Parents of afflicted teenagers often get reassured by supportive, well-intentioned friends and colleagues that they carry no blame for their youngsters' turmoil. Yet if their troubled teens had instead excelled, would friends opine that these same parents deserved none of the credit? You know the answer. In truth, parents assume potent roles in all phases of youthful development. They can shape children in positive or negative ways, and they can also fortify them against or leave them vulnerable to--unintentionally, of course--potentially perilous influences in the community. And yet parental influence goes only so far.

Social scientists typically pursue single-factor correlations, like tendencies toward violence or excessive drinking in teenagers whose parents are similarly afflicted. Measuring how a *multitude* of factors impact specific behavior, however, can become awfully complicated, which may be why you don't often see studies of this sort. We are convinced, nevertheless, that the formula might read something like this: when negative-influence factors are intense, numerous, and long lasting, young ones are at highest risk for falling victim to one or more of the disablers; and when the opposite is true, children are strongly protected against this risk.

The following are factors that can work in combinations to undermine youthful stability. Any given factor might be related to one or several of the others in a cause-and-effect or other manner; and yet any negative factor, like unresolved issues from a parent's own upbringing, can easily get outweighed by ones that positively influence children's sense of self.

Factors Contributing to the Dreaded Disablers

Factors relating to parents

☐ Parental absence due to death, desertion, prison, job, etc.

☐ Addictive/compulsive disorders such as drugs or gambling.

☐ Mental illness, personality disorders, and depression.

☐ Lingering anger toward one's own parents or other kinfolk.

☐ Serious and prolonged financial insufficiency or volatility.

☐ Bitter career dissatisfaction and/or recurring job crises.

☐ Frequent moves due to financial, legal, or emotional issues.

☐ Starting out parenthood ill-prepared for settling down.

☐ Difficulty in expressing feelings and showing affection.

☐ Dislike for children generally and insensitivity to their needs.

☐ Dislike for a child due to looks, personality, handicap, etc.

☐ In adoption cases, unresolved feelings about childlessness.

Factors relating to children

☐ Middle child and mama's boy syndrome, and the like.

☐ Handicaps and health issues that frustrate parents.

☐ Personalities clashing with those of parents and siblings.

☐ Hyperactive, attention-deficit, and neurological disorders.

☐ Traumatic events like accidents and witnessing violence.

☐ Naivete, feelings of inferiority, and pervasive loneliness.

☐ Adjustment, behavior, and learning problems at school.

☐ Need for instant gratification and low frustration tolerance.

- ☐ Refusal to share possessions and agree to compromises.
- ☐ Difficulty in learning from mistakes, failures, and let-downs.
- ☐ Behavior that lends itself to ridicule or rejection by peers.
- ☐ Tendency to take out anger on smaller children or animals.
- ☐ Strong need for acceptance from those outside the family.
- ☐ Obsessive drive to win, achieve, and dominate.
- ☐ Morbid fascination with danger and violence.
- ☐ Serious difficulty in forming and maintaining friendships.

Factors relating to the parent-child relationship

- ☐ Ongoing parental neglect, abuse, and scapegoating.
- ☐ Chronic parental insecurity and inconsistency in leadership.
- ☐ Harsh parental stifling of children's opinions and feelings.
- ☐ Personality clashes giving rise to frequent butting of heads.
- ☐ Punishments that bear no relationship to problem behavior.
- ☐ Overprotective parenting that stifles youthful self-reliance.
- ☐ Clumsiness of parents in dealing with child-behavior issues.
- ☐ Parental role-modeling of inane or irresponsible behavior.
- ☐ Parents allowing children to get the upper hand over them.
- ☐ Parents blaring bigotry and projecting blame onto others.
- ☐ Parents regularly bailing children out of stressful situations.
- ☐ Children getting "things" to substitute for personal attention.
- ☐ Unrelenting pressure from parents to conform or achieve.
- ☐ Children being made responsible for younger siblings.

Factors relating to other family relations and circumstances

- ☐ Long-standing sibling-rivalry battling or alienation.
- ☐ A you're-on-your-own atmosphere in the household.
- ☐ Little interest in or opportunity for family-together projects.
- ☐ Busy schedules crowding out time for family togetherness.

❑ T.V.s, computers, etc., contributing to household isolation.

❑ Little contact with grandparents and non-custodial parents.

❑ Chronic marital stress, ugly divorces, and custody fights.

❑ Information gaps, misconceptions, and poor verbal skills.

❑ Situations where step-parents or step-children feel left out.

❑ Us-against-them alliances leading to discord and alienation.

❑ Isolated, overburdened, and undervalued single parents.

❑ Endless feuds with extended family members or in-laws.

Factors related to the community

❑ Neighborhoods that have little sense of community.

❑ Families frequently moving in and out of neighborhoods

❑ Community-based poverty, hopelessness, and gang rule.

❑ Populations ravaged by war and religious or ethnic unrest.

❑ Natural disasters that devastate entire communities.

❑ Environmental pollutants affecting health and behavior.

❑ Powerful allure of gangs and up-to-no-good peer groups.

❑ Powerful allure of charismatic gurus and cult leaders.

❑ Drugs, alcohol, and unsafe sex at unsupervised parties.

❑ Juvenile justice systems becoming tangled webs.

❑ Ads with instant-gratification and you're-not-OK messages.

❑ Society's valuing competition more highly than cooperation.

❑ School behavior issues overshadowing the academics.

❑ Anxiety and confusion in preparing for career choices.

❑ Pressure in society to lust after money, power, and prestige.

If these aren't enough potentially negative influences, you may find even more in the esoteric. For example, when otherwise calm youngsters get hyperactive, some look skyward and find the full moon confirming their suspicions. What is more, astrologers for centuries have warned followers about the dangers of certain planetary alignments; and preachers regularly sermonize as to the powerful pull of the Evil One.

But not to worry. For each gray-cloud factor darkening the formative years, there are lots of positive ones prepared to offset it--ones we'll discuss through the book. So don't fret about lasting harm resulting from isolated traumatic events such as reasonably amicable divorces, occasional parental outbursts, and mistakes in judgment. In a supportive atmosphere, young folks can bounce back over and over and learn lessons from it. Our huge concern is for families in which misguided parenting or a stress-filled home atmosphere becomes a way of life. Here, negative influences related to family-member interactions lean heavily upon the scales; and these youngsters are especially vulnerable to the clutches of the dreaded disablers.

All modern families, especially the stressed and splintered ones, are adversely affected by the way our society functions now, which is in stark contrast to how it did a few generations ago (See Chapter 2). To be sure, there were horrifying conditions way back then; but on the whole, the society of yesteryear was a good deal more family-friendly than it is today. And make no mistake, these way-of-life changes are big contributors to the upswing in youthful malaise. For this reason we strongly urge you to preserve blocks of time for family-together activities like group projects, distraction-free weekly discussions, and family outings.

Negative-influence factors such as genetic predispositions cannot be ignored, but children in emotionally blessed homes are highly resistant to their lie-in-wait tendencies. Schizophrenia was once deemed to be a product of parenting, pure and simple. But studies now point out genetic links that appear very frequently in those beset by the disorder, leading some to declare that this malady will put its curse on every so many predisposed youngsters no matter what their parents do. Yet the researchers appear not at all inclined to look into how loving, cooperative relationships might be able to overcome genetic anomalies. We don't need any studies, to be sure, to convince us of the power of positive parenting. We have seen it over and over in our years of professional work.

The great news is that parental efforts can counteract any number of influences that affect children negatively. And yet some parents never stop to ponder whether their manipulation, overprotection, or harsh treatment might be doing more harm than good; thus the light must go on in their head before they can realistically move to ward off the disablers. Also, parents can nip an ocean of issues in the bud, such as by giving extra attention to insecure or isolated children. And hopeless-feeling parents who seem to have run out of issue-resolving ideas need to know that this is never the case. They just have to remain patient as they continue to search for proper guidance and wisdom from their own inner resources.

I was raised in isolation by a lonely, bitter mother, and I started having suicidal thoughts from an early age. By my mid-twenties I had survived a number of suicide attempts, and the closest I came to getting the deed done was when I swallowed a whole bottle of pills, drove to the beach, and sat in my car waiting to die. I awoke later on in the hospital with I.V.'s in my arm and promptly went berserk as I had once again failed in getting over to "a better place." Soon after this I decided it was time to seek after some serious help, and a caring and patient therapist got me to feel better about myself and about life. I've been married and divorced twice, and my three kids are almost grown up now. They've had their problems, but thank God they seem to look at life as being a worthwhile venture.

Court reporter, mother of 3

Professional counselors help families climb their way back away from the edge, but one way for you to steer clear of the edge in the first place is by generating and maintaining dialogue in family hour sessions. Therapists work tirelessly in encouraging family members to talk openly and honestly with one another; and if they can manage get dialogue to work its magic in homes torn apart by strife, then *you* can surely work a smaller miracle using dialogue in your stable or at least safe-distance-from-the-edge household. It's always good to start from where you can't even see the cliff in the far-away distance.

You can use family hour sessions to address every negative-influence factor on these lists. For instance, while you cannot wish away natural disasters and genetic anomalies, you are able at least to soften their impact by having everybody speak candidly about them. Sibling rivalry and problems related to discipline can be confronted head-on and in some cases eliminated entirely with family meetings; and issues such as a shortage of quality family-together time, gang influences, and a whole bunch of others, simply appear to vanish when you meet on a regular basis as a family group. Still other problems, like the dangers of substance abuse, get the double-whammy in family hour. Parents and young people can talk this issue over in lots of detail; but even when they fail to touch on the subject directly, the family hour experience is in itself a super drug-abuse insurance policy.

For families where young people may already be burdened with one or more of the dreaded disablers, regular weekly meetings might help in a number of ways. Some problems may simply disappear as family members express feelings, clear the air about misconceptions, and practice becoming more helpful and supportive with one another. And when outside intervention or treatment is already in the picture, your sessions can aid in accelerating the process of recovery. Then your family can continue to serve as a support group long after these youngsters have gone out into the world to find their own path.

At this point we come to a more in-depth examination into each of the dreaded disablers and how they become influenced by specific negative-influence factors. Then we explore the ways that dialogue, generated in family hour sessions and elsewhere in your household, can aid in preventing and overcoming these potentially destructive influences.

DRUGS

I'm a pharmacist, and it pains me deeply to realize that some of the drugs I prescribe might wind up in the hands of juveniles who abuse them. Of course all these pharmaceuticals might also get abused by more than a few grown-ups, but that is yet another story--a really long one. And of course these young people will soon be grown ups themselves. For this reason I spend time volunteering at several middle and high schools talking realistically about the various benefits and dangers of drugs. These youngsters sure have some great questions.

Mother in two pharmacist, two child family

A comprehensive list of substances used and abused by youngsters might require almost daily revisions. Problem-prone substances typically get ingested, injected, or inhaled; and, among other things, they may:

- ☐ Bring about a "who cares" emotional disconnectedness.
- ☐ Induce mood changes ranging from euphoria to stupor.
- ☐ Lower inhibitions, leading to violent or reckless behavior.

- ☐ Create overconfidence that leads to unwise choices.
- ☐ Help one stay awake or go to sleep, or aid in concentration.
- ☐ Effect rapid weight gain or loss, or add muscle mass.
- ☐ Mask symptoms like physical pain or emotional distress.
- ☐ Enhance performance and endurance in competitive sports.
- ☐ Bring emotional gratification, as with eating disorders.
- ☐ Cause serious damage to the brain, body, and/or psyche.
- ☐ Lead to physical addiction or psychological dependence.
- ☐ Cause an imminent health crisis, including risk of death.

Factors Involved in Problems with Drugs

The "I'm not OK" syndrome

The more we get all stressed out, the greater becomes the appeal of drugs; and stress on young people comes from dysfunctional and fractured families, a porous safely net in the extended family and in the community, ruthless competition in school and in the peer group, the quest for perfection in looks and style, double messages everywhere related to sex, T.V. shows and magazines promoting superficial values, advertisers trumpeting instant cures for things you never knew ailed you, etc.

Monkey see, monkey do

Prescription and over-the-counter drugs are consumed in staggering quantities in our society; and children notice their parents and other adults forever reaching for something to eat, drink, smoke, swallow, or otherwise cram into their systems. This tends to be underplayed in our polite society, but in fact young people in large measure are just following suit. Teens, however, are famous for copying their parents in a way that puts their own stamp on it; and therefore they end up with precious little input from scientists, medical experts, pharmacists, or F.D.A. watchdogs with their peer-encouraged substance experimentation.

The laws of supply and demand

Drug companies spend a princely sum getting their message delivered, while their shadow-world counterparts rely first of all on word of mouth, and then later on the power of addiction. Yet what they both do well is to conjure up new cravings; and when a demand for a substance grows, entrepreneurial types always find a way to deliver. Illegality is never a big obstacle, as the financial incentives lead to ever more creative methods of staying one step ahead of the long arm of the law. What is more, addicts go to absurd lengths to support their habits; and those lacking the financial wherewithal will drift off into small-time dealing, identity and money theft, prostitution, trading services for drugs, etc.

Influences from outside the family

Young people almost always start using and abusing drugs at the urging of or in the company of others. This involves alcohol, tobacco, street drugs, medicine cabinet drugs, or products stored in the laundry room or under the sink. Experimenting typically has its origins among closest friends, with romantic partners, or in the peer group; and lots of teens learn that drug use not only boosts group status, but also helps cement bonding. Then too, we know that peer group influences are stronger now than in the past.

Relative paucity of educational and treatment programs

Yes indeed, we get frequent "Talk to your kids about drugs" and "Just say no" messages in the media. Catch-phrases such as these cost very little to produce; and at the present time, the lion's share of anti-drug tax dollars are being funneled into law enforcement rather than into education and treatment. When educational programs are given more attention and money, such as has been the case in youth-targeted anti-smoking campaigns, encouraging results tend to emerge.

Dialogue vs. Problems with Drugs

That familiar public service catch-phrase "Talk to your children about drugs" would be better worded "Talk *with* ...." because the former smacks of lecturing, while the latter clearly points to the need for a dialogue. You may give lots of accurate, detailed data to youngsters, but if the atmosphere feels stilted, you won't know how they process it all internally; nor will you get lots of questions and comments, as would be the case in family hour homes. To be sure, arguments might spring up in these families, but a vigorous debate is far better than awkward silences.

The finest anti-drug talks, however, are the ones in which this dreaded subject never even comes up. These are your family hour sessions that focus on anything and everything. They offer a large dose of prevention, since family hour youngsters feel safe in expressing their ideas and feelings to receptive family members, even if the discussions at times might become testy. This is more satisfying and less time-devouring than your running about spying on and grilling youngsters who show possible signs of drug activity. But even family hour youngsters get curious about drugs; and if they do dabble, they will likely possess extra layers of protection against tendencies in the direction of addiction and psychological dependence. Youthful substance abusers typically suffer from a lack of honest, heartfelt communication with family members, and many of them experience significant inner turmoil.

It certainly is an excellent idea to bring up drug issues from time to time in the weekly meetings, and possibly even to devote a whole session or even several to the subject, depending on young ones' ages and circumstances. Please get ready, however, to talk openly about your own experiences with tobacco, alcohol, caffein- ated beverages, and medications--both prescribed and over-the- counter. In addition, it will help you a lot to study up on those sub- stances young folks will be apt to come across, including designer drugs that are so popular at parties. What is more, your research should send you out searching for objective data rather than mere propaganda material.

"Just say no" is a well-intended message; but it is simplistic and it also carries the implication of a finger-wagging parent in the picture. The most effective parental anti-drug arguments are ones focusing on specifics; so in your family meetings you might wish to point out, for example, that:

☐ Juvenile facilities teem with those "too clever to get caught."
☐ Pals offering drugs never mention dangerous side effects.
☐ Drug ingredients vary greatly, as do unintended overdoses.
☐ Mixing drugs can be as deadly as drinking and driving.
☐ No one starts using drugs expecting to become an addict.
☐ Nicotine, crack, meth, and heroin *routinely* cause addiction.
☐ Cigarette and crack smokers are *both* drug addicts.
☐ Gasoline and glue are risky even if *accidentally* inhaled.
☐ "I'll stop soon" never includes visions of painful withdrawal.
☐ "What's in it?" is better asked about drugs than mom's stew.

DELINQUENCY

Our fifteen-year-old began hanging out with a bad crowd, and then he got caught "borrowing" a car for joy riding. In the probation plan we agreed to hold family meetings, but Michael stubbornly refused to open up. We soon felt like giving up; and we would have, except for the fact that we had no real choice. Then Michael started expressing all sorts of resentment toward his mother and me over things we had no idea about, such as his sister's getting a favored status and better treatment, and his never getting to spend enough special time with us. We hope he'll get himself straightened out, but there's no doubt that we understand him quite a lot better now. The funny thing is that his sister is now starting to get all bent out of shape over his getting all the attention. We just may have to hire personal companions for both of them. (Just kidding.)

Business executive,
father of two teens

Delinquency is popularly seen as a community-based phenomenon, but destructive behavior in the home qualifies as well. Youngsters with an intact conscience feel ashamed following malicious acts, while those with enormous pent-up rage or a growing personality disorder tend to justify their actions and derive a sense of satisfaction from their various misdeeds. Among other things, youngsters who are delinquency-inclined may:

- ☐ Place others in harm's way, regardless of conscious intent.
- ☐ Harass those viewed as, weak, odd, foreign, inferior, etc.
- ☐ Steal, cheat people, and damage or destroy property.
- ☐ Humiliate others to impress peers or demonstrate power.
- ☐ Manipulate the vulnerable, ignorant, innocent, or gullible.
- ☐ Risk lives or property through reckless, impulsive behavior.
- ☐ Bully others into gratifying sexual, sadistic, or other desires.
- ☐ Get pleasure from tormenting humans, animals, or insects.
- ☐ Deliberately attempt to damage other people's reputations.

❑ Inflict harm on others through jealousy or quest for power.

❑ Actively seek out socially or legally disapproved activities.

❑ Shirk responsibilities and turn away from those in need.

❑ Consistently disregard the feelings and needs of others.

Factors Related to Problems with Delinquency

Misplaced anger

By nature, anger tends to burst outward, and extroverted young ones let it fly. Enraged parents may "dump" on these small folks, who in turn "dump" on siblings, classmates, or strangers in forms that include bullying, intimidating threats, thievery, property damage, etc. Misplaced anger can also be seen in outer-directed youth who suffer from poor impulse control, built-up frustrations, or general immaturity.

Misplaced emotional gratification

Delinquency springing forth from emotional deprivation is typically the go-it-alone type, and the harm done to others is often a result of the offenders' attempts to find gratification. The sexually indiscriminate and predatory fall into this group, along with the Peeping Toms and exhibitionists, obscene phone callers, celebrity stalkers, shoplifters, identity thieves, etc.

Follow the leader

Youngsters tend to emulate and follow those they admire and find to be charismatic, and this leads many potentially salt-of-the-earth citizens to go astray. In this group are small ones from underworld-connected families and crime-ridden neighborhoods, those reared in anti-social and anti-family cults, and hero-worshipers of delinquency-prone siblings or pals.

The need for close-knit group companionship

When youngsters feel poorly connected to family, they tend instead to connect with peers; and the greater their alienation, the more apt they are to find trouble. But since family unity has been declining across the board in recent times, even children from stable homes could be susceptible to the lure of gangs. And as a result, some otherwise decent young people get involved in dealings they would never consider on their own.

The root of all evil

In our materialistic world, delinquent behavior is often motivated by the lure of money and its buying power. Folks from all walks of life steal out of anger or a sense of emotional deprivation; the underdogs find various ways of buying sneakers they see on T.V.; youthful addicts become dealers or sell sexual favors to feed a habit; those impatient with the corporate-ladder system become scam artists instead; and those who note our society's economic abundance paraded past them by advertisers, might feel driven to get a piece of the action any way they can.

The legal-system maze

Privileged youth at times get to bypass the juvenile justice system entirely, the underprivileged learn to play the system cleverly, and a good many others slip unnoticed between the cracks. With endless bureaucratic and legal maneuvering, and the mixing of vulnerable youngsters with more hardened types, relatively few juveniles get the help they really need.

Dialogue vs. Problems with Delinquency

A powerful delinquency-prevention step is to learn to tolerate youthful expressions of anger. Some parents say "I don't mind them getting angry if they do it in the right way." So when *you* get steamed with your one-and-only, does your voice remain subdued and your language respectful? Now we do not approve of youthful insults, taunting, condescension, or other forms of verbal abuse-- merely the spontaneous airing out of upset feelings. Of course no one enjoys getting verbally blasted, whether it be from somebody higher or lower in rank. If it's from the big boss, prudence dictates that you listen patiently; but when your little ones get hot under the collar, it may be tempting to stifle them with warnings and lectures about showing respect or simply to shout them down.

Indignant little ones certainly would want you to cave in to their wishes, but even if you don't, they will nevertheless appreciate your attentive ear. Also, there is great value in listening to the real message of the anger. Therapists know very well that a sudden eruption is always more informative than a month's worth of chit-chat. As therapists ourselves, we don't know of a solitary delinquent whose parents had both tolerated and listened closely to their unhappy messages.

Another delinquency-squelching tactic calls for your acting preemptively once you notice any danger signs; and trouble-prone youngsters leave clues all over. They may shift the blame, remain sullen, clam up, break toys, break promises, act deviously, offer up far-fetched excuses, give doubtful accounts of their whereabouts, or spend inordinate amounts of time in the company of peers. As you dialogue with these youngsters, you need to listen and to offer support; but get ready to speak your mind frankly about how their behavior concerns you. But in any case, do not get suckered into their sob stories or other manipulations.

Last but not least, the spirit of unity created in family hour sessions and in family-together activities acts likes a powerful antidote to the delinquency-breeding process. This is one brand of preventive medicine that tastes delicious.

DEPRESSION

My teenage years were a living hell, as my mother wouldn't get out of bed for over two years, and we catered to her every need. She finally snapped out of it after my big brother shocked everybody by getting into trouble, but after that she would never talk about those missing years. Actually, she would not talk about anything at all other than surface issues. This experience taught me about never allowing my emotions to build up inside. So when I heard about family meetings, I got right onto it. I get depressed at times--and that really scares me--but I discuss it in our meetings, and I hope I'm not boring everyone else. Mother could have discussed her situation as well, and it makes me sad that she didn't.

Mother with both foster and natural children

Following unhappy events, it is not at all unusual for young people have brief depressive episodes, and these most of the time fade away pretty quickly with the passage of time. There is a real reason for alarm, however, when sadness lingers on and on, and then gets to be chronic. Depression can evidence itself in:

☐ Intense self-criticism, self-loathing, or self-abusive actions.

☐ Ongoing lethargy, loss of appetite, or sense of being adrift.

☐ Gloomy outlook on relationships and on life in general.

☐ Neglect of appearance, possessions, or health needs.

☐ Regular cravings for sugar, caffeine, or other stimulants.

☐ The use of humor to get a brief respite from dark thoughts.

☐ Frequent crying spells or pervasive, unexplained agitation.

☐ Secretiveness regarding thoughts, feelings, and behavior.

- ❏ Diminished interest in favorite hobbies and activities.
- ❏ Precipitous drop-off in academic performance.
- ❏ Voracious overeating--often a sign of feeling deprived.
- ❏ Suicidal passing thoughts, urges, plans, or attempts.

Factors Related to Problems with Depression

The invisible maelstrom

Most observers tend to take people at face value--literally! We all learn to put on a predominant outward expression from an early age. Thus bland-looking folks get overlooked, smiley-faced ones find lots of pleasant interaction, and scowlers tend to scare others off. Yet there is always lots taking place underneath, and a good deal of it is unpleasant. Lots of smilers have a roaring furnace below, but only a therapist might be tempted to poke a stick at it. This contrasts with the sad-faced, who are forever being urged to "turn that frown upside-down." Observers, of course, just wish to see the happy look, and not a hysterical or maniacal one.

Swallowed anger

The same family dynamics that propel outer-directed youth toward an aggressive posture have the opposite effect on the introverted. Thus they don't erupt or cause trouble, but instead they submerge the anger. This process is further aided by "Don't you dare give me that look" remarks. This can lead to internal gloom and symptoms like overeating, loss of appetite, facial tics, sluggish metabolism, lack of motivation, and sleep issues.

Negative feedback and isolation

Lots of children beaten down by regular belittling go on to become expert self-belittlers, and isolation spawns children's fears that they are unworthy of adult-world care and attention. Also, isolation and weak communication provide young ones with a dearth of constructive feedback, and this vacuum provides a fertile breeding ground for glum opinions about themselves and society. Then without intervention, this darkness tends to stick around.

Impossibly high standards for achievement and responsibility

High achievement and the assuming of responsibility--what could be wrong with these? Much can go wrong when parental or youthful expectations are unreasonable and unrealistic, and when pressure from any direction stirs the pot. Youngsters terrified over being outdone by others or falling short of achieving perfection are at grave risk for self-destructive thoughts or depression; and those feeling responsible for other people's happiness may end up in a similar morass. Parents' success-mongering and guilt-trip tactics can play a major role in these syndromes.

Masking the symptoms

When taken in for treatment, some depressive children get talking therapy; but more are seen primarily to monitor the effects of medication. When mood and behavior-altering drugs burst onto the scene a while back, they were touted as an adjunct to dynamic therapy; but they have mostly come to replace therapy altogether, and thus they cut short the opportunity to seek out underlying factors and to get upset feelings released. What is more, family therapy, a highly effective tool for combating youthful depression, is at present a relatively rare form of treatment.

Dialogue vs. Problems with Depression

All children start out life expressing feelings and needs with great gusto. Their wailing might not be pleasant to the ears, but it does help to maintain internal equilibrium--in fact, infants seem to get depressed mostly when they suffer continuing neglect. Later on, little ones learn to put their distress into words, but their need to discharge emotions lasts a lifetime. Children raised in dialogue, which welcomes spontaneous expression, are unlikely to slide into a prolonged slump. This holds true even when the parents themselves tend toward depressiveness; but only if they come to view their mental and physical lethargy as internal problems rather than to project it all onto the world around them--a world where oodles of wonderful things are taking place all the time.

Physical and emotional isolation contribute heavily to the formation of depressive tendencies; so your family hour sessions, where the interaction can be lively, are a big insurance policy protecting everyone--especially the younger set--against the forces of gloom. Here, your little ones' upset feelings are not simply tolerated, but are seen as having value. This squeezes out the potential of feeding the inner demons, which require repressed emotionality in order to thrive. Then too, family hour leaves absolutely no room for derision, intimidation, self-pitying remarks, parental or youthful pressuring, lecturing, or other less than helpful inputs--all of which can sow the seeds of a depressive system.

Finally, if you suspect that your young one may already be caught tightly in the grip of a gloomy syndrome, please be careful about coaxing or prodding troubled feelings out into the open, as this will most likely get met with flat resistance. Instead, steer your discussions into emotionally comfortable territory, have some fun together, give encouraging feedback and support, and provide the excellent example of letting your own feelings flow. You can also talk at times about what you suspect might be behind their gloom, but do so without any expectation of a response. And when your young one finally does erupt over some issues large or small, be sure to bite your tongue and simply listen.

DROP-OUT

Our second boy has been overweight since he was four, and he started stuttering at about the time he first went off to school. Needless to say, he was a loner and got a lot of teasing while growing up. We always encouraged him to join into activities, but to no avail. Now he's twenty-three and spends most of the time in his room fooling around with his computer. We think it's a good sign that he talks to others over the internet, but he won't go into any detail about it. Some friends say I should kick him out of the house, but the very thought of all the things that could happen to him makes me ill. We began holding family meetings as a means for helping him to open up, but he stopped coming after the first time. Now both of my teenagers are dragging their heels about attending, and they complain about Derek's getting all of our attention. Right now I'm searching for a support group, as I am at the end of my rope. How I wish we could start all over again.

Homemaker, mother of 4

Drop-out is largely viewed as a breaking away from school, family, or mainstream society; but it can also be a state of mind. Most drop-outs, and especially those who are out on their own, are at great risk for physical and emotional ills; and lots of them are burdened with one or more of the other disablers. Among other things, potential or actual drop-outs may:

- ☐ Get labeled as a troublemaker or black sheep of the family.
- ☐ Live with a feeling that they are a burden on their parents.
- ☐ Take up with anti-social gangs or anti-family religious cults.
- ☐ Quit school in frustration, and with no realistic alternatives.

❏ In an alienated state, use the house mostly as free lodging.

❏ Withdraw into a world of fantasy-laden internet ventures.

❏ Drift from job to job, uninvolved and vaguely disgruntled.

❏ Sponge off parents and duck school and career decisions.

❏ As a runaway, live on the streets or in chaotic relationships.

❏ Live an underworld life of hiding out and/or incarceration.

❏ Travel widely, scraping by from doing odd jobs or begging.

❏ As a psych patient, live home, in a facility, or on public aid.

Factors Related to Problems with Drop-out

Intolerable conditions in the household

Conditions such as physical, psychological, and/or sexual abuse; biting poverty; chronic hatefulness; substance abusing and emotionally ill parents; and other dysfunctional family behavior can readily propel teens toward ill-fated relationships or simply toward running away. With precious little preparation for a steadfast, self-sufficient life, they often end up on society's fringes.

Alienation from family and/or society

Here you find young folks who have contempt for their parents' values, play the role of black sheep, fail to meet parents' lofty expectations, get discouraged in marginal or fractured families, or simply can't stand a step-parent. These and other similar types all are ripe for the plucking by anti-government militias, racist groups, doomsday religious cults, and underworld networks.

Weak links to nuclear and extended family

Young adults with fragile family ties may start out nicely on their own, but many get knocked flat by the inevitable setbacks of independent living, such as job loss, relationship failure, or a major health crisis. And sensing that family members might lack the interest in or ability for providing support and help, they can easily get lost in the shuffle.

Unreadiness for a self-sufficient life.

Various categories can be found here--emotional instability and fragility; all-consuming anger; marginal intelligence; extreme immaturity; pathological overprotection; head-in-the-sand naivete; willingness to trust anybody and everybody; long-term, paralyzing depression; functionality-impairing drug and alcohol addiction; and neurological, physical, and other handicaps that drastically narrow career opportunities and impede social adjustment.

Problems handling career and financial decisions

Youngsters at sea over budgeting or terrified about career choices often find the home to be a cozy hiding place, particularly if their parents tend to be coddlers. Then others with tenuous job situations and no reserve funds are just one paycheck away from running back home or landing in the street, particularly when they have young mouths to feed.

Dialogue vs. Problems with Drop-out

Family ties will always remain strong unless long-festering domestic turmoil or alienation nibbles away at them; and drop-out prevention is at its zenith when you continue on, through peaceful and dreary times, with dialogue-laden family meetings along with other family-together activities. This is particularly true for homes severely tested by financial stresses, marital break-up, long-standing bickering, adolescent crises, and other misfortunes.

If you see your young ones slipping into the drop-out zone, whether or not they are still living in the house, open up discussion without delay into sensitive areas, no matter how painful it may be for all; and keep in mind that these young folks need your unwavering support and loyalty--even though you may have a strong distaste for some of their actions. At times their floundering might be difficult to watch, but your patience will be rewarded as you maintain broad-net support and a standing offer of constructive help, if and when they request it.

When all your attempts at dialogue have failed and drop-out is here, please refrain from what-could-have-been agonizing, the blame game, and bouts of self-flagellation. Praying fervently and crying on the shoulders of loved ones are fine, but you might also work on letting go--e.g., of long-held bitterness on your part, of rigid views on youthful values, or of reluctance to admit errors. This is also an excellent time to lay out the groundwork for reconciliation and re-inclusion. Even if your young ones' actions dismay you, keep in mind that they will evermore be your closest kin. And as you hold out welcoming arms, dropping out may soon change to dropping in. Then one day in the future, your former drop-outs may in turn extend their arms to you in your own time of need.

SECTION IV

ENRICHING YOUNG LIVES THROUGH FAMILY HOUR

CHAPTER TEN

HELPING CHILDREN REACH
THEIR CREATIVE POTENTIAL

*We try to reserve one family meeting each month
for putting on talent shows, and recently our nine-
year-old Seth planned on performing several magic
tricks. First he did some card tricks, and they had
just limited success; and then he announced as his
grand finale that he had made his report card disappear. The other kids laughed hysterically, and I
must admit I had a difficult time wiping a smile from
my face. I told him that it was all terribly funny, but
now was the time to make that card reappear. So
with a straight face he told me he hadn't yet learned
that part of the trick (more laughs). After the meeting I took him aside, and after a measure of cajoling
he finally figured out how to reconstitute the vapor-
ized card. It really was not as bad as I had feared,
and in retrospect I could see that his quick thinking
and showmanship were quite clever.*

Teacher, mother of 5

A forlorn wish of countless "ordinary folks" is to have been
blessed with a few ounces of God-given talents that creative mas-

ters have in abundance. They would be far better off, however, to give up their wishing and instead get in touch with the buckets of talent they already have within. This treasure trove so often stays underdeveloped because our society tends to discourage creativity, particularly in the formative years, when so many young people are encouraged by well-intentioned grown-ups to walk along safe, mainstream-endorsed paths in every phase of their lives. After all, who knows where creativity will take you?

> *In one of our once-a-week get-togethers, our eight-year-old Joanne talked excitedly about this dream she had the night before about playing the piano, and then she paused and asked if we would allow her to take lessons. Her dad and I quickly agreed, so now she is playing in front of audiences and is even thinking of possibly making it a career. I had never given it much thought before, but now I firmly believe in the power of dreaming.*
>
> *Systems analyst, mom of 2*

About Creativity

To most people "creativity" conjures up images of the arts, literature, and inventions--and not of everyday life. Yet the truth is that every aspect of daily living is a wellspring of potentially creative endeavors. We'll define creativity as using your own ideas to end up with something of value--practical, artistic, or both. On the artistic side we have such as painting, music, dancing, stage plays and cinema, literature, and crafts; and practical works include machines, tools, structures, new materials, need-filling services, and money-saving or efficient ways of doing anything. Creative ideas help resolve problems like getting a closet to yield greater storage space, or working out compromises with an obstinate young tyke.

Some creativity needs mental pump-priming, and some comes in a flash; but as a rule, a fair amount of effort is required for putting innovative works into their polished, usable form.

The imprint of creativity is found everywhere--in the ancient pyramids and aqueducts, in modern skyscrapers and super-jumbo jets, in art galleries and museums, in machinery and gadgets, and through the pages of history and science books. But creativity is not the inevitable result of strenuous, unflagging work, nor has any Thomas Edison type ever been able to teach it to others. We are all simply blessed with this gift at birth. So if you would want your children to fulfill their creative potential, you will need to get busy on two fronts: first, take care not to throw roadblocks in their path; and on the doing side, expose them to a wide variety of ideas and experiences. And you can accomplish all this without turning them into misfits or "starving artists."

Certain creative urges are so powerful that they will in time burst forth despite disdain from every direction--but that is the exception. In a supportive environment, children select from a large menu of ideas and experiences offered by parents, writers, teachers, and radio and T.V. personalities, among others. Then as time passes and they become more self-sufficient, some future shining lights apprentice with mentors, while others study the ideas and works of those they admire. But a true measure of their creativity is seen in the final product. The genuinely inventive may start off mimicking whatever captivates their fancy, but sooner or later they branch out into unchartered territories, affixing their own individual stamp on a work, or "speaking with their own voice."

It's good to be creative, but not every moment of one's day. Creative thinking and activity, after all, can be exhausting; and we all cherish some time for "zoning out" in mindless fun and relaxation. Furthermore, creative thinking and the products and services accruing from it allow us to get into routines more efficiently, effectively, and comfortably. Examples of this rest in the operating of electronic equipment, adopting well-proven bookkeeping methods, paying heed to the instructions of seasoned supervisors, preparing cookbook meals, reading, listening to music, playing bingo or solitaire, or getting into fixed routines of all kinds. And this is as it should be for much of everyday life.

It's good to be creative, but not if it involves a questionable purpose, like devising clever ways to con people out of their hard-earned money; getting so wrapped up in theories and projects that bills, loved ones, and your own health get sorely neglected; stubbornly refusing to heed tried-and-true methods for doing a job; or "creatively" putting together a model airplane from a kit--a method that in almost all cases simply won't fly. And dazzled by "new and improved" formulas, we can quickly lose touch with "naturally perfect" remedies that get passed down through the generations. In addition, labor-saving devices can "save" our muscles from doing the work need to stay in good condition.

It's good to be creative, but don't go looking for the magic in it, as every aspect of it can ultimately be explained--even if it's not in plain view. The universe operates on fixed principles of science; and if any part of this system were to break down, a frightful chaos would ensue. So whenever we disregard nature's laws, we will suffer appropriate penalties. Creative folks, then, simply "discover" concepts that already exist, or conjure up new forms of arranging, combining, or otherwise modifying the enormous array of conceptual or concrete materials.

Creativity in the workplace

Certain careers lend themselves to creative impulses that burst forth in abundance--inventor, social trail-blazer, composer, film director, engineer, scientific researcher, urban planner, advertising wonderperson, and trend-setter in any field. What is more, creative thinking can assist schoolteachers, team coaches, battle-field generals, sales directors, interior decorators, workshop train-ers, etc. In fact almost any chore, however routine, has room for innovative tinkering. This might be even more the case today than it was a generation or two ago, as so many strictly repetitive tasks are now fully automated and computerized.

Then again, no matter how much space or encouragement workers are afforded, creativity constitutes only a small portion of any undertaking. After novel projects emerge, loads of time inevi-tably goes into the practical detail work. Then once an idea, prod-uct, or service proves out successful, the higher-ups tend to want to see it repeated, perhaps with a cosmetic change or two, again and again. This is where money comes in. In a for-profit setting, creative ideas are valued mainly for their improving on the bottom line. And in governmental and non-profit arenas, creativity is often brought into play to bolster efficiency or improve service. Directly or indirectly, this may also involve the pocketbook.

Next we come to the self-employed creative types. Among them are fine artists, artisans, musicians, actors, stand-up comics, landscape and building architects, inventors, interior decorators, fashion designers, self-betterment mavens, financial planners, etc. Relatively few of these entrepreneurs strike serious gold; yet when this does occur, they could become tempted to repeat themselves again and again. And for those struggling to make ends meet, the scent of the long green might become a bigger motivator than the cravings of the heart. To be sure many of the independently crea-tive hold down a "real job" as a way to keep the payment-awaiting wolves away from the door.

Creativity as a hobby

Some fascinating hobbies involve a lesser degree of crea-tivity, like collecting coins, antiques, and memorabilia; participating in literature, art, and music appreciation groups; playing board and word-puzzle games; and managing a team in a fantasy-league of sports. While some are content with hobbies such these, others move outward toward ones that demand a higher degree of creative thinking and planning. In this group are checkers and chess, original crafts, science experiments, ceramics, quilting and dress making, found-object sculptures, community theater productions, furniture crafting, home-improvement projects, scout leadership, mentoring, and holiday lighting and decorating.

Leisure-time creativity might demand a good deal of effort and patience, but the rewards make it very much worthwhile. Do-it-yourselfers enjoy their projects immensely, have no supervisors peering over their shoulders, take enormous pride in their finished products, feel no pressures from production quotas or deadlines, bask in the admiration bestowed upon them, and often make extra income in the process. In fact, some free-time hobbies have even evolved over time--a great bonus indeed--into hugely successful and satisfying careers.

Creativity in children

When you watch small ones at play, you have to marvel at their boundless energy, straightforwardness, and wonderment as they discover and learn. But their play also gives you the chance to witness creativity in its embryonic stages. Unburdened by concerns about academic standing, peer approval, or future-life preparation, they give full expression to their imaginations. You see this in their making up silly names, chatting with imaginary friends, spinning tall tales, crafting artworks from blocks and clay, crayon-drawing eerie scenes, tricking friends and family, walking and gesturing in comically absurd ways, etc. Indeed from the earliest age, young people seem to delight in putting their personal stamp upon everything they undertake.

Children's expressing themselves imaginatively, however, is only the sprouted acorn of the adult-life oak tree. The creativity-speckled careers and hobby projects they embrace later on, to be sure, all have their origins in early life experiences. Concert soloists--even those who never toddled around with a violin in hand--were engrossed in the music all around them; engineers typically spent hours making Lego creations or taking appliances apart and putting them back together; artists, never content to draw within the lines, invariably made fascinating choices regarding color and composition; professional social directors were the ones who had a passion for planning and running tea parties attended by all their little friends; and lawyers and labor negotiators spent many hours sitting on a chair staring intently at a chessboard. Of course some in this group also went on to become chess champions.

> *Nancy got her feelings hurt at various times during our family hour sessions, after which she would run up to her bedroom crying. A few of her outbursts were so sudden, in fact, that most of the rest of us had no idea what the problem was. Sometimes the others would even go upstairs to console her. She outgrew this with time, but what she never outgrew was a flair for the dramatic. Now Nancy is majoring in theater at college, and she appears to be really impressive in scenes that feature weeping and wailing. But she's great at comedy as well.*
>
> *Mother of 5 in blended family*

Our society sends out conflicting messages regarding creativity. On the one hand it shines a huge spotlight on trend-setting performances and artworks, and on the people who create them; yet at the same time it places numerous obstacles into the path of these same folks in their formative years.

Roadblocks to Youthful Creativity

Roadblocks put up by school systems

Standardized testing is the gatekeeper for all students advancing from one grade to the next in our bureaucratic school systems. Yet you cannot standardize creativity, and measuring comprehension skills involves some subjectivity. Therefore, memorizing poetry and prose passages, historical dates, times tables, and the like, predominates in standardized tests. Compliance, elegant writing, and helpfulness to teacher get rewarded too; and this contributes to the smooth running of classroom routine. This is really easy to understand at present, as classroom teachers, especially those slaving away in inner city schools, are largely overburdened and under-appreciated.

Yes, there are teachers who encourage youthful imagination, and in certain cases they must squeeze it into their agendas. Then there are the relatively few, mostly smaller schools that put creativity at or near the top of their lists. But most youngsters are rewarded not for how prodigiously they broaden their minds, but rather for how accurately they regurgitate assigned materials; and they are offered instruction not when they are interested in or feel ready for it, but when the school decides the time has come. This presents a climate alien to the cultivation of creativity; so it is no wonder that legions of successful creative folks all confess to having felt bored to tears or totally out of place in their regular classroom setting. And more than a few got thrown out of school.

Roadblocks put up by the marketplace

When did you last see help-wanted ads for portrait painter, political gadfly, philosopher, poet, guru, composer, and innovator of any kind? In a society as money-driven as ours, the classifieds seldom list anything excepting that which helps to increase profits.

Those who reshape society or beautify it through their artworks all burn with ambition to bring their ideas and works to the public eye; and their zeal is sorely needed in doing battle with the enemies of change and innovation--those who respond with heels-firmly-dug-in opposition, sneers, nary a scintilla of interest, or flat-out refusal to help. Those who successfully weave their way through these obstacles are apt to have bulldog personalities and/or ardent convictions about the importance of their work.

Indeed, mainstream society seems intent on clinging onto the status quo and fending off those threatening to stir things up. But the good news is that once changes get established, whether in the way politics operates or the way music is performed, society in time adjusts--until the next threat of change appears on the horizon, at which time the cycle repeats itself again. School systems have to prepare children for a creativity-alien workplace, so their reluctance to encourage creativity is understandable. Then again, the marketplace has always carved out a niche for creativity of the means-to-an-end variety, such as that turned out by costume designers, engineers of every specialty, scientific researchers, and corporate managers.

Roadblocks put up by parents

Those who come up with prize-winning photos, galleried sculptures, and big hit records make their kinfolk really proud. As ten-year-olds, many of these future artists showed great enthusiasm for taking candid photos, modeling clay figurines, or singing along to taped music; and they demonstrated much less enthusiasm for keeping up with their homework and other school assignments. So in addition to getting yelled at or punished, they usually got warned that their "tomfoolery" would never lead to productive, decent-paying jobs. Surely parents would feel a lot more enthusiastic about youthful creative passions if they could be offered the assurance that it would result in success at the marketplace. But unfortunately, we have all heard stories about creative giants who developed an important sideline in scrounging handouts from family and friends, and in ducking the landlord.

Parents who worry about their children's lagging behind in the academic rat-race tend to embrace the memorize-and-shine system; and the mantra that echoes from these homes is "grades, grades, grades." Certain young people spend long periods under house arrest for being classroom sluggards, and others get showered with gifts as "incentives" for getting back on track. Then too, some parents spend long hours every evening prodding their little ones up the learning ladder. So as rote work grabs the spotlight, creativity gets left in the lurch. But for many youngsters, creative urges bubble up from inside anyway. And this may contribute to hot-and-heavy confrontations peppered with barbs like "You're frittering away your life on that nonsense." Then again, for parents with visions of an Ivy-League-school future for their little ones, the constant harping on grades does have its practical side. Yes, the Ivy Bigs are cllearly interested in "grades, grades, grades."

Roadblocks put up by toy and sporting goods manufacturers

In times past, little girls played with cotton rag dolls "manufactured" by a loving grandma, whereas today's electronically-impulsed dolls roll off assembly lines. Modern-day lasses delight (for a short while anyway) in hearing dolly's voice saying she is hungry or sleepy, but their great-grandmothers got to decide those and all other matters of "mommy care" for themselves. Game playing has a similar sort of story. Boys of yesteryoar, swatting at balls with a stick and using lampposts for bases, had command over their own competitive destinies. Modern little leaguers are smartly outfitted in uniforms and gear, and are guided by intense coaches hammering home the finer points of the game; and they also have intense parents screaming out gems of wisdom at them, as well as at the coaches, umpires, and other parents.

Manufacturers of action toys, computer games, and sports equipment do not see themselves as opponents of creativity; they simply desire to make money. And armed with always-burgeoning technologies, many of them have succeeded admirably. But then again, if there were huge profits to be made in promoting ingenuity, they would race up to the front of the line. Youngsters from an era devoid of toy superstores played with found materials, bought or shaped basic dolls and balls, told stories, and played interactive games; and few of them felt at all deprived. To be sure, a gaggle of wonderful creative games and toys are available nowadays, but store owners as a rule promote computer-driven ones that tend to rake in the highest profits.

Roadblocks put up by the entertainment industry

Today's entertainment choices are totally dazzling. Dance troupes, movies and plays, music festivals, sporting events, and theme parks are but a few of the out-of-the-home choices; and in house we find radios, T.V.s, computers, and all sorts of electronic games and other gadgets. Modern youth cannot fathom how their ancestors got by without all the razzle-dazzle technology at hand today. Indeed, folks of yore had none of the entertainment options our children take for granted now, but they were skilled at amusing themselves and highly creative in the process. Today's entertainment industry might be flashy and splashy; but, sad to relate, it is putting the boa constrictor squeeze on young people's capacity for thinking imaginatively.

Like toy makers, youth-oriented entertainment C.E.O.s are motivated mainly by the sweet smell of profits; and the competition among filmmakers and T.V. programmers is particularly fierce. To their credit, certain moguls would love to nudge young folks on to expand their minds and horizons. But then they become sobered by visions of ratings disasters; so they head for the cozy refuge of mediocrity, and the same lame ideas get rehashed over and over. Critics, parents, and community activists complain long and loud, but programming executives have yet to show the slightest inclination to scrap formulas that work every time out--car chases, alien invasion, super-heroes fighting evildoers, tormented hit-men, teen anxiety, sappy romances, sexual titillation, crime bosses, mistaken identity, moronic misadventures, and sequel after sequel of blockbuster hits that will surely bring long lines to the box office.

> *Howard has always been an underachiever, and in spite of all of our prodding, he has never gotten one iota of motivation. However, he spends a lot of time drawing comic strips, creating humor skits, and putting on puppet shows. At least that has to be better than hanging around the street corners with all the local hoodlums. We always had hope of his getting into accounting like his father, but I guess we might forget about that for good. At the rate he's going at present, he may not even be able to get into a community college. Then again, perhaps puppetry will become all the rage one of these days.*
>
> *Party planner, mother of 2*

Molding children into champion skaters or spellers takes a substantial commitment of time and money from parents, who also need patience and perseverance in order to see all these projects through. Then on the other hand, helping young people fulfill their creative potential, wherever their talents may lie, usually requires little time and effort. After all, true creativity is both self-motivated and self-energizing. In fact, if you appoint yourself as taskmaster over a burgeoning creative talent, you risk putting a damper on the enthusiasm that propels it. Rest assured, however, that there are many ways for your being of genuine help. Who knows, you could even become junior partner in a smooth-running child-parent alliance. And aside from the enjoyment you both might get from such an arrangement, it might prove very helpful in greasing the wheels of the youth emancipation process later on.

Promoting Youthful Creativity

Encourage early interests and talents

Youthful dabbling doesn't in every instance lead to creative careers or hobbies, and yet its influence is seen in adult dealings in forms both obvious and subtle. Today's passing interest, after all, may grow to become tomorrow's flaming passion. So the first step for stirring up youthful imaginations is to make a mental note of activities that appeal to your young ones, even ones that seem nonsensical or boring. Interests such as the following might hold a potential for future creative works: science experiments, dismantling household appliances, studying electrical circuits, math problem solving, persuasiveness, deal making skills, word play, public speaking, construction of all kinds, absorption in chess and other strategy games, free-hand drawing, singing and instrument playing, dance, and story and joke telling.

Encouraging small ones' interests and talents does not require loads of effort. Keep your eye on what fascinates them most intensely over a period of time--and try to keep your own leanings out of the equation. Also, don't stew over whether a particular interest may lead to a creative career path, as the future will always bring forth surprises. And there is no need for lavishing praise and encouragement on them; a word or two here and there will in most cases do just fine. Little ones much appreciate your merely taking the time--even in occasional snippets--to watch them as they play and to talk with them about some of their actions.

Provide youngsters with a wide variety of experiences

Your little ones are naturally inclined to involve themselves in certain of your interests such as cooking, music, crafts, sports, handyperson projects, church programs, and gardening. What is more, you may want them to study ballet, try scouting, or take advanced classes at school. Organized activities like these are fine, but creativity can emerge from mere exposure to a wide variety of experiences; and the wider is the range, the more potential doors may get opened up. According to how each young one responds, interests calling out for youthful and/or parental follow-up can get identified. But even among all those activities children pursue further, there is no way to tell which ones will sow the seeds for spirit-fulfilling careers or hobbies. Then again, consider that even their very brief involvement can broaden horizons.

The possibilities for creativity-generating experiences are plentiful, and include science museums, art galleries, theater and concert performances, cultural festivals, historical re-enactments, national and state parks, and weekend and vacation trips to fascinating places. You can also lobby for the viewing of educational T.V. shows over the mindless variety; host exchange students; encourage young people to become pen pals; sample oddball books, music, and movies together; do research on countries and stateside places in the news; and become involved in church-related and community projects that help wildlife, needy folks, the elderly, and the environment. And let's not forget your regular family hour discussions about anything and everything.

Turn youngsters into junior philosophers

Philosophers never tire of posing questions about the purpose of our existence, the workings of nature, and the definitions of good and evil. And while they often arrive at conclusions, they look upon the process of inquiry itself as having great value. This is because people blindly adopting the opinions and facts provided by others will stunt their capacity for doing critical analysis, which can very easily lead to blinders-on living with precious little tapping into one's creative potential. And closed-mindedness, as we saw earlier in the chapter, is an arch-enemy of creativity.

We all have opinions on a broad range of subjects, and we naturally share lots of them with our children. But we should also encourage them to delve into these and other subjects independently, so as to stimulate their reasoning-out capacity. A sound rule of thumb, in fact, would hold that for every topic on which you give them "the final word," you should present them with at least one other for which you don't know the answers. The world is a highly complex place, and our ignorance about it all by far outweighs our knowledge. So be the philosopher and pose all sorts of questions, present a smorgasbord of theories, and assure youngsters that it is OK to remain in the dark. After all, it was believed a while back that television was a clever idea, but also an impractical one. So rest easy in the knowledge that your open-mindedness and strong bonds with little ones will influence them greatly for the good, and that they will discover all sorts of wonders on their own.

Keep creative interests and hobbies out of the "penalty box."

When children misbehave or get poor grades, lots of parents respond by grounding them or canceling privileges--beloved creative interests often taking the biggest hit. Their motivation is simply to get young transgressors to tow the line, but resorting to intimidation as a tool is risky business. For starters, these youngsters are more inclined to wallow in resentment over losing out on their favorite activity than they are to contemplate the error of their ways; and even if the leveraging succeeds, it gets them "straightened out" through fear rather than from having gotten enlightened.

We have observed again and again in our clinical practice that the more children get punished, the more they simmer with anger and start tending to doubt themselves.

This is a good time to review Chapter 8, where we pointed out that punishment can in most cases be avoided through using dialogue and through rethinking the notion of "punishable offense." We further noted that punishments which relate to the misdeeds present an opportunity for children to evaluate their behavior; and creative projects almost never fall into this category. The same is true for failing grades. Yes, academic slackers might spend more time on their hobbies than on their studies, but this does not make hobbies the *cause* of the problem. So make sure that homework gets done first; then, opening up dialogue, go looking into the root factors involved in the academic malaise. Then your hobby situation should take care of itself.

Be helpful to children in their creative pursuits

You will no doubt encourage young ones' interests that delight you, but don't ignore ones that make you yawn or leave you mystified. The following traps need to be avoided: injecting more energy into activities than your small ones do, appointing yourself to be unofficial manager of a youth-initiated project, placing pressure on young ones to accelerate their progress, holding creative interests hostage in cases of below-expectations grades or behavior, using money to influence the direction of a creative undertaking, and poking into any youth-headed activity without indication of wrongdoing. This is a relationship and trust killer.

There are oodles of ways you can help youngsters as they follow their whims and dreams: e.g., by listening to their ideas and feelings about the blossoming interest; giving support, praise, and helpful feedback in ways that don't smack of supervision; voicing your misgivings about projects that appear to be dubious, and presenting specifics on why you think so; getting actively involved as assistants, researchers, consultants, etc.; offering transportation where it is appropriate; providing financial assistance, but only as you get convinced that it will be spent in a productive way; urging youthful investigations into resources that might provide financial support and upgrades for a great new undertaking; and reminding youngsters that they should study up on an area of interest before they put lots of creative energy into it.

Use family hour as a laboratory and showcase for creativity

Any family hour discussion can stimulate creative energies, whether the subject is the purpose of our existence, entertainment mega-stars, events in the news, scientific theories, neighborhood gossip, or the latest in styles. Dialogue not only keeps new ideas flowing on a continual basis, but it also gives young ones practice in processing these ideas and handling critiques from others in the family group. What is more, it encourages them to proffer weighty questions and to strongly trust their own instincts. Also, you might open up discussion into how creative careers and hobbies evolve; and be sure not to soft-peddle the struggles that could come from following a creative career line far from the mainstream establishment. In addition, you might want to ruminate over how innovative thinking has impacted your own life. But most important of all, assure little ones that they all possess creative talents; and point out to them, if you notice some clear indications, a few areas in which you suspect that their talents may lie.

In addition to aiding creativity in general, your family group meetings hold the potential for providing a showcase for youthful talents as was observed in Chapter 4. Your schedule may include debates, political forums, rehearsed or spontaneous dramas, educational presentations, film and book reviews, demonstrations of magic, music and dance performances, quiz shows, recitations of poetry and essays, art and science exhibitions, leadership development programs, stand-up comedy and skits, fashion pageants, and so much more. What is more, youngsters can be encouraged to plan for and act as chair for certain of these meetings. Let your creative instincts be your guide!

> *I wasn't real crazy about getting into our family hour discussions, especially the thing about having to sit next to my bratty younger sister. After us kids complained about the talks being so boring, my parents agreed to have us do some fun things. We all get a chance to select the activity, and my brothers really know how to come up with some dopey ones. My favorite of all is the "Imagination Game," and we do it fairly often. All the cards have a single word on it, and the first person to draw tells a story based on that word. The next family member draws another card, and then must connect the new word with that same story. Then the whole process gets repeated over and over. It's really lots of fun, and it teaches you to think fast. And my sister and I can even tolerate each other now--well, sometimes.*
>
> *Oldest of four children*

All small children are gifted with a powerful, inborn creative drive, and the more motivated and determined among them might later move on toward satisfying careers and hobbies that put their imaginative ideas to good use. Creativity-dampening influences, however, can exact a heavy toll on these little ones all during their growing-up years; but your helpful support for them in all their interests and endeavors can outweigh these influences and open up the doors to creativity even wider. And even when the youngsters fail to go later on into careers or hobbies that give full vent to their imaginations, you will no doubt see their creativity putting in an appearance in one form or another.

We have always encouraged our young warriors to express themselves, and they certainly make use of their imaginations in our weekly family meetings. But then they outdid themselves on a recent occasion when they put on a crazy spoof that made fun of their father and me, and also of their auntie and grandmother who spend blocks of time here at the house. This may sound defensive, but I don't think their portrayal of me was accurate in the least; but then again, my funny bone may need some serious massaging. Next time I would like to see them do a spoof that makes fun of themselves.

Mother of 4 unruly offspring

CHAPTER ELEVEN

HELPING CHILDREN BECOME

POSITIVE THINKERS

We had family discussions for a few months some time ago. I thought it was time to sit down together and talk after I had divorced their father--for a second time! The girls had a lot of anger, and most of it seemed to be directed at me. This was not at all easy to stomach, but I sealed my lips and let them talk it out; and in time they came to have a better idea about my situation. Ever since then our communication has gotten better, and I realize this experience helped me to sort things out. The girls are now out on their own, and they vow that they won't make the same mistakes I did. That is probably all true--so they will make different mistakes instead. And that's all fine, as long as they learn something from the experience.

Business owner, mother of 2

Positive thinking has been all the rage for some time now. Adherents devour books, flock to workshops, and repeat affirmations over and over in search of a sunnier mental outlook. Their motivation? A sense of drowning in an ocean of negativity--morbid thoughts, self-doubting, self-criticism, guilt, resentments, depression, and/or despair. Negativity doesn't spring up all of a sudden, but rather takes years of practice, almost always beginning in the formative years. This means that all those striving toward positive thinking in the next generation will emerge from the ranks of present-day youth who, sad to say, are getting stuck in self-denigrating thinking patterns right now.

So doesn't it make sense to nip any funereal thinking in the bud before it obtains a grimly entrenched foothold? Yes, there are programs, usually school-based, designed to bolster self-esteem-- positive thinking by another name. But these efforts are typically remedial, aimed at little ones already saddled with some degree of inner turmoil; and they seldom get to the root sources of the problem. Common wisdom indicates that caring, harmonious households produce sunny-thinking youth; and that, on the other end of the spectrum, angst-riddled, dysfunctional households give rise to a dark-cloud mentality. And in general this tends to be exactly the case; but high-powered optimists somehow emerge out of conflict-torn households, and all too many caring, close-knit families have turned out depressive, and even suicidal young people. So there is obviously more to the story than meets the eye.

> *When I was growing up, awkward silences were a way of life in my house. Everybody seemed to be unhappy, but nobody ever spoke up about anything even remotely related to "unhappy" issues. I wasn't ever openly ridiculed that I remember, but I wasn't encouraged either. Nonetheless, I came to have a poor opinion of myself, and I got into addictions at an early age. I've had a lot of therapy and twelve-step involvement over the years, and I've always lived alone. Life is an ongoing struggle, but some breaks have come my way too.*
>
> *Semi driver, survivor*

> *When my oldest girl was barely toddling around, we lived across the street from a young couple whose daughter was around five. Every so often we would hear the mother's screaming that could surely have been heard a block or two away, and the message she bellowed out was always the same--"Helen, be happy. Helen, be happy!" Over the years I have at times wondered about whether little Helen ever got to be happy, and whether at this time she cringes whenever somebody wishes her a "happy birthday."*
> *Mother of four (truly) happy children*

Parents don't deliberately set out to plant the seeds of self-doubting and self-criticism in their little ones; in fact, few give it a thought until a crisis jumps up. Parents need not be paragons of positive thinking themselves in order to nip in the bud the cycle of negativity in young children. Even those who struggle with marital wrangling or their own inner demons can keep their small ones on the right track, and they can get it done without compromising one iota of their head-of-house authority. But in cases where a system of negative thinking has already made an appearance, it can get reversed; although this calls for lots of awareness and consistent effort on the parental side. Now dim thoughts cannot be banished altogether, as all children--particularly adolescents--are inclined at times to sing the blues. The problem arises only when gloom becomes overwhelming or hangs around on a regular basis.

On the face of it, the formula for positive thinking seems to be pretty much self-evident: mix equal parts good cheer, optimism, and self-confidence, and voila! Yet a cheerfully intoxicated, "invincible" driver, disregarding scare tactics of seat-belt scolds, may be only seconds away from a head-into-the-windshield crash. This sort of "positive" mind set is obviously one we do not endorse. So let's go deeper, starting with keys to unlocking the door to happy-endings type positive thinking.

Keys to Positive Thinking

Positive thinking is informed

Some stereotypical positive thinkers sashay along smiling in their Brady Bunch world of make believe, and in most instances they harbor a burning desire to be liked. These folks afford everybody the benefit of the doubt, get duped by or just can't "say no" to persuasive or mournful manipulation, and may not notice when a spouse or child gives off distress signals. Then if their world collapses around them, they tend to feel hurt, mystified, or dismayed; and they rarely learn lessons from the experience. Such "positive" thinking is positively dangerous.

Ignorance *is* bliss in benign or protected surroundings, but not if your house sits near a toxic waste dump or if you gobble up, no questions asked, a few feel-good pills given by a friend. Here, you may start out blissful, but you soon become remissful. In this complex world of ours, we need oceans of data about various subjects so as to stay safe. But all too many folks, accepting dubious information as gospel or making naive assumptions, end up feeling dismay later. Dredging up vital facts is hard work and at times may ruffle some feathers, but it does lead to positive thinking that truly serves your best interests.

Positive thinking is non-competitive

A high-flown self-image based on feelings of superiority is precarious. The danger is not snootiness, however, but rather the quicksand beneath one's feet. The clerk smugly lords it over a co-worker, who later gets to be the boss. Positive thinking now leads to frustration and possibly distress, if the new boss has revenge in mind. And being *the* glamor queen at school might be exhilarating until someone even more regal comes along. A shining self-image based on competition is even more perilous when it finds success *at the expense* of others. Getting to the top of the hill by stepping on people's necks might feel triumphant, but the victors must then worry about others not trusting in them, about their victims seeking revenge, about their consciences bothering them (if they possess a working conscience), and about the prospect of other hill climbers planning to step squarely on *their* necks.

Non-competitive positive thinking is generated by and also leads to constructive actions of every stripe, such as sticking with an exercise routine or reminding yourself to do something creative every day. Such positivity flows out of your own inner resources, and doesn't rely on others behaving as you hope or expect. Then too, it rests on positive standards you value, not on relative ones like being prisoners getting the most mail or having the least time left on their sentence. Furthermore, positive thinking doesn't need to be goal-driven at all. Everything may be fine and dandy simply because a rare species of warbler came to visit your feeder, you just ate a hearty meal, and you see your toddler happily tumbling around the yard with a little friend.

Positive thinking is assertive

What you think and how you are feeling are rather closely intertwined. Joyful thoughts come streaming when the home team wins, your biorhythms hum, or your little ones bring home glowing report cards. But when your washing machine, your minivan, and your mindfulness of a vital appointment all break down on the very same day, crankiness can storm in and take over. If you just react to events rather than making as many as possible of your desired ones take shape, achieving an upbeat mood and chipper thoughts then evolves into a crapshoot. So should you get mired in multiple misfortunes, you begin to see the world as a dreary place teeming with miserable luck. With such a scenario, your potential for positivity depends on the fickle finger of fate.

As an ordinary citizen you cannot get quarreling nations to the peace table, but you can shore up your outlook, regardless of your circumstances. If you feel under the weather, you can do all the right things for your body, and then savor the prospect of getting back on your feet. If your T.V. set features politicians talking in riddles, you can switch channels or go out for a brisk walk. And if a career setback hits you smack in the face, you can start out on a search for lessons--and there are always some--to help you avoid a similar fate in the future. In fact there are constructive steps you can take in every quagmire. So assertiveness is the key factor in generating a positive mind-set, not only from the good results you might achieve from your hard work, but also from the very effort to make something worthwhile happen.

Positive thinking involves maintaining your autonomy

Love, respect, admiration, loyalty, trust--all wonderful, positive traits. Yet these traits can also serve as a vehicle for handing over your decision-making power to others. In affairs of the heart, some otherwise smart, self-sufficient people become insecure and indecisive as they strive to placate a domineering and demanding partner. Mentors, therapists, gurus, charismatic leaders, coaches, and champions of causes also possess a potential power over the lives of others--those seeking out celebrity, serenity, salvation, "parental" love, enlightenment, or the joining into a noble movement. The unscrupulously vain, to be sure, are more than willing to exercise this type of power; and thus, many hero-worshipping "positive thinkers" come to discover their fortunes, or in certain cases even their lives, heading down the tubes.

Happy-outcome positive thinking requires you to hold firmly onto your legitimate decision-making authority, with some room to be sure for working out agreeable compromises. Now we realize that you might feel totally safe in the hands of a protective spouse or spiritual guru--and loads and loads of gurus and spouses have noble intentions--but you will actually *be* safer and feel abundantly empowered as you formulate and follow your own agenda and the decisions in relation to spiritual and political beliefs, career opportunities, the purchase of a home, selection of friends, control over discretionary money, etc. And if your "benevolent" spouse gets all bent out of shape over your newly-discovered initiative, then she or he may need some counseling in regard to control issues. Your decisions to be sure will not always prove out to be wise ones; but then again, neither will those of the enlightened masters.

Positive thinking is a formidable asset, but it does have its limitations. For example, it won't help you score well on an exam when you have neglected to study up for it, nor can it help you sell a house if no one shows up to look it over. But in partnership with thorough information gathering, common-sense judgment, persistent effort, and a willingness to compromise, it can help get a great deal accomplished. Positive thinking can help you:

- ☐ Get more work done from having an abundance of energy.
- ☐ Save time by weeding out superfluous task elements.
- ☐ Influence others (non-manipulatively) to be cooperative.
- ☐ Resolve issues that could make gloomy types discouraged.
- ☐ Make steady progress in pursuit of your own best interests.
- ☐ Promote and maintain good physical and mental health.
- ☐ Bounce back from disappointments and traumatic events.
- ☐ Move toward career positions of prestige and responsibility.
- ☐ Give your family, friends, and co-workers an emotional lift.
- ☐ Maintain a predominantly pleasant mood most of the time.
- ☐ Discover opportunities that disgruntled folks might overlook.
- ☐ By example, lead children toward positive thinking as well.
- ☐ Live a longer, happier life surrounded by those you cherish.

We were dirt poor but really close-knit as a family. My father became disabled when I was ten, and six years later I lied about my age to get myself into the Air Force. Next I bummed around for a while, yet I always sensed that things would turn out OK in the end. Now I have a great family and I manage my own business. We have family get-togethers every week, where we talk things over and do some fun stuff. We're a whole lot better off money-wise than when I was a kid, but I also want us to be as close-together as my original family was.

Owner, food franchise; husband and father of 5

The influences promoting negative thinking in young folks are many and varied; and some can't be avoided, like being raised in abject poverty, living in our dog-eat-dog competitive society, and falling victim to random criminal acts and nature's fury. However, you possess the ability to soften the impact of many of these influences, and to eliminate others entirely.

Factors Promoting Negative Thinking in Children

Negativity from parents

Being only human, parents are inclined toward moodiness and temper flare-ups, and can become grouchy when dealing with unacceptable behavior. But sporadic outbursts play only a minor role in fostering negative thinking. The bad-news gremlin is regular nastiness emanating from parents--name calling, harping, sarcastic responses, bellowing, threats, icicle-forming stares, slaps in the face, etc. Furthermore, frequent punishments, even when administered in a serene, businesslike manner, conjure up in young minds a big assortment of poisons such as self-pity, self-criticism, resentment, and devious thinking. Parents such as these, sad to say, cannot see beyond their noses. And no, their becoming more sensitive to young egos would not create spoiled brats. But what it would do is to keep their offspring from spending half their adult lives attending therapy and twelve-step groups and forever repeating positive-affirmation mantras.

Households drowning in unhappiness and conflict

While occasional ups and downs befall every family, young ones suffer few if any ill effects from emotional brush fires that remain short-lived. But when misery becomes a regular visitor or a long-term hanger-on, young folks learn cynical lessons--that intrafamily conflicts never get fully worked out, that affairs of the heart eventually dissolve into mush, and that striving for a better life only brings hurt and disappointment. And even when troubled parents reassure children that a brightly shining future awaits them, these impressionable little ones will no doubt find their parents' unhappiness to be a much more powerful influence.

Weak communication among family members

Households bathed in silence might run harmoniously, but they tend to be a wellspring of unhappy thinking. By nature folks are rather talkative, so a stony parental exterior might well point to inner turmoil--making mischief from behind the scenes. Pervasive silence also deprives younger ones of greatly needed verbal interaction. Zesty interaction not only brings to them treasure troves of information and feedback, but it also serves as a gateway for their expressing opinions and emotions, as well as for their getting fully engaged in resolving issues of daily living. So when communication is scant, little ones tend to arrive at gloomy conclusions about themselves, no matter how well-intentioned their parents may be.

Then too, with scant data and feedback to guide them, youngsters come to distrust their own natural conclusions and instincts, and to end up instead with naive, ill-considered decisions.

Unrealistic standards for achievement and responsibility

You no doubt desire your youngsters to become academic standouts and responsible citizens, but be sure your expectations are reasonable and get conveyed with no sense of pressure. Also watch out for outlandish expectations that youngsters might adopt for themselves. This unrealistic thinking can create enormous internal pressure and huge difficulty in landing in a fallback position when goals remain unfulfilled. This is dangerous territory, as the glowingly positive thinking of super performers can quickly turn to acute depression if they suffer what in their thinking are crushing setbacks. Suicidal ideation is not uncommon in this group, so it is mighty important to keep your avenues of communication in good working order. This is the finest of preventive maintenance.

The perilous ploys

The perilous ploys from Chapter 7 are in great form once again, this time as a spawning ground for cerebral muck. Parental prying promotes youthful secretiveness, evasiveness, resentment, and self-doubting. Pressuring is pretty similar, plus it drives young folks into becoming bull-headed stubborn and into putting extraordinary pressure on themselves. Preaching contributes to a dulled sense of annoyance in young listeners; and, if lecturing gets windy and regular, encourages them to regularly tune others out. Poor-me-ism saddles the younger crowd with guilt and makes them feel responsible for the happiness of others--a can't-win situation. Furthermore, the perilous ploys all tend to place dialogue on the sidelines, leaving little ones severely deficient in relationship-nurturing and problem-solving skills, and making it difficult for them to keep a positive mind-set that engenders self-confidence.

Regulation roulette

These negativity spawners were highlighted in Chapter 8. Management systems featuring rewards and revocations tend to make young ones anxious about meeting behavioral expectations, sneaky in working to subvert the system, whiny and manipulative when faced with undesired consequences, and angry and/or self-deprecating after the fact. Authoritarian child rearing generates a pervasive dread, off-the-wall anger, emotional rigidness, and the tendency to view every situation in terms of who's got the power. And finally, the restrictive approach stirs up massive doses of self-doubting in young ones and keeps them from mastering problem-solving skills. So regulation roulette saddles up with the perilous ploys in an effort to thwart young minds in their quest for straight-forward paths toward a self-confident young adult life.

Traumatic events

This covers a wide range of misfortunes befalling individual families as well as whole communities, and young psyches cannot escape their devastating impacts. Trauma can be precipitated by parents who are mentally ill, neglectful, abusive, drug dependent, disabled by illness or handicap, or who die during the child-raising years. On the youthful side we make mention of deformities, dis-abling accidents, genetic disorders, and horrendous experiences of all kinds. Negativity gets fomented as well by grinding poverty, disease epidemics, natural and man-made disasters, rampaging crime, persecution, enslavement, years-long warfare, terrorist at-tacks, refugee displacement, and lots else. To even survive many of these traumas is indeed a tribute to the human spirit.

Our acquisitive society

Eyes glued to the T.V. screen, small ones learn from a very early age to hound mommy for toys and sugared cereals. Then comes a message that the proper sneakers and acne creams will propel them into the highest circles. Youth-oriented commercials promote greed, competition, surface values, and impulsivity; and they teach young folks that their lives are far from OK. Thus many youngsters blessed with stable families, abundant material goods, and educational opportunities can nevertheless slip-slide on down into a disgruntled, cynical, me-first attitude. Young children adopt a positive mind-set naturally when their family life features tenderness, support, collaborative teaching, free-flowing communication, and room to grow comfortably towards post-teen self-governance. But they benefit additionally from parents' softening the impact of the relentless bombardment by ad makers. This subject is a natural one for family hour sessions.

Our competitive society

In our dog-eat-dog world, young ones bare their fangs from early on. Siblings wrangle over playthings, toddlers tattle to obtain parental favor, and elbows turn into weapons at the supper table. At school and in peer groups, young people jockey among themselves with relation to academic standing, attractiveness, athletic accolades, popularity, leadership, charisma, etc. Victors strut and whoop, and losers fret and fume; but competitors all feel stressed as they struggle to move up the ladder or stew over sliding down. For sure, competition can be an invigorating experience in moderation, but small ones lack the maturity to let regular setbacks and third-place finishes slide easily off their backs. And to repeat what we noted earlier in the chapter, positive thinking based on competition is indeed precarious.

Most of the kids in our high school are way better off than I am, but lots of them seem to love being miserable. They get all obsessive over their looks, and they always want more and more stuff. So this one girl, who is very attractive, is bugging her parents about getting her nose fixed. I've talked with a bunch friends about having family meetings like we do, but they look at me like I've come from another planet. By the way, my nose isn't close to perfect, but it's good enough for me.

Teen in single parent family

Those struggling to attain positive thinking find that breaking negative habits can be a grudging, frustrating process. And as parents, they surely do not want their youngsters to end up in the same struggle. The following are some ways to help instill positive thinking in children.

How to Role-Model Positive Thinking

☐ Think "possible" rather than "could-have, should-have."

☐ Let anger flow, but exclude rash threats and put-downs.

☐ 'Fess up to shortcomings and mistakes in judgment.

☐ Try to chuckle at day-to-day tribulations and at yourself.

☐ Engage in causes and hobbies, but at no breakneck pace.

☐ Appreciate and express gratitude for life's small pleasures.

☐ Look at the "big picture" rather than at a sea of details.

☐ Let criticism sink in before getting all defensive or testy.

☐ Have the sense to bow out of going-nowhere arguments.

☐ Make serious efforts to let go of resentments and grudges.

☐ End political discussions when acrimony starts taking over.

☐ Strive to view personal setbacks as a learning opportunity.

❏ Follow your "inner voice" rather than following the crowd.

❏ Don't let career or hobbies interfere with time for family.

❏ Practice politeness, which begets the same from others.

❏ Give yourself an encouraging pep talk when needed.

❏ See some ups and downs as better than being in a rut.

❏ Maintain sensible eating habits, and stay in decent shape.

❏ See the glass as one-third full rather than two-thirds empty.

❏ Try forgiving your own parents for their "inept" child-rearing.

❏ Let your hair down at times and have uproarious good fun.

❏ See the use of group identity labels as a sign of laziness.

❏ Avoid quick judgments regarding important decisions.

❏ Bring yourself to seek help when things are going poorly.

❏ Remember that we create most of our good or bad fortune.

❏ Keep on tinkering even after having attained excellence.

❏ Consider that living an honorable life is its own reward.

Falling short on a number of these items is no reason for alarm, while fulfilling them is no sign of near-perfection. Furthermore, super-achievers, charismatic personalities, and living saints might not score as well as parents who upon occasion feel really lost or who trip over their tongues. Perhaps most important of all among positive thinking attributes is that you keep your mind open to changing and make consistent efforts to grow personally, however uneven the process may turn out to be.

Role modeling plays a good size role in promoting positive thinking in your young ones, but generating and maintaining free-flowing communication in weekly family meetings and elsewhere in the household is also a powerful factor. Dialogue accomplishes a great many things, and high up on this list is its ability to nourish young minds with a stimulating stream of ideas and with the valuable skill of resolving all manner of interpersonal issues.

How Family Hour Promotes Positive Thinking

Family hour encourages children to trust themselves

Little ones naturally tend to trust their own thinking, and yet their self-confidence can get undermined from every direction from the cradle to the grave--by untrusting, manipulative, ferrous-fisted, and overprotective parents; by education systems that encourage conformity and discourage creativity; by paper-shuffling and mind-numbing careers; and by a society that views our seniors as old-sters rather than as elders. Young adults with a history of follow-ing others' thinking may find satisfaction in their careers and mar-riages, but when adversity strikes, their sense of security can get badly shaken. Having always believed that the "safe" path would remain safe, they now find themselves floundering around as they search for answers after getting hit by job layoff, chronic illness, or divorce. Also, their dearth of puzzling-it-out, trial-and-error experi-ence can leave them flooded with dark, brooding thoughts.

Toddlers gobble up the information and opinions of grown-ups; but as they mature they tend increasingly to weigh facts and opinions for themselves.. Family hour is helpful in this process by encouraging small ones to trust in their own opinions while at the same time remaining open to others' ideas and points of view. In weekly sessions, they get lots of input from family members, and their speaking out in dissent is at least tolerated and at best wel-comed. They are further encouraged to lend an ear to those who disagree with them; but they don't get opinions jammed down their throats, nor do they get badgered for standing adamantly by their own theories This is how self-confident thinking takes root. Then after their apprenticeship in the dialogue of the home, these young folks go out to a life of adventure as they expand their minds and skills, seek new experiences, expect the unexpected, and remain ready for challenges and changes.

Family hour welcomes the expression of feelings

It can be frustrating for therapists to watch clients wander through session after session of story telling and intellectualizing while carefully skirting around their disturbed emotions. After all, therapists realize that superficial expression will not open the door to internal peace. So they confront the surface chatter; and when the emotional floodgates finally open up, they observe relief taking over, along with the beginning of enhanced self-confidence. Emotional gunk keeps sufferers feeling sluggish, contributes heavily to the spawning of gloomy thoughts, and is a huge factor in steering many frustrated folks into seeking out professional help in the first place. In our experience as therapists, we have noted that clients needing extensive treatment had almost all been raised in families that strongly frowned on or even punished them for the expression of anything unpleasant, particularly anger. Then too, there were stone-faced parents who kept everything inside, and through their example, taught their little ones to do likewise.

You need no classroom training for dealing with emotions expressed in family hour. Just listen to spontaneous expression, whether it sounds pleasant or not; and make an effort to grasp the message involved, even when no words are spoken. But put the lid on any companion tactics like threats, manipulation, and guilt-tripping. Also, *do not* take it upon yourself to resolve an emotional person's issues. But if the emotion is anger and it is aimed at you, your big test has arrived. First listen; but what if you feel angry in response? Well, you are not doing a therapist's job, so of course you may express yourself too. But as your anger sizzles, remember the following: no drowning others out, no threats or put-downs on your part, and no pulling rank. Simply get your message over. Following this process as well as you can will help solve problems, bring you admiration--and set a fine example for positive thinking. Young folks in these families won't likely ever have need to repeat positive affirmations, and will only rarely find themselves with need of even brief psychotherapy.

Family hour generates support and encouragement

Comforting and reassurance are vital for creating a positive mind-set in children, who never outgrow their need for tenderness. They get lots of it in twelve-step, support, and therapy groups, and this is a huge reason why these groups are so popular. But sad to say, many group regulars had far too little tenderness in their families of origin, and they are likewise lacking in hugs and "atta-boys" in their present-day homes. Now this is not to imply that members of helping groups all live in emotionally distant families; however, it does indicate that their households most likely offer only a limited supply of distraction-free quality family time.

When you remain steadfastly supportive of your little ones, especially if you take a dim view of what they are up to, they will no doubt reciprocate, even though it might take some time for this to materialize. In family hour they might at times whine, complain, engage in put-downs, and pout on the fringe of the group; but their receiving practice in the give-and-take of talking and collaborating along with other family members will draw them inevitably into a more powerful sense of kinship. This is similar to how it occurs in twelve-step, support, and therapy sessions. Sometimes support and encouragement might get expressed through words, and at other times by a knowing smile or a brief touch. But in every case, these words and gestures go a long way toward helping generate an optimistic mode of thinking in children.

Family hour helps clear up confusion and resolve issues

T.V. sitcoms are chock-full of madcap miscommunications, much to the delight of the audience; but everything turns out O.K.

in the end. Real-life snafus, however, are usually not funny at all and don't always have an aw-shucks conclusion; nor are they the exclusive province of turbulent homes, as even the most nurturing, sophisticated households seem to experience miscommunication blips on a regular basis. With all too little quality family time within reach, many parents spend a great deal of it in putting out verbal brushfires among siblings, in the parent-child area, or on the adult-adult level. Such turmoil is often minor in nature, but when it is left unresolved it tends to cluster together and form an ominous cloud over the household. And the grayer the cloud, the gloomier gets to be everyone's thinking.

To an outside observer, some of your family meetings may appear to be chaotic, especially when feelings flow and arguments fly. But when you apply leadership skills to put a halt to manipulation, harassment, round-in-circles arguments, and imminent mayhem, some pleasant things happen. For starters, those who erupt emotionally tend to obtain a sense of relief, and their venom might vanish like a puff of smoke. In other scenarios information enters in the picture, compromises take shape, and apologies lighten the heavy air. Isn't this sounding like group therapy? Therapists face the challenge of dredging up long-buried emotions, reconstructing defeatist thinking, and correcting naive assumptions, among other chores; while you need only contend with the here-and-now--in no way a simple process. Yet even if you flounder at times along the way, bear in mind that you are helping to cement a positive frame of reference into malleable young minds, which makes you a more powerful and effective influence than all positive-thinking seminar leaders and writers combined.

Family hour spawns cooperative interactions and projects

Even when parent leaders don't place cooperative projects on their family hour agendas, all the verbal interaction itself has a clearly cooperative aspect; and this is a very good thing at a time when a we're-in-this-together spirit has diminished sharply in our modern households. In Chapter 2 we noted that family members seldom collaborate any more in home projects, in contrast to families of decades back; rather, a fiercely competitive spirit flourishes today throughout society and in our homes as well. We well know that siblings can be naturally competitive, but nowadays the rivalry among family members seems to be more intensified because of societal pressures--to be most popular, best groomed, cleverest, most powerful, etc. Then again, modern youth do sharpen cooperative skills, but typically in the peer group and in team activities. Even here, though, the cooperative aspect is strategic, designed to advance competitive aims.

The simple act of sitting around next to one another is an exercise in family togetherness. Then, most family hour dealings work in a variety of ways to bolster a cooperative spirit. There is exchanging information, sharing experiences, seeking and offering help, telling stories and playing fun games, putting on educational and drama presentations, and even having heated arguments, as long as bitterness and chaos stay away. What is more, once feelings get unburdened and some clarity enters thorny issues, family members tend to feel more solidly bonded. There are even board games than encourage and reward collaborative efforts, and family-group work projects can work wonders for a sense of oneness. Yes, you can tell children all day how wonderful they are, but there is nothing better than working and playing together for the sowing of the seeds of positive thinking.

Family hour stimulates healing laughter

Some say that stand-up comics keep others in stitches in order to keep themselves from being consumed by dark thoughts. And it seems that this formula is working, since some well-known octogenarian comedians delightfully keep 'em rolling in the aisles. Indeed, humor appears to have a naturally anti-depressant quality; and this is why it increasingly gets "prescribed" today by medical specialists to alleviate physical symptoms and promote a brighter outlook. Also, humor is a tonic for people experiencing stress and facing peril--hence all the jokes told to preface podium speeches and the wisecracking that permeates suspense films. But looking past its many health benefits, laughter simply feels wonderful; and as we noted in starting the chapter, the happier you feel, the more readily positive thoughts flow.

If your family is naturally inclined toward humor, family hour sessions might on occasion escalate into a laugh riot. In this case you may encourage the good feelings; but be sure to keep horse-play and joke fests from becoming mean-spirited, haywire, or disruptive to planned agenda items. If on the other hand your family tends more toward solemnity, you might deliberately insert humor so as to keep the atmosphere cheerful. You may, for an example, put the likes of joke sessions, nonsense games, and charades on the agenda. (See the Help section for ideas.) But do act quickly to squelch "fun" that causes chagrin to others. Humor is also a temporary treatment for delicate situations, such as when discussions get boring or edgy, and when awkward pauses get uncomfortable. And let some jokes be on yourself, since this teaches small ones good sportsmanship--a bonanza of positive thinking.

> *In our family we've gotten truly weary of the never-ceasing flow of gloomy and scandalous news in the media, so we've decided to add on the "good news" segment to our weekly sessions. Everyone gets a three-minute time space for items that are amusng, uplifting, educational, etc. It took some time for the family members to get it moving, and we've seen a few instances of bad news becoming disguised; yet*

overall, this experiment has been O.K. At least it keeps getting enough votes to stay on the agenda. And that is "good news" to our ears.

Paralegal, mother of 3

A long while back Giancarlo and I decided for one of our weekly meetings to do a sociogram--people in a group rating everyone, themselves included-- on a smorgasbord of personal qualities. I had participated in one on the job, and it proved out fascinating. Our kids at that time ranged in ages from eight to fifteen, and so we saw lots of possibilities for their responses; so we constructed it to try to eliminate elitist elements and to make sure that all the kids would be apt to get some positive feedback. To my surprise and delight, they all took it quite seriously, and the results were amazing; but best of all was the question that asked as to which youngster was best at helping others. Two got all the votes split between them, then a lively debate ensued, with each of those two arguing eloquently a to why the other one was the better helper. You might say it ended in a tie. Every once in a while I think back to that occasion, and each time it's like I have just seen a three-hankie movie.

Insurance agent, mother of 6

CHAPTER TWELVE

HELPING CHILDREN

BECOME SELF-RELIANT

At one of our family sessions Andre said that for his seventeenth birthday he would hope for a car--and it needn't even be a new one! I know that his father would have agreed to it without any conditions, but I specified that he must take responsibility for all the insurance and for repairs. He started to squirm, so I asked him how he could afford his car without any income. This led into complaints about how all his rich friends have cars, so I suggested that he might start cultivating friendships from among the under-privileged. Soon after this, one of his chums drove into a parked car after having had a few drinks, and suddenly the grumbling stopped. He recently got a part-time job and is saving up money, and lately we have not had to nag at him about wearing his seat belt. I suspect that the car issue will be resurfacing soon--real soon.

Dance therapist, mother of 3

All parents dream of seeing their little ones arrive at young adulthood standing firmly on their own two feet, while at the same time maintaining a close, loving relationship with family members.

Some parents go on to see the dream come true; but others, alas, watch it deteriorate into a nightmare. The delighted parents hear that dame fortune has smiled upon them, while the dismayed ones get consoled over their terrible luck or the overwhelming influence of defective genes, bad news pals, or a cold-hearted society. Yet while pure chance and unavoidable circumstances will enter into the picture on occasion, the fact remains that all parents possess the tools needed for guiding youngsters steadfastly toward a satisfying, self-sufficient adult life.

Self-reliance should never be measured based on surface features. One young adult still living at home may in fact be comfortably independent, while another with a decent-paying job and a nice apartment may be hanging on by a thread emotionally. Also, your average jack-of-all-trades can be far more resilient than the entrenched bureaucrat who doesn't have a clue about functioning outside the system. Indeed, the truest measures of youthful self-sufficiency are to be found within. So now let us examine several inner-strength characteristics that help build foundations of rock-solid stability. While there are many other such attributes, the following list provides some of the more typical examples.

Young Adults and Self-Reliance

Young adults typically rejoice over their new-found freedom that springs from moving out of the parental nest, and they seldom spend much time contemplating the factors that go into their being able to stand comfortably on their own two feet. The following is a list of many of these factors. Young adults demonstrate a healthy measure of self-reliance when they:

☐ Enjoy moderate to excellent self-confidence.
☐ Handle obligations well, but also know when plate is full.
☐ Fulfill responsibilities and promises guided by conscience.

- ❏ Budget wisely, opting to do without rather than amass debt.
- ❏ Beware of get-rich-quick schemes and glossy sales pitches.
- ❏ Evaluate trustworthiness from people's proven behavior.
- ❏ Think realistically re: vocational and personal ambitions.
- ❏ Trust that hazy-looking career goals will crystallize later on.
- ❏ View work, financial, and personal setbacks as temporary.
- ❏ Learn to take practical steps in search of wants and needs.
- ❏ Reach for help when things get too stressful and confusing.
- ❏ Ponder advice, then make decisions after weighing options.
- ❏ Recognize and quickly reject manipulation and intimidation.
- ❏ Move on quickly rather than risk abusing others' hospitality.
- ❏ Open eyes to "the ways of the world," and move cautiously.
- ❏ Enjoy times with friends, but also cherish times of solitude.
- ❏ Refuse to cave in to that can't-live-without-someone feeling.
- ❏ Rather than blaming others, seek remedies for misfortunes.
- ❏ Don't cling to stale relationships out of fear of the unknown.
- ❏ Throttle budding obsessions, compulsions, and addictions.
- ❏ See anxiety and sadness as clues to solvable problems.
- ❏ Neither desire nor expect parents to subsidize their budget.
- ❏ Prefer solutions over extrication from self-created messes.
- ❏ Don't cave in to parents out of fear of disappointing them.
- ❏ Depend on selves--not folks or others--for direction in life.

A few years ago my eleven-year-old was with me at my office, and he had a dental appointment for later that afternoon. There was a bus line going directly to the clinic, but he felt anxious about doing the trip on his own, and asked me to drive him there. I was just on the verge of agreeing, but then I realized it was time for him to try out some independence. It worked out just fine, and we never had that type of problem again. He's been living on his own now for

some years, has moved around to several states,
and has always worked for himself. I don't know
whether that bus situation played any role in his
growing independence, but I do believe our family
meetings made some contribution.

Civil servant

Human history is replete with tales of company-store servitude, blind obedience to charismatic leaders, total subservience to a domineering or culturally favored spouse, and legalized slavery; yet it is each human's natural birthright to grow up strong and free. Autonomy, however, doesn't guarantee happiness; but then again, happiness depends on a roll of the dice without it. Now while the concept of self-reliance is quite easy to understand; there is, sad to relate, loads of confusion over the role parents play in helping children navigate the long journey from utter helplessness to total self-determination. And this "big mystery" deepens even further in today's ramble-scramble society.

Dubious Ideas on Youthful Self-Reliance

Parents can teach children to take care of themselves

Parents can give scads of information as to how the world works, and lots of advice on how to adapt to it; but this kind of help merely plays a supporting role. Self-sufficiency is not a how-to-do operation, but rather a grab-bag of skills you master in the process of actually doing.

Parents can role-model self-reliance for their youngsters

Parents serve as role models in relation to character, interests, attitudes, habits, etc.; and they can also model an inclination toward self-reliance, but never an actual blueprint for it. Have you ever heard of a professional dancer role-modeling her little daughter into becoming a prima ballerina?

Children become self-reliant by being given responsibilities

Doing assigned chores can help one turn into a responsible person, but it doesn't teach *self*-responsibility, as this develops from within. Getting tasks done is a key to a well-ordered life, but some highly reliable, productive workers act dependent and helpless in their personal lives.

Children become self-reliant through mastering skills

Learning to grow food, repair cars, handle money, and run computers are skills that make it much easier to find a place in the world; but they do not shape self-sufficiency--they serve it. Then too, there is no hands-on skill that can keep young adults from being controlled by guilt-tripping parents.

Self-reliance emerges out of firm-handed parental control

Young adults whose parents had run a truly tight ship tend either to stay unswervingly obedient or to strive to control others. The self-sufficient, on the other hand, obey others when it makes good sense to do so, or when the consequences for disobeying would be severe; and they prefer to take care of their own needs rather than order others around. Self-reliance and control or self-control, to be sure, have little in common.

Achievement and good behavior foster self-reliance

Excellence in comportment and studies head most parents' wish lists, yet they have little to do with self-reliance. Some super-scholars get all lost in the hurly-burly of the "outside" world, and a soaring score on the conformity scale can actually be a handicap along the road to self-sufficiency.

Protection from danger is a key to self-reliance

And the earth is really flat. Tots need lots of sheltering; but when the sheltering fails to ease off as youngsters grow physically and emotionally, these offspring become insecure and tend to shy away from making difficult decisions. This knocks self-sufficiency completely out of the box.

Self-reliance comes naturally as children advance in age

The *capacity* for self-sufficiency enlarges with the passage of time, but its fulfillment is the result of young people's own self-determined endeavors; and it tends to be more harmonious when parents remain supportive and helpful along the way. If age were the main determinant, why then do some folks in their forties and fifties (and even older) look to others on a regular basis for even the smallest decisions?

> *Cody, our only child, kept getting into conflicts with his teachers, and we naturally gave him the benefit of the doubt. By the time he reached the seventh grade he was transferred into classes for discipline problems, and he was also becoming a handful in the house. Teachers kept suggesting counseling, and we finally felt so desperate that we agreed to it. We were told to cease rescuing him, but when we did this he had frightful tantrums and made us feel really guilty. He's now twenty-two, is still at home, and only works sporadically. We know we've made a mess of the whole situation. We recently went back into counseling, and told Cody he must join us*

if he wants to remain at home. We keep on hoping
that he'll get straightened out.

Too-much-love parents

Browse through the parenting literature all you please, and you will find precious little with regard to the emergence of youthful self-sufficiency. And we're not talking about little ones making the successful transition from the parental nest to their first grade classroom. More on that later in the chapter, but first let us unlock the "mystery" of how self-reliance unfolds.

How Youngsters Attain Self-Reliance

The formula for youthful self-reliance is not a complicated one. Small ones grow toward independence as a result of making decisions and plans on their own, and then acting on them. This process involves their seeing others' examples, making trial-and-error and educated guesses, learning lessons from errors in judgment, honing skills through repeated self-determined experiences, and gathering confidence from the simple act of standing firmly on their own two feet. Now some young folks may be self-reliant, but they are also miserable in their personal lives, so we refer here to their gaining autonomy in an internally harmonious fashion. Self-reliance unfolds smoothly and happily when youngsters:

Experience a solid foundation of nurturing and guidance

Most experts-in-the-rough start their careers feeling rather unsure of themselves, their destiny getting placed in the hands of those more skilled and experienced. The early-stage confusion of fledgling chess masters, courtroom attorneys, and operatic divas gradually evolves toward a confident grasp of fundamentals when their mentors, whether pleasant or crusty in manner, demonstrate sensitivity to their wants and needs, and patience with their early-stages floundering. Furthermore, top-drawer teachers delight in the progress their young proteges keep making toward self-determined functioning.

In contrast to career trainees, newborns rely on others for all of their needs, and their apprenticeship lasts for about two decades. This makes all you parents the most important trainers on earth. Affection and attention are necessary all through the formative years, but most of all during infancy; and this gives small ones a solid foundation for standing tall when it comes time for them to start out on their life's journey. As wise parents you will adapt your teaching to young folks' interest levels and personal maturity, then you become increasingly less didactic as children come to formulate more and more of their own plans and decisions.

Gain gradually-increasing freedom of choice

People oftentimes begin their mastery of a wide range of skills through the study of technical language, history, rules and regulations, procedures and short cuts, etc. Yet it is all just words until they obtain some hands-on experience, and generally in this order: observation, dry-run practice, solo work under strict supervision, increasing autonomy, and finally, total freedom of action--consultation being offered according to need. This is particularly important for skills that involve dealing with safety risks, such as skyscraper construction, surgical performance, child seat design, and air traffic control. Successful adaptation to the world outside of the parental home, by far the most complex of all skills, entails the gaining of competence in confronting and dealing with potential risks from every conceivable direction.

Growing youngsters get loads of advice on how to live life, and they also get to observe whether or not adults abide by their own teachings. Youthful choices should begin rather early in matters of least consequence, and then gradually expand through the years subject to ever-diminishing supervisory control. Small ones experience spurts in physical and emotional growth, followed by periods of readjustment or even regression; so their readiness for greater decision-making freedom will therefore have a somewhat irregular pattern. The overall picture, however, should indicate a steady rise in self-sufficiency, culminating in almost total decision-making autonomy as the date targeted for the departure from the parental nest approaches.

Assume chief responsibility for dealing with consequences

Employing brute force or intimidation with impunity, having a clever lawyer, or running amok in a state of anarchy permits one to make choices without having to pay the piper. Irresponsible behavior like this is called license; and it can be scary, particularly if the one with an "unrestricted license" has cruel intentions and is headed your way. Assuming responsibility for the consequences of all your choices is not only morally correct, but it is also a sign of personal maturity. Those who hold themselves accountable on a regular basis are inclined to think before they act, and thus are likely in most cases to consider doing what is right.

Small children, as is only natural, insist that their goof-ups could not have been avoided or that "they" were to blame; so you have the task of guiding them gently toward ownership of all their actions. Encourage self-reliance by not letting them wheedle their way out of icky situations; by giving them, perhaps after they stew a bit, a major role in forging solutions; and by withholding your defense of them until after you have investigated complaints of outsiders. Also, carefully avoid the perilous ploys and regulation roulette, the villains featured in Chapters 7 and 8. These tactics tend to sabotage self-reliance by getting children tangled up in self-pity, self-doubting, brooding resentment, manipulation of a parent's behavior-control system, dread of parents' intimidation, foot-dragging resistance, guilt-tripping, etc. In scenarios like these, youngsters tend to lose sight of the important issues at hand and their natural consequences.

Use parents as consultants, support givers, and helpers

No matter how self-sufficient we become in conducting our affairs, we still need help and reassurance from others. Successful executives tend to delegate duties to capable aids and to take counsel from trusted advisers; and even most go-it-alone people tend to seek out the listening ear of true friends when the sledding gets slippery. Then again, some folks are independent-minded to the point of qualifying as modern-day hermits. They are seldom motivated, however, by love of solitude, but rather they oftentimes have dread about being controlled by or betrayed by those around them. Mature self-sufficiency entails confidence in your own deliberation and decision-making processes; and it also leaves considerable room for others to act as assistants, burden sharers, and support and sympathy providers.

Early self-determined decisions, such as restaurant menu choices and some clothing options, have little risk to them. Then as small ones spend more time at school, visiting friends, and doing other out-of-house activities, their plans and decisions, along with the burden of dealing with the aftermath, should increasingly become their own. However, there are important roles for you to play--e.g., as financial backers, resource locators, transportation providers, and schedule coordinators. But perhaps the most crucial role of all--especially when teens are involved--lies in the area of communication; and it might involve such as helpful info, suggestions, feedback, support, or encouragement. And contrary to popular wisdom, youngsters *do* want frank discussions with parents--arguments and all--during this crucial time.

I lived in foster homes from a very young age, but I never felt sorry for myself, as I had some pretty caring folks around me. I was a good student too, and that helped. But knowing that I had no family to fall back on, I learned to stand on my own feet. From hard work and squeezing my pennies I got financial independence, and my second marriage has given me emotional security. My daughter is a student in college now, and she's a self-sufficient type as well; but hopefully her independent spirit is based a lot more on her natural instinct, and a lot less on fears of ending up on the street.

Computer troubleshooter

But wait! These days things seem all topsy-turvy. Instead of focusing increasingly on their youngsters' upcoming departure, oodles of parents are joining into battle with them over self-determined choices. Seventeen-year-olds, as an example, ought to be largely independent in operating their personal affairs; yet we see so many of them confined to quarters for lengthy periods, wearing beepers to monitor their whereabouts, or hearing "no" echo over and over in their ears. Then we venture over to the flip side--many still-at-home young adults dabbling at schooling or career opportunities; but in truth devoting themselves to partying, hanging out, or staring intensely into television or computer screens. Typically, these offspring receive free room and board and have only vague plans for the future. And ironically, some of the parents were at an earlier time "warden" types who eventually just gave up.

Personal accountability is another area in which things appear upside down. Micro-managed youngsters, hell-bent on beating the system, rarely learn lessons from their actions, and neighborhood bullies get absolved by "boys will be boys" parents. What is more, youthful misbehavior gets explained away by a chorus of adult voices citing poverty, dysfunctional families, brainwashing by advertisers, rich-kid syndrome, permissive parenting, obsessive-compulsive tendencies, divorce, psychiatric disorders, television and computer addiction, chemical imbalances, peer pressure, junk food excesses, pornography, Satanic influences, and much, much more. Then when laws get broken, otherwise toe-the-line parents get all snarled in legal maneuvering. All this prepares young folks for an adult life of blaming, self-excusing, and litigating, where the phrase "I did it" makes their attorneys cringe.

Handing out punishments that are totally unrelated to misbehavior is yet one more way to toss obstacles into the pathway of youthful responsibility-taking. The more youngsters get tangled up in the web of behavior-control systems, the less likely they are to ponder the wisdom of their own actions. Behavior-control parents also get tangled up in the system while they run it, and this leaves them scant time or energy to dwell on the self-reliance issue. Ask these parents how children get readied for a self-managed future, and they will cite several factors, but not likely the one that towers over all the others--that they advance from complete dependency to complete autonomy by being given ever-increasing freedom of action coupled with responsibility for the results. And the reason behaviorist parents will ignore this factor is that it goes counter to their system. Yes, micro-managed youth <u>can</u> get to self-reliance--not through their system, however, but in spite of it.

Indeed, lots of parents appear confused when it comes to promoting youthful self-reliance, so one would expect alarms to be sounding in the parent education world. But no. Many educators have gotten all occupied with helping parents extinguish behavior-management brushfires that they also might have lost sight of the big picture. What is more, they may become stuck on the horns of a dilemma. How can they be helping parents obtain leverage over wayward teens, then at the same time be urging them to diminish their control? Then again, some writers indeed address the issue of letting-go, but typically in the context of parental trepidation over handing small ones over to preschool staff, grandparents, or camp counselors. Scenarios like these, to be sure, are merely the start of the letting-go process.

So why has youthful self-determination become such a hot potato for all too many parents in these modern times? No single answer looms large on the horizon, but clues are to be found here, there, and everywhere.

Factors Giving Today's Parents the Letting-Go Blues

Dangers awaiting in the outside world

Handing little ones over to daycare workers may be scary for parents, but the idea of sending them out just a few years later into the murky outside world can be truly terrifying. And the list of perils is a really lengthy one--drugs and alcohol, eating disorders, sour-influence friends, financial scams, cults, gangs, hate groups, A.I.D.S., compulsions, abusive and abrasive relationships, random violence, depression, homelessness, etc. Then going beyond any dangers like these, there is the perception that the world ouside of the family circle is a substantially unfriendly place where one can easily slip between the cracks. To be sure, young folks may meet many of these same dangers while still living at home, but parents understandably look at their home-sweet-home environment as a buffer zone that minimizes these risks.

Modern-day education and employment

Way back when, youngsters got schooled near their home and as a rule moved on to family-together or home-town careers in farming, the trades, homemaking, or factory work. These days it is altogether different. Overcrowded local schools have become bureaucratic and impersonal, and out-of-the-area and out-of-state universities hold appeal for youth smitten with wanderlust. Then young adult offspring move into careers that take them all over the map. Parents today are resigned to telephone and other electronic chats, and to holiday visits from their grown-up youngsters; yet even when all-together events take place, certain parents strain to grasp particulars of highly technical careers, and wish a translator were on hand. So it's easy to see why many of them might prefer to prolong their children's adolescence indefinitely.

Shattered and scattered family life

In the olden days two-parent families were the rule; households often included grandparents; and uncles, aunts, and cousins lived only a stone's throw distant. And as depressing as it was to watch a youngster succumb to disease or trudge off to war, there were always lots of kinfolk around to comfort and console. These days, by contrast, families are way more shattered and scattered. Many non-custodial parents are a plane ride away, grandparents reside in sunbelt retirement or in nursing homes; and for the adult children who happen to stay back in the old home town, their parents most likely have relocated to another locale. Modern family members make herculean attempts to remain connected by telephone, e-mail, and as-frequent-as-possible vacation visits and reunions; but the family solidarity commonplace in a long-departed era has diminished considerably. This is what parents of growing youngsters have to look forward to in these times.

Parent-child power struggles

Today's parents have the notion that when small ones get out of line, some action must follow at once, typically in the form of house arrest or the loss of possessions or privileges. These punishments--often euphemistically named "consequences"--open the door to arguing, and then the battle of wills may get into full swing. Parents that fall anywhere between total rod-rule and total cave-in are susceptible to this syndrome. Legitimate arguments over punishments should not take more than a few minutes; so if it goes on after that, it is merely a matter who has the greater perseverance. No matter how it finally winds up, everybody loses. The misdeeds at issue slip out of focus, time and energy all get wasted, good will is squandered--and this exercise in futility does nothing to prepare offspring for an adult life of proper self-reliance. And then parents, seeing the lack of preparedness in their young ones, feel reluctant to encourage their move toward self-rule.

Fear that little ones might become traumatized

Many "enlightened" parents, mindful that early life traumas can lurk menacingly in the subconscious for an entire lifetime, go tiptoeing around the little ones lest they unwittingly create psychic damage. And when it comes time for youngsters to venture out all starry-eyed into the dog-eat-dog world, even greater psychic perils await. So these parents naturally feel anxious about loosening up their reins. Foot-dragging on occasion may be on the subtle side, as illustrated by a vague apprehension as youngsters go out with friends, streams of concern-laden questioning, emphasis on risks involved in new undertakings, and making home living comfortable to the degree that the youthful adventuresome spirit might become seriously dampened.

Fear that already weak communication will weaken further

Many parents and teenagers have little to discuss beyond safe topics like household schedules, T.V. programs, the weather, current events, gossip, and sports. The generation gap at work?

Not at all. Instead, try placing the blame squarely on a scarcity of family-together time, which includes a dearth of shared activities. Devoted parents, lamenting the fact that communication falls short of the ideal, at least console themselves that their teenagers are still around. All too soon, however, their nestlings will be flying off, and then parents worry that the present-time dialogue gulf will expand into a bottomless chasm. This fear becomes even larger in homes where vague resentments linger around, or even a small degree of alienation has already crept in. As a result, the parents in dialogue-deficient households might feel increasing resistance levels as the time for emancipation draws near, showing this typically in non-verbal ways such as hang-dog looks, anxiety, and failure to react with enthusiasm about youthful moves toward greater self-governing.

Have our modern modes of living, then, made it practically impossible for young people to undergo a smooth transition from dependence on parents to reliance on their own inner resources? By no means; and as usual, the key to solving this dilemma rests in the cultivation of dialogue.

Dialogue: The Glue That Binds Teens and Parents Together

Throughout the chapters we have seen how dialogue is a large factor in all areas of concern regarding family relationships, and one of the most crucial of them all is the unfolding of youthful self-determination. When parents and their young ones slowly but inexorably separate from one another with regard to authority, the free flow of dialogue can and should continue right on unabated, shifting only in content and level of sophistication as young people become more mature and worldly wise. So in one sense parents and their children gradually become disengaged from one another, yet at the same time they remain firmly united. Dialogue does not keep them problem-free, but it does permit their large and smaller conflicts to simply come and go.

What concerns many parents and makes them reluctant to loosen up the reins is that they know precious little about what is going on in the lives of their teens, particularly in areas of potential danger. So dreading the worst, they slip into a "no, no, no" mode. By contrast, small ones raised in dialogue-rich families tend to be more open about what they are thinking and doing, and this naturally carries over into the teen years. (Of course they don't tell all, nor should parents expect them to.) This creates a positive-direction domino effect: the more parents know, they more they tend to trust (except in worst-case scenarios); and therefore, the more apt children are to keep on the right path. Furthermore, parents who have an excellent idea of what young people are thinking, feeling, and doing are well positioned to help and support them when they grapple with day-to-day issues or even with crises; and this even further reinforces the positive cycle.

We saw in Chapter 6 that dialogue is highly adaptable, but its survival depends on your rejecting tactics such as harassment, intimidation, guilt-tripping, and condescension. Furthermore, dialoguers listen reflectively and are aware that hogging the floor is a no-no. These rules of verbal etiquette are the same for everyone, adults and children alike; but you cannot expect seven-year-olds to grasp this right away. With your patience and proper example, however, they will eventually come around. Dialoguing folks may differ with regard to experience and wisdom, and may rank higher or lower in status at home, school, or the workplace; but as is the case with rules of the road for automobile drivers, they all need to have equal standing in any discussion.

The level-playing field feature inherent in dialogue makes it especially well-suited for parents and adolescents, since the latter might be more than a tad sensitive about authority and status. But unfortunately, the potential for parent-teen dialogue in all too many homes remains largely untapped. Teens, to be sure, are naturally outstanding with dialogue, since they spend hours chatting on the phone and in person with close pals. Adults tend to view rapport among teenagers as reflecting their shared peer status; but in fact some teens also shoot the breeze with their parents for hours at a time. Granted they do not share peer concerns together, but they instead share interest in lots of topics, including the family-related themes that continue on for life.

Yes, the potential for parent-teen dialogue is extensive, but today's household members are tightly scheduled in outside activities; and then when they are at home, time that in years past went to open-ended family discussions and interactions now gets gobbled up by T.V. watching, electronic gizmos, computers, telephone calls, radio listening, drudgery chores, the need to zone out, solo hobbies, etc. This is where regular family hour, which offers carefully safeguarded quality time, comes to the rescue.

The seven-year-old twins are our youngest, and are they ever spoiled rotten! They have been skipping in and out of our weekly meetings for more than a year now, but lately I have been trying to get them to take a little more responsibility for their behavior. Whenever they are not blaming each other for everything, they are whining and making excuses. The older ones come to their rescue, but I have started putting my foot down. Rudy even posted a big sign reading "Tell me your solution first, and then I'll listen to your problem." The twins started coming up with some silly sounding solutions just so they may get their gripes on the table, but at least it's a start; and it gives the other kids a good chuckle. I believe they are perfect for putting on a talent show.

Homemaker, mother of 5

Family Hour: A Bastion of Parent-Teen Dialogue

Everybody knows how "normal" it is for teens to keep their parents at arms length. So following this logic, it must be abnormal for them to remain close during these years! This of course is nonsense. No, it's not too easy for parents and their teens to talk frankly, just as it's not too simple for people to maintain a normal weight during middle age. But just because a drop off in communication and a surge in body weight can happen easily, it does not make them normal or desirable. The sad thing about the truism of the parent-teen gulf is that it tends to keep some parents from trying to keep the lines of communication running smoothly. So yes, all parents should strive to generate and maintain fluency between themselves and youngsters from the first "goo-goo, ga-ga" at the crib until "keep in touch" echoes at the doorway; and participating in family hour sessions is the best way we know of to do this.

We have seen examples of family hour helping in a variety of parent-child dealings; but with regard to the unfolding of youthful self-sufficiency, it plays the unique role of enhancing a smooth transition between youngsters' reliance on parents and reliance on their own resources. Also, family hour is well-suited even to teens who feel rather touchy about house rules, since dialogue and parental authority do not mix. But whether relationships are cordial or cool, parents are wise to keep in mind teenagers' interests and needs both in the choice of agenda and how the discussion gets framed. As Chapter 4 demonstrated, the possibilities for setting the agenda are as extensive as your imagination will allow; and a generous mix of serious and fun topics in most cases serves you best. The following are a few suggestions:

❏ Debates, educational sessions, cooperative projects, etc.
❏ Story telling--happenings that others may not have known.

- Quiz and talent shows, stand-up comedy, charades, etc.
- Gripes and good will--no interrupting, and using time limits.
- Sessions in which parents may speak only when spoken to.
- Sharing news from the workplace, school, peer group, etc.
- Compiling family history, and suggestions for preserving it.
- Drug use and abuse talks--no parental preaching allowed.
- Forums on everybody's hopes and dreams for the future.
- Examining talents and interests as career possibilities.
- Frank discussions, as long as things don't get out of hand.
- Any type of program planned and conducted by teens.

> *Lurellen is a high-school senior now, and lately she has been assuming the complete leadership of one family hour session per month. I don't agree all the time with her methods and tactics, but she appreciates my waiting until after the meetings to discuss it with her. Boyd, on the other hand, is a sophomore, and he shows no inclination whatsoever toward the leadership of family hour sessions, but that's really okay. He's a strongly independent young man, and that's the main thing.*
>
> *Day care owner, mother of 2*

If your adolescents are family hour veterans, their roles in the sessions have very probably transitioned smoothly from their preteen years; but if this experience is new to all, please be realistic about teenager participation. If they refuse to show up, remind them of how they might miss out on lots of important family news; then again, if they attend but appear emotionally far away, remind yourself that they are without a doubt getting something from the experience. Consider some of the above-listed ideas--or a few of your own--for your agenda, and this might also be a great time to look back on the nuts and bolts of dialogue in Chapter 6. And it's also a good time to convey to teens that you support them always and that your assistance will be available to them any time there is a genuine need. This helps to lay down the groundwork for mutually satisfying adult-adult relations in the years ahead. We cover this in greater detail in the final chapter.

After their little ones have flown the nest, all parents seem to have at least a few regrets--about having displayed insufficient affection, having spent too little time doing fun things, having been too soft or too strict, having eaten too little ice cream together, etc. Well, one way to nip regrets in the bud is to speak about heart-felt subjects now in your family hour sessions. For sure not every issue can find resolution, but you will be amazed to see how easily certain concerns just seem to melt away after you engage in honest and open discussions. One matter your soon-to-be adults will have few if any regrets about later on is your having encouraged and helped them as they traveled the long journey toward young-adult self-sufficiency.

SECTION V

LONG-TERM BENEFITS OF FAMILY HOUR

CHAPTER THIRTEEN

RECOVERY BEGINS AT HOME:
THE KEY TO INNER HARMONY

Dalinda was five when I got divorced, and right off she became all clingy. In time I started wondering if she would ever get beyond it, so I began getting the urge to push her away. Then, however, I began to realize that she would settle down as soon as she was ready, and not one moment sooner--and that my pushing her away would make matters worse. Then when I got my life back on the right track, she followed suit and got to be more relaxed. Later on she became a vocal leader in our family meetings, and now she has friends following her all around in high school. I'm sure glad I dug down deep and found a bit of patience way back then.

Interior designer and mother
in a blended family

What a wonderful thing, this capacity we have to heal our emotional wounds. We suffer frights, frustrations, and emotional fractures, yet we bounce back again and again; and we can grow from these experiences when valuable lessons are learned. We refer to this as "primary recovery." But a different kind of recovery has become popular recently--the self-policing steps folks adopt to keep their self-destructive urges in abeyance when their healing process comes up short. We call this "secondary recovery."

Primary recovery

This is the emotional self-healing just outlined, and for the most part it is an automatic process, much like the physical body's ability to repair hair-line fractures and fight off infections. Parents promote primary recovery in small ones by providing them with a nurturing, supportive environment; and then by granting to them ever-increasing freedom of choice coupled with the responsibility for dealing with the upshot of their choices. But even the most well-adjusted young folks on occasion lose face in competitions or lose their heads in romantic entanglements. Yet when few if any psychic wounds go on festering in the long term, they are benefitting from primary recovery--and their subsequent behavior will always give clues as to how well this is working. When primary recovery takes place routinely, it becomes a life-long asset, rendering secondary recovery in most cases entirely unnecessary.

Secondary recovery

This is the squelching of dysfunctional behavior that arises out of the inability to achieve primary recovery. (A physical-body equivalent is noted in the thwarting of coronaries in chronic heart-disease patients.) When stresses overload their system, afflicted ones pursue satisfactions in substitute ways like overeating, substance abuse, gambling, or lashing out at the fragile and vulnerable. Such behavior never resolves core issues and often creates new ones--e.g., health, relationship, financial, and legal. Some go on to embrace aberrant behavior of a less annoying or dangerous type; while others, seeking support from the outside, learn to keep their impulsive appetites in check, thus achieving an "in recovery" status. Recovery periods tend to continue on indefinitely because underlying issues seldom get resolved, and this leaves the threat of relapse forever waiting ominously in the wings.

> *I've been attending eating disorder groups for some time, and it never ceases to amaze me how everyone talks of growing up in families sadly deficient in heartfelt sharing, encouragement, and support. We get lots of support in our groups, but I feel doubtful as to whether many of the members carry this practice over into their present-day family situation. For this reason, I started getting our family together for weekly meetings, and that was around five months ago. I had to crack the whip at first to get my stubborn kids to come; but it was definitely worth it, and they have started opening up little by little as time passes. Any time I start feeling dismayed, I stop to realize that I don't want my girls to have to struggle with food or other issues the same way that I have. I have told some of my group members about it too, and they smile and say it sounds great, but I don't get the feeling that any of them intend to follow my example and round up their family members.*
>
> *Transcriber, mother of 3*

Everyone suffers from at least a smidgen of impulse-ridden behavior, which goes on to become problematic only if it follows a regular pattern, is hard to resist, and causes significant annoyance or trauma to oneself or to others. From the impulse-ridden menu, therefore, we exclude eating, drinking, and spending sprees that spring up only rarely under loads of emotional stress; and we also leave out rituals such as compulsive hand washing and neatness, so long as they wreak little or no havoc on intellectual, emotional, or social functioning.

One might easily get the impression that the incidence of impulse-impelled behavior in our present-day society has greatly skyrocketed, given the recent proliferation of inpatient treatment facilities, half-way houses, and twelve-step programs. Well, such behavior does seem to have increased quite a bit, but don't lose sight of the fact that sufferers in times past mostly fought their demons in isolation. However, what is true beyond the shadow of a doubt is that obsessive, compulsive, addictive, and other impulse-ridden disorders are a matter of great concern in our modern society, and that most parents have some worries that their little ones could in the future fall victim to one or more of them.

What causes deep-rooted impulse-ridden behavior? In the "good old days" of simplistic explanations, inveterate drinking and gambling were in most cases viewed as moral failings. We have since become more enlightened, but there still exists a good deal of confusion about the underlying causative factors. Most experts agree, however, that various factors work in concert to engender problem behaviors. The following is a sampling.

Factors Influencing Impulse-Ridden Behavior

Chemical Imbalances

Attributing impulse-ridden behavior to chemical irregularities mght offer comfort to the guilt-riddled, such as the parents of youthful drug abusers. Yet even assuming that these imbalances are very powerful, what brings them into play to begin with? "The experts don't know" is a standard response, but one thing we suspect Is psychic malaise. Frightening situations, after all, generate loads of adrenaline; yet if we freeze up with fear, we don't put the blame on the adrenaline. So isn't it possible that a stressful psychological atmosphere *creates* chemical changes that, just as with the adrenaline, are designed to help us find solutions?

Genetic factors

Genetic traits leave some folks more susceptible than others to drug abuse, alcoholism, violence, and other impulse-ridden behavior. But how great an influence do these traits exert? Some experts suggest that they are irresistible; but if that were true, then armies of genetically disposed yet sobered-up inveterate drinkers would still be raising their glasses. Furthermore, these tendencies become identified in people already in trouble; and we know of no studies in which hereditary factors are sought out in random samplings of the general population. We suspect, therefore, that many youngsters carrying the gene for violence may never fall under the microscope because they are blessed with nurturing parents and never get into trouble.

The power of addictive substances

Cocaine and heroin, and let's not leave out highly addictive nicotine, can ensnare even those from homes full of love and dialogue. Youngsters from these families, however, are less likely to abuse drugs in the first place, and more able to kick the habit once addicted. Any drug can be kicked once the abuser gets past withdrawal, and lapses typically are the result of urges to revisit all the *satisfactions* associated with the substance.

Influences in the community

Our high-stress society is a really big factor with respect to impulsive behaviors. Emerging adults enter into a highly competitive society bursting with temptations and way short on social and emotional support systems, and often far from the parental cradle. Captivating advertising and entertainment stimulate instant gratification; keep reminding young people that they are never O.K. just as they are; and they foist on them, from the playpen to their day of emancipation, ridiculously high standards of glamor and status. What is more, they deliver conflicting messages as to body image, food, sexuality, aggression, and the handling of money. We have observed in our years of clinical practice that little ones from rock-solid, well-informed families tend to be pretty resistant to factors in the community that influence impulse-ridden behavior.

Influences related to child-rearing

Chemical shenanigans, genetic predispositions, addictive properties, community-based factors, and even rotten luck all contribute to impulsive behavior; but nothing can even come close to rivaling the impact of one's family of origin. Young ones from dysfunctional homes are influenced both by the unhealthy interactions and also by the impulsive-behavior example found so often among their parents. In twelve-step and therapy sessions, tales of dreary and scary early life experiences appear to be the norm; and those who speak of an idyllic childhood are usually suspected of living in denial. Parents never wish to foist impulse-driven disorders upon their small ones, but they open up the door nonetheless by being personally or maritally miserable, emotionally volatile or aloof, insecure or inconsistent in parenting, or tangled in the perilous ploys or the "game" of regulation roulette.

> *I have been depressive ever since I can remember, and my worst fears have been that my youngsters might follow on the same path. Recently my oldest boy--the bedrock of the family--got arrested for drug possession, and after I stopped getting hysterical I knew that now it was time for us to get some family therapy. I certainly need the help, and Tony will be agreeable, especially if it helps keep him out of the system. I realize that I should have gotten real help before having had children, but I'm going to do all I*

*can now to see if we can get some of our problems
straightened out--even if it's a painful process.*
                                   Homemaker, mother of 4

Modalities for treating impulse-riddled disorders are emerging rapidly as the ranks of those in need of intervention continue to swell. Many programs, in particular those in extended-stay rehab facilities, combine elements from a wide range of modalities. Here are some broad categories.

Treatment Modalities for Impulse-Ridden Behavior

Physical-body approaches

Drying-out programs typically take a whole-body approach, offering the likes of special-need diets, vitamin and drug regimens, Yoga and aerobic exercise, acupuncture, and chemical-imbalance treatments. Also included in physical-body remedies are extreme measures such as stomach stapling and castration. Professionals who stay exclusively with physical-body therapies are typically behaviorists who have little or no interest in approaches that address underlying causes of aberrant behavior, nor do they see the value of verbal interaction as an important agent of change.

Spiritual approaches

While meditation is used to relax body and mind, it is also touted for its potential in spiritual growth. Twelve-step programs enter the spiritual realm by urging participants to hand their lives over to a Higher Power and to take a regular moral inventory; and church sponsored programs place very heavy emphasis on taking the righteous path to overcoming addictive-compulsive behavior. Also, we all know of religious conversions that result in immediate and dramatic changes in outlook and behavior, and free many, at least for some while, from their troublesome impulses.

Verbal interaction focused on problem behavior

The talking approach, as long as it steers clear of intellectualizing, can trigger emotional catharsis, openness to receiving help from others, and the taking of responsibility for ones actions. Twelve-step programs put emphasis on sharing, mutual support, and mentoring; while discussion groups specialize in free-flowing interaction, which may on occasion become confrontational. Discussion leaders in some settings hold the "facilitator" title; and in others, "therapist" is the handle. Behavior-focused verbal interaction is a mainstay of prison-based, psychiatric-inpatient, and court-mandated programs.

Behavior modification

Behavioral specialists, seeing no good purpose for dredging up buried memories and emotions from a troubled upbringing, strive instead to reshape attitudes, patterns of interacting, and the process of choice making. Clients are encouraged to extinguish self-defeating behavior patterns, challenge irrational beliefs, and avoid behavior-triggering occasions. Positive affirmations these days have moved beyond the behavior-therapy venue to popularity among the general public. Behavior-treatment specialists tend to be more didactic than interactive, and they are typically referred to as trainers.

Underlying-issue resolution

Psychoanalysts, clinical therapists, Gestalt specialists, and others in the professions encourage clients to let out their feelings related to long-smoldering psychic wounds and to learn some self-awareness, all designed to help them let go of their unhappy past. Many people seek this kind of dynamic therapy for issues such as marital distress, parent-child turmoil, or chronic anxiety or depression; and they often have impulse-driven behavior as well. These therapists, however, do not treat this problem behavior in isolation, but rather they view it as being symptomatic of deeper unresolved issues. This is the psychologically whole-person approach

Twelve-step loyalists proudly speak of how their marriages, careers, and even their very lives have gotten saved through their program's precepts and the caring support of their fellows. Many treatment programs, especially those privately run, claim excellent success rates; and psychotherapists routinely find a correlation in clients between their excellent overall progress with treatment and the diminishment of their impulse-overrun behavior. Even people initially mandated into treatment in numerous cases wind up being true-believer converts. In truth, any form of assistance can benefit a few or many, depending to a substantial degree on the skills and caring instincts of the leader, and also on the steady work of those seeking help for their demons.

Yes, treatment for impulse-riddled behavior could turn out to be a life saver, and yet questions remain nevertheless. Twelve-step programs, a bulwark of long-range help, have never opened themselves up to studies about effectiveness. Centers claiming a high success rate usually focus on relatively short-range sobriety; and since insurance coverage--if any--is so often limited, enrollees are all too soon on their own again with only community-centered programs providing backup. And similarly, those who successfully complete court-mandated treatment go back, with scant supports, into the hazardous zone. Then finally, dynamic psychotherapy--in our opinion the most effective treatment of them all--can be a time-consuming and expensive undertaking.

Treatment programs focus almost exclusively on troubling behavior and steer clear of underlying causes. What is more, they offer to enrollees no hope at all of getting freed for good from their addictive and compulsive cravings. What is more, no matter how much success various programs may claim, overall rates of back-sliding in fact seem rather high. Lots of twelve-step dropouts just can't remain clean and sober; but even among the faithful, lapses aren't at all unusual. Follow-up studies on abusers leaving court-ordered treatment are hard to find, but the hordes of returnees into the penal system indicate high rates of relapsing. And high-profile private treatment programs make headlines when celebrities slide off the wagon again and again.

Life-long struggles to establish and maintain sobriety make for a huge impulse-riddled population; and to make matters worse, wave after wave of coming-of-age youngsters keep adding to their numbers. This is not a very rosy picture. Some parents become convinced, as they cross their fingers, that such a fate could never befall their innocent ones; and still others live with dread, and as a result become super-restrictive. The "Talk to your children about drugs" slogan is really great in theory, but if children and parents don't already communicate regularly and openly on a wide range of sensitive issues, then drug-related talks initiated by parents are in many cases not likely to get too far.

Don't get discouraged by gloom-and-doom statements like "There is no telling which children might become victims of drugs." This is a case of head-in-the-sand thinking. The truth is that you *can* immunize young ones to a significant degree against impulse-ridden behavior even without the requirement that your household be essentially problem-free. Yes, small ones can emerge virtually unscathed after facing a marital break-up, major illnesses, natural disasters, school issues, and other crises. This takes place when the overall home atmosphere is a nurturing, empowering one; and when problematic events are dealt with in a constructive way and with a sense of hope.

Since searching for recovery from impulse-riddled behavior can be a long, frustrating journey all through one's adult years, it is really important for your little ones to learn recovery skills as they grow and mature. Then they can look forward to a future featuring bumps in the road that are for the most part easily repaired.

> *I have had more foster children that I can count, but my favorite of all was Rodney. He came to me six days old, drug-addict for a mother, and he just cried and cried all of the time. So I held him and hugged him as much as possible, since I knew those drugs had messed up his system so badly. Finally, about four months later he suddenly stopped crying and seemed as normal as a young fella can be. At age six he moved on to a long-term foster home which adopted him on down the line. He's at high school now and in honors classes, and he comes by once in a while to see me and give me a big old hug. He sure doesn't remember much about living here, but his family talks about it, and I know he feels a lot of love way deep down.*
>
> *Foster mom of umpteen kids*

How Children Acquire Primary Recovery Skills

When newborns feel distressed in any sense, they scream until help arrives on the scene. This both signals their wants and purges their systems of tensions. Colicky babies cry non-stop for a seeming eternity; then when their discomfort eases up, parents often marvel at how unscathed they appear to be from all that suffering. The crying, however, is not a feature of their suffering, but rather a feature of it's resolution. And when you put up with all the screaming and then strive to puzzle out and respond to the young child's needs, you are practicing preventive medicine on a very big scale. This is stage one of primary recovery.

As they grow, little ones increasingly use words to convey their fears, emotional pain, and fondest desires--thus diminishing their need to screech. Listen reflectively (see Chapter 6) as they emote and plead their case; but quickly short-circuit harassment, guilt-tripping, and other tactics designed to weaken your resolve. You may decide not to give in to their wishes nor to assist them in their plans, or you may decide to lend them a hand. Yet in every instance you will be partnering up with them as they learn primary recovery skills.

When children suffer trauma from becoming lost or injured, they are routinely encouraged to let the words and tears flow out, a signal of recovery's getting well underway. The relatively small traumas they face on a frequent basis are lesser in magnitude, but the same dynamics are at work. Instead of being helped to open up, however, all too many of these young ones are now expected to shut down--by being told to stop acting like a baby, being pesty, or taking up valuable time. This can result in their swallowing feelings or expressing them off-the-wall--that is, over-dramatized and in inappropriate situations. Then by the time they reach adulthood or perhaps even sooner, they turn into candidates for impulse-ridden behavior. And no, we are not asking you to coddle them--just to spend a few moments listening to their feelings.

Some recovery-skill challenges cannot be avoided, like the death of a loved one or a pet, learning disabilities, searing poverty, and divorce; and even while parents are standing close by, small ones nevertheless suffer injuries and emotional traumas. Then as they carry out more self-determined choices, the risks are increasingly beyond the parents' control, as indeed they ought to be. Yet confident, supportive, parents know that their little ones are taking bumps in the road as lessons in the primary-recovery-skill learning process. Overprotective parents, by contrast, work to dampen the mastery of these skills. It can be stressful to watch your fledglings struggle and make mistakes, and it is not an easy task to tolerate youthful outbursts, especially if you are the target; but your reward will be in seeing the little ones grow to young adulthood with scant if any need for community-based recovery programs.

A loving, stable home atmosphere is certainly crucial to the fostering of primary recovery skills; but unless children are allowed and encouraged to express themselves spontaneously, the opportunities for their learning primary recovery skills can very easily get compromised. Here is where dialogue-laden family hour sessions enter the picture. Family hour serves as a laboratory for nurturing primary recovery skills in growing youngsters, and thus it holds the potential for rendering infertile the breeding grounds for addictive and compulsive disorders. This is tons of prevention.

> *In our family meetings the rule is that if you want to complain about something, you need to talk about your feelings as well. Usually this leads into anger, but one time our little one, seven-year-old Dennis, said that his complaint about his brother made him happy. When we finally got it clarified, it turned out that he was happy his brother was in trouble for the breaking of an antique lamp. This led to some fiery debate over the whole incident, and it then became clear that Dennis had thrown a ball in the direction of the lamp, which led to his brother's backing into it. So Dennis went from happy to unhappy.*
>
> *Professor of government*
> *and mother of 4*

Let us now examine several areas where impulse-riddled behavior runs rampant, some underlying issues that influence this behavior, and how government and the broader community react to and cope with it. Then we show how the dialogue generated in family hour, along with the nurturance and support of members of the household, helps young people become powerfully protected against it's ravages.

How Family Hour Combats Impulse-Ridden Behavior

Eating Disorders

Bulimia seldom puts in an appearance in famine-plagued lands, where food never has the chance to get taken for granted. Our food-rich society, on the other hand, is a veritable cafeteria of eating disorders. Beginning with infancy, feeding is synonymous with nurturance and security; so those who stumble on this initial hurdle tend to search for goodies, typically sweets and fats, when they feel lonely and/or anxious. Then their will gets further sapped by incessant advertising for tasty, fattening fare. Some fall into yo-yo dieting and bulimia when they get frustrated over their excess poundage; and anorexics, obsessed in their mania over thinness, tend to wrestle with power and control issues. Binge eaters, regular over-indulgers, and yo-yo dieters seek help at "fat farms" or in sessions at Weight Watchers, Overeaters Anonymous, or similar programs. Anorexics and bulimics can be found at inpatient facilities, outpatient treatment clinics, and twelve-step groups.

Family hour vs. eating disorders

Regular overindulgence and eating binges typically make their appearance in conjunction with depression, emotional neediness, frustrations, and/or isolation. Family hour combats this syndrome through words of endearment and encouragement, supportive comments, and reflective listening, just for starters. But even heated words can be part of an overall nurturing experience, as is the case for encounter and therapy groups. The only family group members likely to feel lonely or unloved are those swimming in an ocean of self-pity; but when their tactics of manipulation come up short, they very gradually begin blending in. All family hour small fry have their unsettling times, but they are more likely to reach for help and support than for platters of food. Then as young adults they look at waif-body expectations as strange and unhealthy, and they are unlikely to tolerate careers that saddle them with perfect-figure pressures.

Substance Abuse

Abuse-prone substances, both legal and illegal, are readily obtained and way too often mixed inadvertently in potentially dangerous combinations. Physical or psychological dependence can result from a large menu of substances we take into our systems, and incessant drug commercials erode our already poor tolerance for any degree of pain or discomfort. Users may be fleeing physical or emotional stress, seeking nirvana, rebelling against parents or society, or mimicking what "everybody else" is doing. Alcohol, our drug of preference, tends to unleash inhibitions and promote sociability, risky actions, emotional release, or the need to escape; and addictions are reinforced by the furious tugging of withdrawal symptoms. And unfortunately, despite a tremendous proliferation of treatment programs, substance abuse appears to be streaming further and further out of control.

Family hour vs. substance abuse

Featuring freedom of expression, stalwart communication, and steady support, family hour protects against substance abuse in the same manner that it does for eating disorders, but with one added benefit. Drug abuse often starts in the peer group, but family hour youngsters are simply not suited for blindly following other folks, peer or parent. When sessions get focused on drug use, be prepared to talk frankly of your personal experiences with alcohol, tobacco, medications, and perhaps even taboo items. This moves the talk along, whereas lecturing douses it. The greatest deterrent of all, however, dwells in your regular family hour sessions. Since dialoguing youngsters feel free to speak out, their misery tends to be short-lived and their rebellion isn't apt to get out of hand. This decreases the chances of their reaching out for mind-altering substances. Also, as in-the-know young people, they well realize that drug-induced euphoria comes with serious risks.

Materialism-Related Problems

Our "gimme" society is ideal for money-related impulsivity disorders. Children growing up short on monetary and emotional enrichment often equate material plenty with love and happiness; and those whose "stuff" substitutes for quality at-home time come to crave endless goodies. Angry young people may take the illicit route, naive and impulsive types turn to spree spending and wild business ventures, and insecure magical thinkers often find gambling irresistible. Credit card abuse is rampant, theft and financial trickery come in endless formats; then there is the keeping up with and getting ahead of the Joneses. And be aware that many financial wizards, however masterful they may be, are driven by hidden insecurities. Those in financial straits find a haven in Gamblers or Debtors Anonymous, but have you ever heard of programs aimed at the obsessive amassers of money and goods? Not at all likely, as they tend to become admired and envied by most everyone.

Family hour vs. materialism-related problems

The relentless pursuit of all things material is a pitiful substitute for internal peace and harmony, and for loving relationships.

The good news is that family hour promotes these and other price-less non-material assets. These youngsters come to value happi-ness and fulfillment way ahead of big cars, headline grabbing, and power over others; and this leaves them well protected against all impulse-propelled ills of a monetary nature. Then to protect them even further, you can broach topics such as the lure of advertising; financial schemes and scams; pressure in the peer group to keep up with the latest fads; and the exercise of due care in budgeting, credit card use, and checkbook management. Also, be willing to talk about lessons you have learned from credit card use and the sting of having gotten conned; and please take a look at how your choices of residence, vehicles, clothing, and possessions of every kind have been based to any degree on prestige value, or on the desire convey a specific image of yourself.

Sexual Disorders

The sexually obsessed act out in fashions that betray their beliefs about being outsiders to deeply shared love. The message of flashers is " I'm certain you don't want to see me, but I will force you anyway;" voyeurs say "I'm sure you don't want me to see you, but I'll sneak me a look anyway;" molesters lure innocents to rip off gratification; and rapists do the same, but viciously. Social pariahs all, they keep on reinforcing their pathetic ineptitude for engaging in give-and-take love. Sex addicts, a more socialized lot, find that no amount of cavorting can satisfy longings hidden deeply within. The hysterically prudish go the other way, in many cases dreading that sex could rip open old wounds or leave them vulnerable. Sex also serves as a manipulative tool, as with incessant teasers and those who barter with sexually gratifying favors. Sexual offenders engender community and household uproar, so they often end up pressured into going after twelve-step help or psychotherapy; and for habitual offenders or those committing heinous acts, treatment

most often takes place inside a prison or in court-sanctioned facilities. As one might imagine, the odds for success are long ones.

Family hour vs. sexual disorders

Jokes about sex in family sessions teem with superficiality,
and sexual issues that arise regarding family members usually call
for private handling. But when this subject comes up, don't lapse
into beating around the bush or droning--clear signs of your lack of
comfort. This squelches free-flow discussion. Give young people
space for talking; but then when the situation allows, don't hesitate
to supply simple facts, without moralizing, on topics like AIDS and
unwanted pregnancy. And if you voice your dismay over inappropriate sex, strive to balance it out with your enthusiasm--genuine,
not staged--over the joyful kind. Nipping sex-connected impulsive
disorders in the bud, however, has everything to do with nurturing.
Since sexually aberrant behavior serves as a substitute for emotional intimacy, make a point to grace your sessions with loads of
tenderness, encouragement, heartfelt emotionality--and possibly
most important of all, your undivided attention.

Anti-Social Behavior and Violence

The anti-social and violence-prone, typically brought up in
abuse, neglect, or emotionally sterile atmospheres, live a dog-eat-
dog existence as bullies, gangsters, scam artists, etc. Sociopaths
learn to say and do all the right things to move smoothly in social
circles, but they typically leave a trail of devastation in their wake.
The violence-prone include "decent folks" whose "Mr. Hyde" side
emerges when provoked or "under the influence." Then there are
cause-driven crusaders and vigilantes, revenge seekers, and vol-
canic spewers. Angry outbursts, fueled mainly by deep-down fear
or emotional pain, may provide momentary relief, but this behavior

wreaks havoc on family relationships. These types possess poor frustration tolerance and little insight, and rarely seek out help on their own. The violence-prone might attend anger-management or twelve-step groups under duress, such as the threat of divorce or legal action; or they can get corralled into treatment in the criminal justice system. And many of them do an excellent job of faking it through these systems.

Family hour vs. anti-social behavior and violence

The accepting atmosphere of family hour, periodic grumping and grousing notwithstanding, is no breeding ground at all for the anti-social personality. Family hour instills in young people a sense of personal value, leaving them with little interest in the use of intimidation or frightening outbursts as a way of keeping others in line--favorite tactics of the violence-prone. What is more, abusive types haven't a clue about resolving issues through dialogue, the staple of family hour. Small ones who regularly attend family hour meetings see their anger welcomed when spontaneously expressed, but not when manipulation or browbeating sits behind it. Also, family members know that sticking to issues is more productive than engaging in insult-sprinkled personal attacks. So these young people get two huge benefits from expressing their feelings: a sense of relief, and the opening of doors for resolving issues.

Maladaptive Behavior

This grab-bag category includes accident-prone behavior, self-mutilation, exaggerated orderliness and cleanliness, non-stop prattling, anxiety attacks and phobias, and suicidal thoughts and urges. Maladaptive behavior incubates in homes that feature battling, harassment, silence, enormous pressure to excel or assume responsibility, coldness, and other dysfunctional behavior patterns.

Many loners and black sheep are found here. Obsessive thought and compulsive rituals serve to keep the conscious mind occupied while truly scary emotions threaten to burst out from below, which is not unlike whistling in a graveyard at night so as to dispel a fear of ghosts; phobias and panic attacks serve similar purposes, the latter showing great internal pressure and also serving as a warning; and suicidal thinking shows pressure having reached an intolerable point, and with anger turned inward. Therapy programs as well as Neurotics Anonymous are often summoned to the rescue; and in risky situations the afflicted, for their own protection, might even require hospitalization. Therapy regimens for these sufferers usually focus heavily on medications.

Family hour vs. maladaptive behavior

The roots of psychologically and socially maladaptive behaviors obtain scant nourishment in family hour houses. Non-stop babblers crave attention but don't think others will offer it willingly; so they rip if off verbal-diarrhea style, which turns others off--thus confirming their worst fears. These unfortunates don't likely live in family hour homes, where listening is just as important as talking. Compulsions, phobias, and panic attacks all point to great fear of one's own emotions, which explains why unpleasant feelings get so dammed up. Family-hour-veteran children feel at ease venting their ideas and emotions, and this is because parent leaders both accept and encourage such expression. What is more, these parents are careful not to over-pressure small ones, and they further watch for signs of youngsters putting pressure on themselves. All this nips potential self-loathing and suicidal urges in the bud. One family hour feature is especially potent in squashing all things maladaptive. This is the serious matter of having fun. This includes being downright silly, playing light-hearted games, staging comedy routines, and the like. And no, this is not a frivolous waste of time, but rather a large dose of preventive medicine--the kind on which you cannot overdose.

> *Some of our family meetings have an weighty feel, and some get very silly, like our every other month costume party. Outlandish dress is the order of the day, and we have to remain "in character" for all the hour--or however long the affair goes on. One time recently our eleven-year-old Jayson came dressed as a hitman. My wife and I were taken aback at the start, but we decided to wait and see what he would do. By coincidence, however, I was in the role of a cop for that session, so later on I arrested him. He then demanded to see a lawyer, but we didn't have any lawyers in the costumed group. We all enjoyed some good laughs about it after the time was up. I hope Jayson takes on the role of judge some time soon, so he can get to decide his own fate.*
>
> *Civil engineer, father of 4*

CHAPTER FOURTEEN

COME-AND-GO PROBLEMS:
THE KEY TO FAMILY HARMONY

*Ellen and I each had children from a prior marriage;
and when we met, one from each group got into an
all-out war. We thought about going for some family counseling, but then we finally decided to have
all of us sit down together in order to air out all the
upset feelings. The two girls shed tears and voiced
their complaints, and my fiance and I needed to bite
our tongues so as to not even appear to be taking
sides. The session seemed worthwhile, so we all
agreed to keep on meeting like this for an indefinite
period--not just because of the problem that got us
started, but also because it just seemed like a good
thing in general. Their squabbling continued on for
months to a lesser degree, but then the marriage
came along and all of a sudden their fighting disap-
peared like magic. And in time these girls have become pretty close friends.*

Middle school athletic coach

How wonderful it is to be in perfect health. Yet nobody has
really perfect health, do they? We have all at one time or another
suffered with coughs and colds, aches and pains, and other afflic-

tions and annoyances too numerous to list. In robust individuals these usually minor but occasionally serious health issues simply visit for a while and then go away. It's amazing how the physical body strives continuously to repair itself, and succeeds again and again for those in so-called "perfect health." But for the less fortunate, the road to health keeps getting strewn with obstacles; and this opens up the door wide for debilitating conditions like arthritis, osteoporosis, glaucoma, crippling strokes, and incessant, insufferable pain--and also for life-threatening conditions such as cancer, emphysema, and heart disease.

Perfect family harmony is also an illusion. Blissful newlyweds may all dream of it, but some instead get saddled with mind-numbing misery. Now there *are* couples who seem to possess the magic formula; but in so many cases they are heavily into devices that guarantee peace but greatly diminish the vitality of their relationship. Among the better known devices we see submissivenes, superficiality, avoidance, and appeasement. Strong, steady, emotionally vibrant families surely have their share of ups and downs, but their downs wind up getting resolved at the time or fade away gradually. Yes, the physical body works relentlessly to heal itself, and the family body has just the same inclination. Yet in oodles of households the healing process somehow fails to take hold, and the reasons for this are many.

Factors Contributing to Chronic Family Discord

Unresolved psychological issues in parents

Emotionally ill parents and those burdened with continuing psychological stress usually manage, without conscious intent, to ensnare their little ones into dysfunctional family interaction. Then again, even parents who have never been labeled as "psychologically disturbed" are capable of stirring up trouble, as we note with demanding perfectionists, blamers, carpers, control freaks, poor-me folks, grudge-holders, and the super-sensitive. Then if both of the parents are laden with heavy emotional baggage, the chance for major household conflict rises significantly. Self-awareness regarding personal hang-ups is an asset, whereas parents who give full throttle to their dysfunctionality pose the highest risk.

Lack of suitability or preparedness for parenthood

Starting a pregnancy at a highly inopportune time, getting married when one is emotionally or financially on shaky grounds, caving in under pressure to the marry-and-have-kids expectations of society, and slipping unprepared into step-parenthood are a few of the possibilities here. Also, some people assign a low priority to child raising as they get wrapped up in careers, hobbies, social or civic involvements, causes of all kinds, or their own misery. Then too, some otherwise affable, functional people are simply inept at dealing with little ones. Inadequately equipped, dedicated, or prepared parents so often go on to contribute heavily to dysfunctional family interaction.

Unfortunate, unforeseen circumstances

Disasters more often hit vulnerable families, but rock-solid ones are never immune. Incarceration, desertion, and mountains of debt can crack a family's foundation; ongoing health problems, crippling accidents, and kidnappings can strike anyone, anywhere; and communities on occasion devolve into military battlegrounds or targets of nature's fury. Even if parents have made no contribution to a misfortune, their frustrations might leave them embittered, blame-seeking, and emotionally isolated. And even when matters later return to normal, certain of these families run into trouble trying to repair the damage to their relationships.

The close quarters of family life

When friends, neighbors, co-workers, or schoolmates suffer a falling out, they can usually find ways of staying pretty much out of one another's way; but since the home is a confined space, young ones get no comfortable refuge from a big-people shouting match. Then too, icy silences slice through the household air like a kitchen knife, affecting even those outside of the "arctic circle." Households generally have a prevailing atmosphere, and when it is distinctly on the unpleasant side, family members typically look to the outside for tender, supportive relationships. This leaves the house as a base of operations for those caught up into the spirit of battle, a prison for those too young to escape it, or a place to just "crash," eat on the run, do chores, etc.

The family as a dumping ground for misplaced anger

It is tempting to dump anger onto safe targets, and household members are the safest of all in the short run. The long-term harm inflicted on family relationships, however, makes this a dangerous practice. Mr. Big screams at a worker, who goes on home and sends misery down the line until the family mutt gets kicked; stressed-out parents chit-chat with neighbors, and then go grumbling all around the house; a boy with low self-esteem bullies his little brother; and some siblings, swallowing resentment meant for parents, lunge into hateful exchanges with one another. It is said that some parents can "be themselves" only in their own homes; yet their actions often leave their dismayed offspring wishing that they would be someone else instead.

Naturally clashing personalities

Friendships are based on compatible interests and needs; and if one falls to pieces, another one may be waiting in the wings.

Yet within the household, friendship choices are limited. Siblings, thrown in together through nature's roll of the dice, would in many instances never befriend one another were they not blood related. And infants are routinely welcomed with great affection, yet in the fullness of time, serious personality clashes can surface between the parents and their once cuddly offspring. What is more, some married couples who found a mutual attraction through unfounded hopes and expectations, later on become much more realistic and also more cynical.

Conflicts stemming from the "only human" factor

Some combustible interaction arises out of relationship factors such as sibling rivalry, competitiveness, favoritism, or absurdly high expectations on the part of parents with relation to each other or to their young ones. Other dissension springs from personality traits such as defensiveness, impulsivity, and the tendency toward holding grudges. Then too, family folks develop disgruntlement to varying degrees from the likes of traffic jams, health issues, sleep deprivation, or misunderstandings engendered by faulty or garbled information. And as might be expected, the greater the number of bedeviling factors a family gets, the more likely they are to blur all together into a big bundle of discord.

A shortage of time for family-together work and play

This issue keeps on cropping up because a short supply of family-together time adversely impacts every aspect of household living. What is more, its contribution to family-relationship discord tends to be insidious one. Before our technology revolution came upon the scene, family members spent oodles of time working and playing together, and battling among themselves as well. But their strong bonds of cooperation also aided them in many instances to forgive and forget pretty quickly. The dissension found in today's off-in-every-direction families, by striking contrast, is more typically marked by a vague erosion of trust, lingering resentments, and the dark shadows of alienation.

> *I grew up in a home atmosphere of bitterness. We all saved up our petty annoyances until they finally exploded like a volcano; then the accusations and insults flew around at warp speed. When I got married I vowed that I would never repeat that pattern, but what has happened instead is just the reverse-- I avoid touchy issues entirely. Recently we started having family hour, and the first few sessions went OK. Then two of the kids started battling, and next Wesley started to grumbe about my being way too lenient with them. I felt furious inside, but I just kept my mouth shut, and we agreed to end the meeting before the hour was up. Naturally, no one felt like scheduling another session. I know we need some outside help, but I fear that it will get ugly like it was for me years ago; and I don't want that.*
>
> *Bookkeeper and mother of 4*

Let us now take a look how disharmony shatters the family scene, both in the form of habitual behaviors and as a prevailing atmosphere--and sad to say, the list could be a lot longer. You will notice that certain of the examples contain none of the nastiness typically associated with dysfunctional family life.

Elements Found in Chronic Family Discord

☐ Chronic sarcasm, insults, name calling, cruel jokes, etc.
☐ Condescension, criticizing, supervising, and moralizing.
☐ Round-in-circles arguments where no one is ever "wrong."

- ☐ Theatrical wailing, throwing objects, storming off, etc.
- ☐ Periodic screaming matches fueled by piled-up grievances.
- ☐ Lingering negativity from grumbling and gloominess.
- ☐ A prevailing me-first atmosphere, with no cooperative spirit.
- ☐ Episodes of accuse-and-defend, yielding no resolutions.
- ☐ Anxious tip-toeing around and grinny-face superficiality.
- ☐ Relationships riddled by avoidance, apathy, or alienation.
- ☐ Relationships choked in smothering over-involvement.
- ☐ Misunderstandings that lead to petty or big-time squabbles.
- ☐ Regular spying and grilling, and tactics used to combat it.
- ☐ Manipulation like guilt-tripping, trickery, and false promises.
- ☐ Attention-seeking ploys like clowning and mischief-making.
- ☐ Sympathy-seeking ploys like self-pity and playing "victim."
- ☐ Protracted parent-child battles over rules and enforcement.
- ☐ Chaos on the parenting scene due to ineffective leadership.
- ☐ Cultural alienation resulting from shortages of quality time.
- ☐ Regular cut-throat competition and one-upmanship.
- ☐ Frequent get-backs on a score that never gets evened.
- ☐ Fierce pressure to succeed, along with great fear of failure.
- ☐ Pig-sty living, featuring little sense of responsibility or pride.
- ☐ Festering addictive, compulsive, and psychiatric problems.
- ☐ Crisis-to-crisis living, with no foresight or lesson-learning.
- ☐ Physical violence, sexual abuse, and other such horrors.
- ☐ Anti-social activities--e.g., drug dealing and gang warfare.

For fifteen years Nick and I had a bizarre marriage, but my fears over the broken-home thing and about finances kept me on board. Then I finally snapped after one of his drunken rages, so I tossed him out. Three months later I heard that he was not doing so well, so I went and gave him a pep talk. But he got worse, and then one day he came crying for me to take him back. The kids thought I was totally nuts, but I told him I would give it another try, but under two conditions: that he give up drinking and that he give me the final say-so on decisions. He agreed, and now four years later--much to my surprise--he has stayed sober and seems comfortable with my ruling the roost. He devotes all of his spare time to making furniture, and has become really good at it. We hold occasional family meetings now, but it is hard because the kids are always off somewhere. The funny thing is that when we do sit down to talk, no one says a word about the old problems, so it's like it never happened. I guess I should have been the head honcho in the first place--but hey, it's better late than never.

Nurse's aide, mother of 4

When relationships in the household get bogged down with never-ending conflict, family members might easily get resigned to the prospect that things will never change for the better; and they might even give up trying. But it is never too late to change; and most parents--even the cynically battle-hardened--will jump at the opportunity once they are provided with much-needed information and support. After all, apparently intractable folks are no different from anybody else in longing after affectionate, harmonious family bonds; and in fact they typically search for supportive, understanding relationships away from their homes in their choices of friends, social activities, and helping groups.

Family hour sessions can be a forum for bringing positive changes to the family scene, and this process will be made easier when conflicts are fairly isolated and short of the level of mayhem. Don't expect to solve all issues, but do concentrate on two important leadership tasks: extracting the very lifeblood from destructive interactions, and increasing the flow of dialogue. Everybody participates in dialogue, even if they have relatively few interests and values in common; and in fact family members dialogue together on a regular basis in non-sensitive areas of discussion. Your big challenge is to help keep dialogue flowing even when the waters of verbal interaction flow into dangerous areas.

Some parents report a boost in harmony after just one or a few family hour sessions, particularly when a specific problem, no matter how trivial in character, gets resolved or eased up. Some families, however, find it tempting to disband the discussions once tensions have eased; but why should anyone settle for an upgrade to "not as bad as it was" or "now tolerably OK" status? Now at this juncture it would be prudent to continue on, as family hour's benefits increase greatly over the long haul--in the prevention and solving of issues, as well as in the enrichment of everybody's lives--in particular the lives of growing youngsters.

Conflict-Abating Benefits of Regular Family Hour

Many root causes of discord get eradicated

The right to speak one's piece applies equally to all family members, and the desire to find a receptive audience for spontaneous emotions plays no favorites based on age or status in the household. These rights and needs, to be sure, are an essential component of family hour; and accordingly, household members aren't likely to let resentments simmer away, nor are they likely to be ridiculed for bringing them to others' ears. Spouses who feel ignored or unable to get a word in edgewise will make a foolproof case for themselves in their sessions, parents who tend to lecture to children ad nauseam will get hooted down, and an angry slap to the face will hopefully be caught in mid-air. Also, parents will blow a timely whistle to put a stop to persistent whining and wheedling.

Then there are all sorts of other trouble-making elements that will be picked off as they find their way into the discussions--e.g., guilt-tripping, manipulation, name calling, intimidation, drowning others out, threats, and non-stop talking.

Potential disharmony gets nipped in the bud

Even in households where verbal talents abound, tempers can flare up suddenly as the result of miscommunication, preconceived notions, hastily reached conclusions, and biases. Way too often somebody's words get taken out of context, misunderstood, or distorted; and motives get misinterpreted. Veteran family hour participants of all ages learn to sniff out badly mangled interaction in a flash and to make efforts to clear matters up; then as a result, needless wrangling is averted, or at least it gets eased way down. Then in a rippling-out effect, the lessons of straightforward family hour communications get carried over to household relationships across the board.

Conflicts are kept from spinning out of control

It doesn't take long for certain household flare-ups to escalate into the stratosphere. Therefore, you will need to become an early expert in two leadership skills. The first step is to intervene quickly and with an even hand when discord starts to get destructive or chaotic; and the second is to listen patiently to contentious words and feelings that might turn out to be cathartic or might become helpful in solving problems. Being firm while maintaining a cool head is not so easy, but a tad of practicing will get you there; and remember, there is always safer ground to head for if discussions fizzle or reach an impasse. Also, if chaos threatens repeatedly, resolve to establish more structure in your sessions so as to avoid hot spots of potential volatility.

Many issues get actively resolved, and others just disappear

When grievances get aired out with the help of family hour dialogue, all sorts of good things might occur, like apologies, compromises, a softening up of mutual expectations, or a better grasp of the issues. But perhaps the very best solutions of all come in a spontaneous way. Family hour veterans get accustomed to seeing disharmony, some of it long-entrenched, disappear like magic after participants let their emotions flow or put their deep-felt worries and desires into words. Furthermore, those who silently simmer in resentment and self-pity almost invariably begin loosening up as other family members benefit from discussing issues freely in their presence.

> *My wife and I are both from eastern Europe, and it is natural for us to do some big yelling. Our earliest family meetings felt much too stiff, so we decided to get back to our family roots. The format is now one of open expressing, but with certain basic rules--no threats, no insulting, and no cursing. We feel really serious about the enforcement part of this system-- on every person, including my wife and myself--and violators must remain silent for the rest of the hour. Sometimes we have debates about what is a threat or an insult--or even a bad word--and because she has more formal schooling than I do, my wife holds the final decision on all that.*
>
> *Grocer, father of 6*

In some cases, despite your finest efforts, family conflicts might go on unabated; or you may find yourself so caught up with the swirling of negativity that you cannot manage your leadership role adequately. This might signal the need for professional help. In addition, if you become truly frustrated, confused, or dismayed, you should definitely consider moving in this direction--and without delay. Family therapists are likely to be highly objective since they arrive on the scene from the outside; and they come with a sense of confidence about getting issues resolved, bolstered by an array of proven problem-solving strategies.

Most family therapists are sensitive, carefully trained, and competent. But, as in any profession, a minority turn up unhelpful even when family members are ready for change. Phony credentials are one issue, but the problem is more apt to lie in the outlook and personality of the therapist. Being human, therapists might be biased due to unresolved personal issues; and those with a strong desire for control find the therapist role as a ticket to "hog heaven." The most popular means of control is in taking a parental role with clients, thus fostering dependency--just what clients *do not* need. These therapists may advise clients, for example, to quit their job or to stay in a relationship. It's a good idea to get references, and then to do your own detective work by quizzing prospective therapists on their attitudes, experience, and treatment methods. And if this elicits defensiveness or annoyance, it might be a sign that the help you need is to be found elsewhere.

Even when therapists are free of control issues, helpless-type clients will try to lure them into assuming a measure of power in their daily lives; and reputable therapists, who refuse to take the bait, instead encourage them to take charge of their own destiny. Even the most brilliant therapists are merely helpers. They make note of strengths to build on, initiate discussion over self-defeating behavior, and give unflagging encouragement and support. The lion's share of the work in family therapy is always done by family members themselves, who often continue making big strides long after they have attended their final session.

Successful collaborations between stressed-out family and capable therapists are a great learning experience for parents, but some of what is learned in therapy can also be learned elsewhere. Reading and attending parenting workshops can help, and engaging in family-together projects is always advisable. But long-term family hour holds the greatest potential of all because it resembles family therapy in certain aspects. In truth, it could even be called "family therapy lite," especially if family relationships are largely on the cordial side and there is flexibility. Intervention techniques can be located all through the chapters and in the Help section, but the most effective ones of all will come from your trial-and-error experimentation. And do not take it on yourself to figure out what is on everyone's mind. After all, skilled behavior modification specialists have disdain for such probing, as they believe that insight is totally unnecessary and all too often misused.

> *I will never forget the family hour session where the two girls were teasing Walter, who then started crying for me to get them to stop it. Suddenly I started shaking, and uncharacteristically I screamed out for everyone to just leave me alone. I went on like that for a short while, and then a dead silence followed. And then I realized that I was acting worse than the kids, and I started to apologize. But Larry, bless his heart, said he could see I had been in the pressure cooker at work lately and that it was good for me to let off steam. Then I started weeping, and they all gave me a lot of comforting. I felt much better after that, and I also came to see that I shouldn't let the stress build up again like that. I have a great deal to be thankful for, and it all starts with family.*
>
> *Bank manager, mother of 3*

Family therapy and family hour are different in all kinds of ways, starting off with "stranger" vs. family-member leadership; yet they often accomplish many of the same things, although in unlike methodologies. So point by point, we will now take a look at how they stack up next to each other.

Family Therapy and Family Hour: A Comparison

Scheduling and cost

Family therapy sessions typically get conducted at the professional's office during regular business hours, which usually cuts into school and workday schedules. Then again, some therapists work into the early evening, so the supper hour becomes the only possible casualty. The fees charged by most therapists in private practice, in certain cases covered at least in part by insurance, are similar to those of attorneys, physicians, accountants, etc. Those working in non-profit and government-run clinics in most instances use a sliding scale, but very few families get quality service for no charge or at minimal cost.

Family hour, requiring no travel, gets scheduled at whichever waking hour is most convenient for all. However, since family members these days have activities to attend all over town, some compromises are usually required. The biggest potential obstacle is that, especially in the beginning stages, you must conjure up the perseverance to wade through everyone's resistance, particularly your own. Then again, the no-cost sessions are no doubt the best do-it-yourself project you will ever undertake.

Training and experience of leaders

Most therapists have advanced degrees and special training, usually balanced between classroom studies and supervised field experience. And some have undergone therapy themselves, although only rarely is it part of one's professional training. Clients at non-profit centers might be treated by seasoned counselors or those in training, but most family therapists have at least a number of years of experience in dealing with a wide variety of problems. But then again, more than a few professionals, sad to say, struggle with issues of stagnation and burnout.

We suggest that you attend family hour workshops should they become available in your community, but you can also savor success at the helm of family sessions without any formal training. Your role as natural leader in the home is a huge advantage. You train and supervise small ones in tasks of daily living, like chores, scheduling, and finances; and you know everyone's behavior patterns in advance, in stark contrast to professionals, who start from scratch with total strangers. You might flounder in your beginning scenes as family hour leader; but this places you in the same boat with therapists, who also must start out somewhere.

Attendance at sessions

A small minority of therapists treat the entire family during every session, and others focus in mostly on the parents, who are in the strongest position to effect changes--except for some older teens, who are soon to venture out on their own. The makeup of the sessions might also vary depending on the presenting issues. Yet far too many therapists cater to the requests of "Please fix my kid" parents, and make children the focus for treatment--meeting with parents in consultations. This approach winks at the broadly accepted concept that problem behavior in youngsters is in most cases largely symptomatic of unresolved adult issues--parenting, marital, psychological, financial, career-related, etc.

While problem solving is a key feature of some family hour sessions, it is for the most part a secondary function. Family hour is first and foremost designed to strengthen and enrich family relations and promote household unity. This is why all available family members should be invited to the sessions. The only exceptions we can think of are the exclusion (hopefully temporary) of children who are severely and chronically disruptive, and of small children whose benefit from attending gets outweighed by the distractions they stir up. So when problems get aired with all family members present, those outside of the "combat zone" have a chance to be supportive and helpful, and this--as with group therapy--performs wonders in promoting a sense of solidarity.

Nature and severity of problems addressed

Some seek out professional help so as to keep small brush fires from turning into roaring infernos; but countless others come in having put up with their inner demons and/or relationship woes for months or even years. And what almost always prompts them to ask for help is a crisis--marital split-up, out-of-control behavior, school failure, juvenile arrest, etc. Many therapists wrap up treatment once the presenting problems get all cleared up; but others work with clients, often delving into issues beneath the surface, to help keep similar issues or still others from causing trouble in the future. Long-range work can also help clients in mastering skills that enable them to live more enriched lives as individuals and as a family group. Therapy here becomes largely teaching.

If you are starting family hour at a point where dissension in the home has been severe for a long time, a truly big challenge awaits, and your patience will be greatly needed. Conflicts will no doubt spill over into your sessions pretty quickly, so you must be nimble and resolute in your efforts to keep them from derailing the whole experience. Airing out upset feelings will be in most cases an essential, but be careful to keep chaos, violence, and dead-end wrangling from entering the scene. (The Help section covers this.) Probing into problem areas is not a good idea until the family hour group gets stabilized; but even then, proceed cautiously and structure your sessions more tightly if circumstances dictate. If, on the other hand, your home atmosphere is rather peaceful, and/or your children are fairly young, you can take your time finding a suitable style and content for your regular weekly sessions. Then you will have the luxury of being able to wrestle with relationship problems while they are still in the early brushfire stage, and are therefore a lot easier to manage.

The work of the group leader

The work of dedicated, self-aware family therapists can be more than a bit stressful. They attend to the feelings and needs of others while placing their own off to the side; then they demand a great deal from themselves, but refrain from leaping in and putting pressure on clients who may be struggling in their attempts to find the proper direction. And for therapists who find themselves harboring expectations over how much progress their clients "should" make, or who lead unfulfilling personal lives, the danger of professional burnout lurks right around the corner. Then too, the professional community endlessly debates the efficacy of one treatment modality over another. A theory that appears to enjoy consensus, however, is that highly effective therapists have a loving, optimistic nature and a genuine desire to help.

Family therapists don't become members of the treatment group, but instead stick exclusively with the leadership role. You, on the other hand, are both a leader and a member of your family group; but not both at the same moment. And a big goal of yours should be to spend as much time as you can being simply one of the group. Therapists keep regular tabs on clients' state of mind; whereas you simply keep the family group interactions on the right track, resting assured that individuals will thrive when the interaction proves out interesting and productive. When individual family members are visibly upset or voice complaints, you can step in to offer help; and you can expect others to return the favor when you get stressed out, as *your* emotions and needs matter as much as anybody else's. And while you might never get to be as skilled in taking on dysfunctional behavior as is a trained professional, you can take enormous pride in being a specialist who keeps any dysfunctional behavior from getting conjured up in the first place.

> *When we started our family meetings it was rather chaotic from the opening bell, so I soon got up and walked out. But my best friend, who told me about family hour in the first place, appeared to be having success with it. So I decided to give it another fling, but this time I started out by asking the kids for their input; and to my surprise, they all agreed that I was always complaining but that I never did a blessed thing about it. In addition, they said that I only paid attention to them when they were battling or mired down with problems. So I asked them to talk about some cheerful happenings that were going on, and that started our policy of devoting the first portion of every session to happy thoughts and good news. It was a little strained at first, but then somebody told a joke, and we were off and running. Now some of the sessions don't even move into problems areas, and the kids appear to be getting along better overall. But the most amazing thing is that my best pal now comes to me from time to time seeking some guidance in dealing with her kids.*
>
> *Veterinarian, mother of 3*

> *I received some counseling a while back and was advised that my attempting to resolve the children's problems was never going to get me anywhere. So now we do family hour, and it is quite a relief to just let them complain or cry, and I remind myself that I don't have to come up with a solution. And now we have kept the griping to no more than three minutes devoted to every issue. What a shock it was when Shawna offered some help to her brother--a sworn*

enemy--with his school lessons one day recently. Also, I noticed that Anthony isn't stuttering quite as much as he used to, and that his father is expressing himself more than he did before.

Social worker, mother of 2

CHAPTER FIFTEEN

MEET TOGETHER, FEEL COMPLETE TOGETHER: THE KEY TO FAMILY UNITY

When I was growing up we put on spirited debates after Sunday dinner, but at that time we didn't call it family hour. My dad was chief moderator, but mom appeared to have the final word with respect to important matters. But in any case, we all turned out to be good debaters. Even now when we celebrate holidays and special occasions, the feathers might start to fly at the drop of a hat. The very nice thing, however, is that there are never any chafed feelings left over after our debates because we can all see that--no matter how ludicrous my brothers' opinions may be--our love for one another is more important than for whom we voted for and why. And yes, I've come up with a few off-the-wall opinions too.

Lawyer, mother of 2, with a third bundle of joy coming

An indomitable spirit dwells in third-world villagers who end up in refuge camps and then hasten back to visit their bombed-out rubble to scour the land for scraps of building materials, never giving up hope. So where is that same spirit in the alarming numbers of gifted folks in our bountiful society who are at this very moment contemplating suicide? One answer may rest in something these hapless villagers appear to possess in greater abundance than do our privileged but painfully distraught countrymen--a powerful and pervasive sense of family unity.

As a concept, "family unity" sits up there with motherhood and apple pie; but in our modern world it all too often remains just that--a concept. As we saw in Chapter 2, there was greater family solidarity in olden times than there is now; and this unifying spirit came about naturally from the projects family members performed together, like tilling the soil, plying trades, and making from scratch countless items that are store-bought now. And since high-speed travel and high-tech entertainment existed only in their fantasies, they also played together a lot more than we do now.

> *My grandmother often talks about how her family all used to go out singing Christmas carols during the holiday season, and how they always had different parties to attend in the neighborhood. It makes her sick to see parents these days having to check over their little ones' Halloween apples for razor blades, and sort through their M & M's for pills and pebbles. She's pleased, however, that we all sit down for our family gatherings every week, and then she joins in whenever she is around. But she will not likely get us to go out caroling with her and her group.*
>
> *Temp worker, mother of 3*

The term "family unity" is pretty much self-explanatory, but not every form of unity is desirable. For example, we definitely do not recommend the following:

☐ Pervasive agreeableness due to fears about intimidation.

☐ Blindly following the lead of persuasive family members.

☐ Joining forces to harm others, steal, damage property, etc.

☐ Engaging in smothering relationships that stifle individuality.

☐ Abiding a hateful marriage, even after fruitless counseling.

☐ Catering to family members out of guilt or a need to please.

☐ Using domineering tactics in order to keep others in line.

☐ Getting enmeshed with others in love-hate relationships.

☐ Huddling together in refuge from a "perilous" outside world.

☐ Overindulgence that kills youthful drive for self-reliance.

Our high-technology age features a big bounty of services and goods, but someone forgot to issue a warning label: "Caution, this product might lead to a decline in family unity." Now when a structurally weakened family get fractured, we place the blame all around--on peer pressure, the allure of drugs, declining moral values, etc. To be sure these issues are all valid, but they are immediate causes, not underlying issues. And to study no deeper than what shows up on the surface is like hearing old timers blame the "evils" of punk rock on youngsters' letting their hair grow long.

Throughout history we have witnessed the furies of nature and humans disrupting ordinary folks' efforts to lead a tranquil life. High on this list are wars that result in an inevitable displacement of families; and widespread plagues, famines, storms, and floods devastating entire communities. Our urban (and suburban) high-tech way of living, by contrast, has impacted families in altogether different ways, a host of them clearly but subtly negative. But unlike wars and natural disasters that savagely tear into the fabric of family and community life, the negative influences of modern living have sneaked in through the side door while we gaze at the latest contraptions rolling off the assembly lines.

In these modern times of ours, exciting new careers have emerged, but they rarely find kinfolk working side by side. What is more, one family member might not have much grasp at all of another's job function. We can now travel to anywhere in a flash, yet this transportation marvel has also permitted grown children, non-custodial parents, and extended family members to relocate to far off places. Electronic entertainment has become truly fascinating, but it does not allow family members to interact with one another like they did so regularly in the past. And suburban living, with its endless sea of cookie-cutter housing, has created an impersonal lifestyle that finds families only superficially acquainted with most of their closest neighbors--except when disputes arise.

In distressed families, emotional ills and relationship woes tend to run rampant, and this unfortunately contributes to disunity. But nowadays, as a result of family-alien technological advances, many of our rock-solid homes also suffer from at least a smidge of the disunity bug. A large portion of these families do experience a sense of togetherness, but one that isn't nearly as strong as it can and should be. And now, sad to say, this situation has turned into a calmly accepted way of life--a "necessary evil."

I am ashamed to confess that once I stood by while another boy punched my brother out; and my dad, who was reared in that old stick-up-for-your-family school, wasn't at all pleased when he got the news. I long ago forgave myself for this foul deed, but the dismay about our family's lack of cohesion remains. Years of spiritual seeking have helped me to feel a greater sense of kinship, and my own kids--now all grown up--appear supportive of one another; yet I still wish they would keep in touch with each other more than they do. But we all share in many blessings, and for that I am eternally thankful.

Semi-retired musician

Examples of diminished family unity

☐ Family-together work and play projects are in sharp decline.

☐ The term "chores" now refers mostly to solitary drudgery.

☐ Most in-depth family confabs relate to problem situations.

☐ Family-together meals and gatherings have become rare.

☐ Children are often unfamiliar with their parents' careers.

☐ Outside activities regularly get priority over family projects.

☐ Misinformation and miscommunication are now rampant.

☐ The T.V., computer, and gadgets isolate family members.

☐ Television has assumed a prominent role as babysitter.

☐ Helping groups now provide intense, family-type nurturing.

☐ Grown children and extended family often live far apart.

☐ Siblings are now less inclined to stick up for one another.

☐ Never-leave-home pets get lavish care in many homes.

☐ Family history is preserved chiefly in genealogy charts.

☐ Daycare centers do what extended-families used to do.

☐ Nursing homes now do the same for the elderly and infirm.

My mother was a large, unhappy woman, and her moments of joyfulness seemed all too fleeting. She used to scream a lot in a loud, irritating voice, and I would find a place to hide when screaming started. I became devastated when I found out one day that the neighborhood kids referred to her as "mamma hog with her little piglets." I haven't had much contact with my brothers for a really long time, but my sister and I visit each other on occasion. Holidays are really painful for me, as I see all my co-workers celebrating with their families. At least I have fairly good health and some enjoyable hobbies.

Computer data analyst

In Chapter 3 we looked into our fervent need for emotional intimacy, and how people go searching it out elsewhere when they find too little of it in the home setting. Schools, the workplace, the 'hood, and the internet are among the favorite searching grounds; and those with unmet family-solidarity needs understandably feel drawn to organizations that cater to people of similar backgrounds and interests. Then too, a powerful spirit of familyhood is an inevitable component in performance and teamwork-focused groupings like sports teams, entertainment ensembles, military units, police squads, and submarine crews. Close emotional bonds develop in settings of this type because the participants share common goals and endeavor as a group to get them accomplished as they spend substantial blocks of low-distraction, quality time together. This is the same brand of teamwork that was taken for granted in families just a few generations back.

Having a strong sense of community is greatly rewarding, and all except the most alone of lone wolves experience it in some measure. But bonding that unifies family members is one of life's essentials. Families afford us the nurturing and guidance needed for adapting into society, and they continue on for all of us, through the generations, as a base of operations and as an anchor. Long after your involvement with most neighborhood, school, and group friends is over; your parents, siblings, children, and grandchildren remain somewhere in the picture. And even after family members have long departed from this life, they continue to be present, with rare exceptions, in memory and in spirit.

In this modern-day era of tortured and splintered family life, people in record numbers are seeking out healing in twelve-step programs, therapy and support groups, and rehab centers. Some impulse-ridden behavior can be controlled by pharmaceuticals and retraining; and inner torment may soften after long-buried traumas get exposed to the light of day. But the bonding with kindly therapists and/or fellow group participants is also a sizable factor in the healing process. This very same caring, support, and potential for problem resolution is also available at home, but family members seldom spend sufficient quality time together to tap even a fraction of its enormous potential.

The scientific advances that make present-day living more convenient, productive, and fascinating are not only around for the long haul, but in reality they seem destined to keep on expanding. Yet there is no reason to turn back our calendars in order to revive a powerful spirit of family. We can hold tight onto our T.V. sets and computers, and maintain our busy schedules; but we also need to preserve a modicum of distraction-free family-together time. Now in times past, family members labored and recreated together out of economic necessity and a shortage of other options; whereas in modern times, quality family time tends to be a catch-as-catch-can proposition. So when we get deeply involved in other projects, the quality family time can quickly vanish into thin air.

To echo a concept that goes way back to Chapter 1, family hour is an efficient and effective use of quality time in today's busy households; and when you put it rock-solid on your schedule, you can be certain it won't get lost in the shuffle. We have seen many benefits of family hour, such as its enrichment of little ones in their formative years, its working relentlessly to prevent and ease relationship woes, and its enhancement of communication all across the board. Now we can see where it leads in its most far-reaching application--to a powerful spirit of family unity that not only buffers every member of the household during the epoch of raising young ones, but also ripples way out into the post-parenting years, to the next generation, and even beyond.

Family hour functions as a vehicle for discussions, creative activities, home improvement work projects, forums for the voicing of grievances, and much, much more. And when family members spend good quality time together over the years, from bellowing to whispering to everything in between, a strong bond of family unity will be the result. Household unity is, in fact, a natural condition in every household, and it takes regularly dysfunctional relationships and/or a shortage of time and energy for family-group discussion and activities to put fractures into it. Performance group members get emotionally bonded by spending long hours working intensely together, but family bonding comes much easier. Family members have so many matters in common, such as the sharing of a home, cultural and legal ties, family history, participation in child nurturing and guidance, and a variety of beliefs and attitudes--appearances oftentimes to the contrary.

Relationships with grandparents and other extended family members all fall under the broad umbrella of family unity, but we'll concentrate here on two aspects: the sense of togetherness which grows as your young ones grow; and this same spirit that prevails after your child-rearing days are finally over, keeping you and your emancipated offspring in close, loving contact.

Our grown children all have their own families now, but we have stuck with the tradition of family reunions each year. Fortunately, we all live in the same general area of the country, and when money is too tight, we all camp out in the designated host's back yard. This is a load of fun for everybody, and I only hope that our grandchildren will do the same thing a generation from now.

Retired recreation specialist

Family Unity in the Child-Rearing Years

In this the final chapter, our book has now come full circle. The Cornerstones of Confident Parenting were the centerpiece of Chapter 1, and now turn up as the key element in family unity, the main theme of our final chapter. In Chapter 1 we saw the promise of enhanced parental confidence based on the tenets of all four of the cornerstones working in unison, and now we see the results of these precepts over time.   Confident parents are solid achievers, and their engineering an atmosphere of family solidarity is clearly one of the most important achievements of all. So let us review all the cornerstones once again, this time with an altered focus.

Pursue your own and your children's needs with equal vigor

This may seem simple, but the parenting literature is proof of how tricky its application can be. Enlightenment-era writers put an emphasis on children's needs and took those of parents largely for granted; and many of the latter soon fell into anxiety, confusion, and guilt as they approached young ones more sensitively. Next, along came a cadre of behavior-oriented writers who had become alarmed over floundering leadership in the home, and they set out to arm parents with no-nonsense management tactics. But if the child-centered writers harbored pie-in-the-sky attitudes about their effect on parents, then parent-focused behaviorists had pie-in-the-sky attitudes as to their effect on both children *and* parents. In the resulting disaster, children cried, argued, lied, wheedled, sneaked, and played victim; and the parents, who had before felt guilty over imagined traumas to young psyches, now had guilt over real traumas caused by the behaviorists' tactics.

Since the unintended calamity engineered by behaviorists, parenting writers and trainers have pretty much skirted around the more significant issues involved in child-rearing, and have stayed mostly with detail work. Typically they counsel parents on handing specific troublesome behavior, or they focus on narrow areas such as how grandfathers can help bolster a middle child's self-esteem. All this makes parenting seem more like an affliction than a great adventure, and leaves parents relying more on their advice givers and less on their own common sense. No wonder parents end up confused as they attempt to do what is best for their little ones and for themselves.

Confident leadership is a necessity in order for family hour to succeed, and a key element in this leadership is your attending to the feelings and needs of little ones as well as to your own. All family members are urged to express themselves in the sessions, and even if youngsters don't prove out to be adept listeners at the outset, they will follow your example--eventually, or perhaps even before eventually. Issues will not always get resolved to the satisfaction of everybody, but the freedom to speak freely and the sincere attempts at addressing issues go a long way toward fulfilling the needs of children and grown-ups alike. All this opens the door wide to a spirit of family unity. This might be a good time to review Chapters 5 and 6.

Propagate free-flowing communication in the household

Effective communication has been a popular item for some time now. Some workshops mold you into a confident speaker or a skilled negotiator; others unleash your power of persuasion; and still others get you and your helpmate to talk and listen attentively, pinpoint issues, and master conflict resolution. But unfortunately, writers appear not to be willing to touch the subject of parent-child dialogue with a pole of any length. Yes, parents have been taught effective listening techniques, but no one has yet written a manual for little ones urging them to return the favor. And the take-action-right-now parenting writers seem to view parents as being way too vulnerable and fragile to withstand volleys of spontaneous youthful expression. And to repeat once more--no, they are not!

The "Effective Communication Between Parents and Children" book may show up some day, but meanwhile family hour will carry the standard for encouraging constructive verbal exchanges and weeding out the destructive variety, which eat away at family solidarity when they take place again and again. As you and your small ones practice conversing openly and honestly with one ano-ther--and the formula differs little from that of couples communica-tion--you need no longer agonize over saying the wrong thing; nor need you fret any longer that temper flare-ups may lead to drastic consequences. All this paves the way toward a wonderful spirit of family solidarity. Throughout the book, but especially in Chapter 6, you will find help for generating and maintaining dialogue.

Promote a cooperative spirit among family members

The more parents attempt to get young ones to cooperate, the greater the resistance. Why? Because as soon as pressuring springs into the picture, frustrated parents are no longer searching for cooperation, but instead for *submission*. Genuine cooperation involves a mutual agreement to strive together towards a common goal. Cooperation isn't always cheerful; but it does find everybody focused on the task at hand, such as piling up sandbags to keep a swollen river from running amok. Families in this modern time no longer find the abundant opportunities to participate in cooperative projects because technology has taken over so much of what our ancestors accomplished together. Then too, our society worships competition, while cooperation has now become a lost art. What is more, groups that rely on teamwork, like business partnerships, athletic programs, and military combat units, develop cooperative strategies primarily as a means to a competitive end.

Devoting family hour time to cooperation-boosting activities such as board games, dramatic productions, and science projects is great; as are resolving problems together, working out compro-mises, and giving one another a helping hand. Yet no matter what takes place in your sessions, a cooperative spirit will flow naturally and abundantly. So simply engaging in dialogue--no matter where it leads you--is an exercise in teamwork on the discussion and/or activity level; and what is more, the very act of sitting together as a group, even for those who have little to say, is a cooperative experience from the very start.

Preserve blocks of time for family togetherness

In the parenting literature there are many lists of excellent ideas for interacting with little ones, but where are all the excellent ideas for preserving the quality time you'll need for nurturing these interactions? The fact is that countless great ideas never come to fruition because the time needed for them simply doesn't show up, especially when it involves teenagers. To be sure some writers do advocate family meetings; but they typically offer scripted formats that give dialogue little room to flourish, and they never appear to address the question of what to do when young ad-libbers choose to go off script and just talk (horrors!) spontaneously.

One final time we exhort you to accord family hour a place of honor on your household's calendar. Everybody's resistance to attending, and most of all your own, may at times give you fits, but your perseverance through this resistance and other rough spots will bring you mega-dividends. In these times of holding down two jobs and juggling hectic schedules, we definitely consider weekly family hour to be the best way for fostering family cohesion during the child-raising years and beyond--and we trust you see the logic in all this. If you get stuck or discouraged, please leaf through the chapters as often as needed, and keep trying out new approaches until you find what works best for you and yours. You will end up feeling delighted that you did.

> *My husband often goes on business trips, so when*
> *we started out doing family hour, it was pretty much*

the children and myself. Then when he did join us, he seemed awkward most of the time because he had never gotten into the swing of how we related to one another in the discussions. Finally a serious fight erupted about it, during which he vowed never to attend another session. But before very long he came in and apologized, and that led to our figuring out different ways for him to get to fit in better in the weekly sessions. An example was that he took up the planning and leadership of some sessions. And furthermore, he made a vow to rework his business schedule in order to spend more time at home, and he also expressed a desire to do more family things during his at-home time. So far so good. I greatly appreciated his doing all of this, and it reminded me again that he's really a very decent man. And one more thing: he's finally talking more about the finer points of his job. None of us ever understood much about just what he does. Some of the stuff is really hysterically funny.

> *Scouting activity volunteer*
> *and mother of 3*

Family Unity in the Post-Child-Rearing Years

If family solidarity has blessed your household during your child-rearing years, it might be relatively simple, although never a sure thing, to maintain a grip on that spirit in the grown-up-children era. But if togetherness has proven to be elusive while the youngsters have been maturing, it is never too late to recapture it at the present time and keep it safe for the future. Furthermore, there is hope for those of you enjoying harmony in your present household yet feeling dismayed over long-time strife with and alienation from kin from your family of origin. We now leave you with four keys for the fostering of family togetherness all through the post-parenting years and with nuclear and extended family members.

The adult-adult relationship

You didn't want your parents treating you like a child when you were twenty-three, and your young ones will not want it either when they reach that same age. Long, long after youngsters have achieved independent-adult status, overprotective parents might continue their hovering, domineering parents might keep on trying to control, and insecure parents may cringe when their former junior partners treat them as equals. Then on the other hand, some adult children resist letting loose of their home-fires comforts, and others find their parents wanting to reverse the roles and become dependent on them.

Transitioning from parent-child to adult-adult status isn't an overnight or even an over-one-year process, but one that ought to evolve gradually from an early age and be mostly established by the time youngsters leave home. For family-hour versed offspring, adult-adult relations are within easy reach, since one of dialogue's key features is equal rights for all discussants. Your young adults may still solicit your advice, and they will surely relish offering *you* advice in areas of their expertise. Being fast friends with them will be a pleasure, and it will put the icing on the cake of your successful child-rearing mission. At this time, as you will no longer retain legal or personal responsibility over them, you can watch the saga of their young adulthood unfold, and also at key times play a large supporting role in their adventures out in the world.

The trouble-shooting family meeting

When a family with growing children stumbles into frequent bickering and a dark cloud of ill will hangs around, their discomfort might possibly propel them toward wanting to talk things out--or in some cases seek professional help--so that everybody, especially the impressionable little ones, might find peace of mind. But when long-time hostility pervades relations between emancipated young folks and their parents, siblings, or other kinfolk, the motivation for getting matters cleared up may be weaker, as the involved parties are most of the time busy with their divergent lives. In retrospect, some long-estranged kin have confessed, in embarrassment, that they had even forgotten what the issues were that they had gotten so upset about in the first place.

In trouble-shooting family meetings, it's usually a good idea idea to get right to the heart of the issue. Regular and conference telephone calls may help up to a certain point, although in-person discussions are always preferable. Let emotions flow, apologize if appropriate, and confess how much a close relationship means to you. If the issue is an isolated one from way, way back, see if you can get the books closed on it; and if the area of concern is ongoing, such as extreme competitiveness or battles over politics, you might all agree to henceforth stay far away from the danger zone. But even if issues prove difficult to resolve, your addressing them with good will might ease tensions noticeably.

Being a friend-in-need

During the child-raising years the primary roles for parents are as nurturers, teachers, and guides. The friendship bond is a secondary one at this time, but in stalwart families it grows deeper over the years. The adult-adult relationship described a page ago is in essence a friendship, and the test of its strength comes when a young adult offspring goes to parents for help--or in some cases when the roles get reversed. A youthful help seeker, for example, might be looking for relationship or other advice, an opportunity to vent feelings, reassurance, financial aid, or a safe haven.

When your adult children become friends-in-need, you are a friend-indeed when you: refuse to support (with money or otherwise) self-destructive habits or irresponsible behaviors; investigato the facts before staunchly defending an offspring who is having a relationship or legal problem; dispense advice based on objective facts in a situation rather than on preconceived notions; dispense money based on need and expected responsible use of it, and not with an attempt to manipulate; and refuse to permit aimless, self-indulgent young-adult offspring to live in the house rent-free for the indefinite future. As a parent of grown children you are also being a true friend when you: listen closely to upset feelings, particularly when those feelings are directed at you; offer encouragement and support for youthful plans and projects, even if they don't get you excited; and offer thoughtful advice and feedback, even when it is not exactly what they would like to hear.

Having a wonderful time--so glad you're here

For those who greatly cherish one another's company, the frequency of family get-togethers depends to a large extent on the distances between them, the cost of travel, and the availability of time. Yet even when relationships are luke-warm or stress-laden, many families visit back and forth as regularly as clockwork. This constancy could be motivated by--among other factors--the tug of guilt, a sense of obligation, or the desire to maintain appearances. And in spite of the uncomfortable atmosphere, this same process gets repeated over and over. How can anyone derive satisfaction from such a situation?

Trouble-shooting sessions spring to the rescue when awkwardness in family gatherings stems from unresolved issues; but certain discomfort might be a simple matter of everybody's having gone in different directions and now having relatively little in common. Fortunately, this should get resolved quite easily. Details of family history that might otherwise get lost forever can be coaxed out of family elders, adults may delight in retelling their escapades as little imps, and everyone can get chances to swap old tales that bring to the surface long-lost memories. Grist for your discussion mill may also be located in current events such as school, careers, hobbies, friendships, and extended family relationships; and also in future possibilities, like everyone's dreams and plans--including how they expect to get there. Then there are oodles of fun games and activities that can joyfully rekindle the spirit of yesteryear. And you might like to use these precious occasions to tell others in the family how much you love and appreciate them.

> *We have nineteen grandchildren, and for the summers we often have a few of them--preferably from several different families--staying over for at least a week even or longer. At one point my husband and I launched the practice of sitting down with them on the very first day and discussing what everyone has been up to, and this has now become a regular feature of their visits. On occasion they come out with some gossipy stuff about their parents, but we try to discourage that. One of the older kids recently expressed an interest in doing a family tree, and now we are talking seriously about starting the research needed for it. Three of our children have shown an interest in sharing the work toward this end. I sure hope we don't find any reindeer thieves on the Finnish side of the family.*
>
> *Retired real estate appraiser,*
> *mother of 7 grown children*

Advertisers shell out mega-dollars to display images of all the things people yearn for and desire more of--e.g., convenience, laughter, prestige items, popularity and sociability, and the easing of pain and discomfort; furthermore, they cleverly appeal to a longing for greater family unity by picturing everybody seated together at mealtime, gathered attentively around the living room, and having rollicking fun times on family vacations. Images such as these undoubtedly help sell many goods and services, or else we would not continue to view them. But if every household were the scene of family meetings, ad makers might have to stick more to the easing of aches and pains, as family members would not be yearning for greater family unity--they would be busy enjoying it!

*Recently we had a photo shoot for our family, and it included five generations, I'm delighted to say. My grandmother on occasion goes on about the stories she used to hear from **her** grandmother concerning the war between the states, and I realize that some of **my** grandkids might live to usher in an era where everybody will be speeding around in personalized space ships. This is such an amazing world we live in. Our entire extended family has seen its share of ups and downs, and even a tragedy or two; but the unhappy times have been substantially outweighed by the joys of everyday living.*

*Granddaughter, daughter,
mother, and grandmother*

HELP SECTION

TROUBLESHOOTING

No matter how smoothly family hour sessions work out for you in the long haul, there is always the possibility of your running into situations where you become really stumped over what to do, or even feel like tearing all your hair out. Nipping problems in the bud is certainly far better than endeavoring to put the wheels back on after they have fallen off; so just ahead we'll present you with a listing of potential troublesome situations, along with various ideas for coping with them--a family hour first aid kit, so to speak. These suggestions will hopefully help you get over the hump--but please look to your own creative energy as well, as you will likely run into issues we fail to bring up. But even for those issues we do cover, your family situation may have a different twist on them.

Most of the upcoming scenarios have children in mind, but large people will turn out to be guilty parties in some--but hopefully not ones like being a tattle-tale. We recommend that you keep an eye on how family members behave in the meetings compared to with how they conduct themselves on the outside, as this can help you to better understand your group's dynamics. For example, if a small one is equally unruly in the sessions and on the outside, this might not indicate much about your group itself; but if an otherwise angelic child begins behaving strangely in the group, you will know that something is up. This could mean that your sessions are less than scintillating, that your child feels uneasy about interactions in the group, or something else altogether.

So don't get all discouraged if your family group leadership gets a severe testing, and don't be afraid of making mistakes--and also bear in mind that each sticky situation, even hopeless-looking ones, can get solved or at least eased off greatly. The qualities you most need in this regard are a pocketful of patience and a willingness to continue on experimenting until your find the approach that brings success. The following are some of the problem areas you are most likely to encounter.

Conflicts over when to meet

If scheduling problems make it hard to find a suitable time, work on compromises. This could even mean meeting with one or more family members missing (hopefully not the same ones every time). Then if the schedule still doesn't work, it may be a sign that your household is suffering from overschedul-itis. Just think, if not even a single hour each week can be made available for you to be all together, then your family's sense of solidarity may need some major shoring up. So see if you can work it out equitably, but don't fall into the trap of scurrying around to find a new time every week. That would assign family hour an uncertain status and pretty much guarantee that it will soon disappear from the scene.

Refusal to attend

Chapter 4 might help here. Although resistant youngsters usually respond to firm words, *do not* threaten a stubborn holdout. With regard to teens, however, talk about the value of your group, and remind them that if they miss out of items that might interest them, it is their tough luck. And if they do inquire later about what was discussed, invite them to join you next time to find out. Family hour is for the whole family, so be careful about letting AWOLs in on the benefits accruing from the sessions.

Verbal sniping

If only occasional, this can be ignored, but regular sniping has no place in family hour. Stern words often snuff it out, but you might need to place a ban on dialogue-smashing tactics like name calling and put-downs; and you may decide to impose a one-at-a-time speaking rule. If hostilities get severe, you might think about exploring issues behind it, and in this case be prepared for some verbal fireworks. But be watchful over opening up a can of worms before the family hour group has a chance to coalesce.

Physical fighting

This must be stopped immediately. If it is confined to such as shoving and elbowing, keeping your combatants separated will in most cases get the job done. This might be a great opportunity to get the brawlers engaged in a dialogue over issues. And if this fails and the scrapping continues on, you now must take stronger measures, like letting the antagonist(s) settle down for a spell outside the group circle. Then as a last resort, repeat offenders might even need to be excluded from the session.

Chronic unruly behavior

Unruly behavior might lead to your seating the participants away from any sources of potential trouble, or imposing a one-at-a-time talking rule; but exclusion from the group may be indicated if behavior gets to be a serious disruption. Now ousting might be just what some youngsters want, but they could miss out on some fun activities planned by the group, and their failure to cooperate in the sessions may lead to *your* being reluctant to cooperate with them the next time they want a special favor.

General chaos

Scampering around usually involves little ones, and everyone's talking at once is typical of preteens and adolescents. Yet even if you happen to be a laid-back type of leader, you must gain control at once. Rigid structuring can save the day, particularly in family hour's early stages, and there are lots of ideas in Chapter 4. If small ones are the offenders, get them involved in activities they might enjoy, and watch out for any urge on your part to make them sit quietly like little tin soldiers. Also, don't overlook the possibility that they may be too young to participate appropriately.

Chattering off to the side

You might be tempted to try ignoring the chatter, which can indicate that the offenders may be feeling bored or resistant to the group process; and questioning all involved parties could give you your answer. If resistance is the cause, invite feelings out into the open and try to be patient. And if the agenda is boring, take steps to liven up group interaction. Prolonged mini-conversations during group discussions can bode ill for your project, thus we advise you to sit and wait until you have every person's attention before going further with the discussion.

Excessive clowning

Clowning can bring good cheer and liven up the group, but it can also become a problem. Horseplay is trouble if it continues unabated, disrupts your agenda, diverts attention away from your comedian's issues, or moves the group toward chaos. If the comics are a hit with the group, give them recognition, but emphasize how important it is to let the agenda move ahead. Then again you might invite the home-spun entertainers to use a future session or two to put on a comedy show promoting their talents.

Extreme competitiveness

This usually involves preteens or teenagers, but adults are oftentimes in the mix as well, since this may be a trait that runs all through the family. Don't strive to eliminate competition altogether, but rather work to take the edge off by making it more relaxing and enjoyable. We suggest that you keep an eye on competitive interactions both in discussions and in activities, and simply call a halt to ones that begin getting deadly serious. And to avoid problems, you might want to announce in advance that you will do so. What is more, you may want to get the group all involved in cooperative games and projects, including ones in your local community. The Recommended Readings section may give you some ideas.

Awkward silences

This happens most often in the group's early stages before cohesion takes root. Silences of even several seconds can stir up anxiety among the participants, so it is important to insert structure into the breach, and to do so without delay. You can break the ice with snappy comments; and for more frequent dead spots you will get help in Chapter 4, in the Suggested Exercises (next up), in the Recommended Reading section (just after that), or from your own creative reservoir. Awkward silences in a well-settled group might indicate a delicate subject matter; and unless it is vital to get to the heart of the issue, and to get there soon, moving on to a different subject might be your best course.

Sullen or stony-faced silences

This seldom involves more than a single group participant; and among the possibilities here are an aversion to attending, unspoken anger toward other family members, worries about saying the wrong thing, or simply being taciturn by nature. You might set the stage for stoney ones to become more relaxed, but don't try to cajole them into talking. If silences don't disrupt the group, simply get on with the agenda, bearing in mind that quiet folks usually get more from their experience than constant yappers. If, however, a silently sullen atmosphere casts a heavy pall over the scene, you know something is going on, and you might wish to adopt a more confrontational approach. (See the next paragraph.)

Angry outbursts

Your challenge here is to have people express themselves vigorously without allowing mayhem to leap in. Give heed to true spontaneity and get issues out into the open, but at the same time keep everyone on the subject at hand. Then again, step in quickly to quash threats, put-downs, and physical contact; and if the back-and-forth becomes chaotic, allow just one person to talk at a time. Situations like these can be very stressful and might require a fair amount of practice before you get totally comfortable with them. A review of Chapters 5 and 6 might be helpful as well.

Frequent interrupting

Interrupting might be appropriate if it pertains to the topic at hand and shows that the speaker is thoughtful. But you should be intolerant over it if it arrives from out of "left field," as this points to inattention or a lack of respect for the discussion process. Young children are more likely to be perpetrators than teenagers or older folks. Firmness is needed, but don't let interrupters get you huffed up; and place emphasis on the importance of listening. As groups get more settled in, interrupting tends to be less of a problem, although it could indicate a dull or unfocused program.

Tattling and apple polishing

Both tactics are designed to curry parental favor, and these tacticians are apt (hopefully) to be grade schoolers. Be careful not to feed into the tattle-tale's wishes by "weighing the evidence," but you may want to delve into how the involved parties relate to each other both within and outside of family hour. The same is true for apple polishers, as their siblings may easily get bent out of shape over the game playing.

Sarcastic, smart-alecky comments

Occasional sarcasm is usually best handled by paying it no heed; but if it becomes regular and heavy-handed, you need to act decisively. Not only can smart-aleck behavior be highly disruptive, but it may be targeted at scuttling your family meetings altogether. Attempt to find out what is bothering the surly one(s), and also ask as to what they would want to get out of their experience. If these inquiries prove fruitless and the sarcasm continues unabated, you might have little choice but to banish the troublemaker(s) from the group, at least for the time being.

Unacceptable language

Language inappropriate for youngsters should be inappropriate for everyone else too. If children tell of hearing taboo words from parents outside the group, you might--if you choose to--justify having two standards elsewhere; but in the sessions, the rule shall apply to all. Youngsters who cannot or will not control themselves might be encouraged to coin their own heat-of-the-moment words, with the stipulation that they don't sound like any real ones. Then again, if children keep on using unseemly language despite being admonished, you might want to look into the real reasons for this defiance; and there may be at least a few.

Non-stop talking and attention hogging

These tactics, if allowed to continue, can prove highly frustrating to the leader and other group members; so firm, consistent measures are called for. Among these possibilities are strict limits on everybody's turn to speak, as well as a system that guarantees more or less equal time for all participants. If the offenders ignore the rules, they might lose their regular turn for speaking. Non-stop yapping and attention grabbing are signs of feeling ignored or left out in some way, so make sure these young ones receive special attention and recognition both within and outside the sessions.

Conflict over group leadership

A good many two-parent households just naturally seem to wind up with co-leadership for family hour sessions, but this often-times doesn't turn out well, even for couples who get along nicely otherwise. If this is your situation, don't put up with such misery or discouragement; but instead explore options like designating one person as the top banana, alternating the leadership, or assigning specific roles and tasks to each of you. This might very well serve as a model for youngsters in their future leadership for family hour and for other situations.

Marital conflict spilling over into the sessions

Strife-ridden couples cannot permit their conflicts to infect their family hour experience, but neither should they put up a false front. The sessions have a potential, if it is used constructively, for easing tensions; but family hour is not designed for resolving their long-festering issues--professional counseling is required for that. Quarreling couples might tactfully discuss their problems in outline form in family hour (depending on the nature of the issues and the ages of the youngsters), but if they find it difficult to be civil to each other, their obvious challenge shall be to learn to bite their tongues and/or to avoid sensitive topics.

Discouragement

More than just about anything else, when the family group facilitator comes down with a serious case of the what's-the-sense flu bug, family hour can now get ready to be placed on the endangered species list. In most instances this happens during the first month or two, and it may have one or several causes. Your family might have made a rather tenuous initial commitment, your expectations might be unrealistically lofty, your leadership skills could be in need of shoring up, you might own a pessimistic streak which is keeping family hour's long-range benefits far away from your field of vision, or your program could be in need of changes in content and/or style. Reviewing Chapters 4 and 5 might be helpful. Even a vague why-bother feeling on your part calls for quick action, as it can quick-as-a-flash spell doom for family hour in your household. And oh yes, it might be an excellent idea to open up the subject of your gloomy outlook with members of the group. Who knows, you might even get some reassurance and good advice.

SUGGESTED EXERCISES AND ACTIVITIES

One-at-a-time talking

Group members take turns talking, no interruptions permitted; and those who interrupt anyway, especially repeat offenders, may lose their turn. Turns are time-limited, and timekeepers need to be eagle-eyed. Use this when chaos or out-of-control behavior comes knocking at the door, or simply for a change of pace. This strategy may be used for one part of a session, a whole one, or as an ongoing practice wherever the need exists.

Guided meditations

A really swell idea whether or not your group has a hyperactive streak. Might be done on occasion or weekly, and probably should be limited to 15 minutes or less--the younger the little ones, the shorter is the time. For those of you who have never attended guided meditation sessions, make certain the images are pleasant and readily pictured by group members. If you are not sure about going ahead, a book on meditation might help.

Other behavior-calming exercises

This includes routines such as non-verbal communication, the five-seconds-between-responses rule, slow-motion talking and moving, and the game of "freeze." In this game, everybody has to freeze on the spot when that word is yelled out. Participants must hold their positions for a specified duration (for small ones, a short interval is the best), or you may conduct a contest to see who can remain frozen--often in odd, funny poses--the longest. There are scads of other choices for enjoyable behavior-calming exercises, so challenge your group to invent some of them.

The double-talk patrol

Family members gather examples of what they perceive as deceptive double-talk, and the others analyze it. Material might be found in all the media, school, workplace, neighborhood, etc.; and likely targets are bureaucratic word-speak, political campaign talks and debates, television commercials, know-it-all friends and fellow workers, etc. May be scheduled often or rarely, depending on the group members' interest. This exercise helps young ones become more understanding of the hidden motives of the media and other fuzzy-language types, and it further helps them develop a greater appreciation for straight-talking dialogue.

The "retirement" celebration

The "retired" family member (may be parent or child) sits in silence the whole time, while others in the group talk briefly about the honored guest's long, interesting life. Can elicit lots of laughs, but is also a means of getting young folks to ponder the future, as many of the "predictions" will be based on their interests and talents. Caution: this should not become a vehicle for "roastmaster" type cutting, sarcastic, or demeaning comments; so quickly put a damper on such efforts by comedians in the group.

Costume parties

Everyone dresses up, and creativity is the style. Costumes might be standard (e.g., pirate), celebrity-themed, or more fanciful; and they stay "in character" the whole session. Great for nurturing thespian talent, and also great for honing skills in costume design and creation. The small ones might need help with their costumes and with playing their assigned roles, but they should participate in this process as much as possible. Thrift stores may be a treasure trove for material, and a sewing machine is a rather indispensable tool. Also, go dig up old Halloween masks and such.

The reviewers

A group member selects material for everyone to review--a comic book, movie, T.V. show, chapter from a novel, etc.; and next time somebody else does the selecting. Family members are sure to have widely divergent literary and dramatic tastes, which opens the door to (hopefully) civil debate. Also, this allows family members to get to know one another's interests in a new and different way. This activity, even with all it's potential disagreements, works to promote family togetherness.

The ego trip-up

Participants take turns discussing personal experiences of any variety, but they must do so without using the words "I," "me," "myself," or "my." What is more, they are not allowed to finagle by referring to themselves in the third person, by employing the editorial "we" or "our," by saying "You know who," or by using evasions of any other type. Those who flub up lose their turns, but younger ones may be allowed one or more missteps before being shown to their seat. This should be a fascinating, challenging exercise, and one that shines a bright spotlight on self-oriented thinking.

Sociograms

Works out best for families with three or more school-aged youngsters, who are asked to score the sibling group (themselves included) on questions like "Who is the most observant?" or "Who is best at making money deals?" Later on they debate the choices among themselves. The challenge for parents is to avoid framing questions that drip with snob appeal, might cause embarrassment, or may be targeting surface values; and to pick out categories that give every child the opportunity for recognition. This exercise may be repeated using different categories.

Build-a-story

Small slips of paper are put into a pile, each with an easily recognized word on it like "horse," "scary," or "respect." The aim is to spin a short story based on these words without glancing at the slips once the story begins. We recommend giving one slip to little ones, and increasing the number of slips according to the ages of participants, up to a possible maximum of four. This tests memory and imagination, among other things.

Other word games

A great many possibilities. Group members weave a story by having everybody contribute a single sentence; or by having a speaker stop in mid-sentence, the next person finishing up; or by having the next person continue on with a word that is a synonym, antonym, homonym, or rhyme of the last word spoken. Use your imagination to create other such word games.

Tell me true

Three participants at a time, each of whom relates a story portrayed as factual. However, only one is true, and the other two are totally made up; then others in the group attempt to smoke out the truth. In one scenario, they directly question each story teller; and in another, they guess right off. If made into a contest, points are awarded to each story teller for the number of wrong guesses made about her or his tale. Story lines may be related to dreams; goings-on at school and office; favorite movies, television shows, and songs; secret beliefs and activities; stories others have told to them; or anything else of interest. And no, such "fibbing" does not promote devious behavior, but rather stimulates imaginative thinking. (Deviousness stems from dysfunctional relationships.)

Climbing the family tree

Parents discuss and write out everything they know about their family tree, including countries of origin, geographical moves, careers, offspring, other clanfolk, and significant events and dates in all their lives. In addition, they seek contact with living relatives in order to gather up further information and clear up any areas of uncertainty. Then all the data is written down--no reason for being formal--and copies might be made for offspring to preserve. Some families might want to do research on a wider scale or have official family trees prepared. Others may even go so far as to write up a family history book.

Where in the world?

One group participant speaks about a country after having selected the name out of a hat. We suggest giving each country a whole session, allowing a week for preparation, and offering small children the assistance of parents and older siblings. Public libraries are a fine resource, with their atlases, treasure-trove of history, and travel guides in book form or on video and C.D. The internet is also a source of endless information. Presenters start out being didactic, and then queries and discussion follow. A breath of fresh air in a society woefully uninformed about the history and present-day happenings in Slovakia, Slovenia, and Slobovia.

The family forum

The designated speaker for the session argues in favor of a thesis that has either been selected carefully or at random, and has one week to get prepared. Others in the group take their turn speaking in agreement with or rebuttal to the argument, and then the presenter gets to respond. Only one person at a time has the floor, and all remarks except the opening argument are limited to one minute. Promotes debating and listening skills--and civility is highly valued. A format such as this one places the presenter in a relatively strong position.

The straight-talking debate

This is altogether different from political debates you view on T.V. or in the high-school auditorium in that logical thinking and accurate, objective information are valued instead of cleverness. It uses the standard format; but after initial statements, each side must stay on the point last made--no changing the subject, avoiding the question, appeals to bias, or personal attacks. The moderator makes sure everyone follows the rules, and may hand out warnings or disqualifications for violations. This is a challenging form of building straight-talking skills.

Joke sessions and comedy routines

Group participants may choose one-liners or funny stories they have heard or read, or they may make up their own. Comedy routines may make use of costumes, pantomime, props, slapstick, impersonations, accents, etc. Stand-up comics may get audience participation, and everyone in the family is fair game as targets of the repartee. The audience is urged to cheer or hiss as the spirit moves. Time limits might be needed for performances. This is all in the spirit of fun--no mean-spirited remarks, please.

Thanksgiving

This can be an inspiring experience for all families from the devoutly religious to the agnostic, and it promotes positive thinking in addition to a spirit of gratitude. Group participants all take turns voicing appreciation for the various blessing they have received in life, and/or discussing whatever delights them; and no one should feel pressure to speak. This hopefully gets folks to focus on items that tend to get overlooked, such as beautiful skies, the resiliency of wildlife, and small acts of kindness and graciousness. We don't recommend coaching young folks or critiquing others' comments. And if one or more of the participants start to dominate the scene, we advise you to put time limits on talking.

The joint project

This may be anything the group decides upon, and should hopefully be finished in an hour; although it could be spread over two or three sessions. Possibilities include crafts projects, murals, science experiments, jigsaw or word puzzles, games of all types, and home improvement projects. Even if a particular undertaking may seem trivial or may not produce the hoped for result, the very process of working together enhances family bonding.

The family restaurant

The family plans a meal, and everyone takes a role in pre-paring food. Steps are taken to cater to special tastes and make certain the dishes have universal appeal. Clean-up is also a joint undertaking. If recipes are used, look to cook up variations; and if the meal seems to be successful, consider preserving it on index cards. Then if you wind up with loads of successes, a recipe book might be in the offing. This is a variation of the "joint project" just presented, and it obviously stimulates group spirit.

This is merely a small sampling of the copious choices for exercises and activities related to family hour, and the books listed next offer lots more for your consideration. So harvest ideas from some of our suggestions, from various other sources, or from your own experiences and creative repetoire. But whatever you decide upon, be diligent about enjoying yourselves along the way.

RECOMMENDED READINGS FOR FAMILY HOUR ACTIVITIES

BIGGEST RIDDLE BOOK IN THE WORLD, THE -- Joseph Rosenbloom -- Sterling Publishing, NY, NY, 1976. -- While certain book titles tend to exaggerate, this volume lives up to the hype. It gives you everything from really silly riddles to the more sophisticated variety.

BILL SEVERN'S COMPLETE BOOK OF MAGIC -- Gallahad Books, a division of Budget Book Service, NY, NY, 1995. -- A comprehensive guide for mastering mental tricks and ones using coins, rope, ribbon, string, etc.

COMEDY THESAURUS, THE -- Judy Brown -- Quirk Books, Philadelphia, PA, 2005. -- This is the Bible of truly timeless comic moments, using material from all the big-timers. If you could have just one humor volume, this might be it.

EASY CARD TRICKS -- Peter Arnold -- Sterling Publishing, NY, NY, 2002. -- A small volume; and as the name implies, is aimed at younger children.

EASY HAND TRICKS -- Bob Longe -- Sterling Publishing, NY, NY, 2003. -- Like the above book in many ways, but without the use of cards as props.

ENCYCLOPEDIA OF WORLD GEOGRAPHY -- By Graham Bateman and Victoria Egan -- Barnes & Noble Books, NY, NY, 1993. -- Pretty recent volume covering every one of the world's countries separately, re: geographical features, society, economy. Nicely illustrated, and with appeal even for those who usually don't keep atlases in their bathroom reader collection.

FAMILY FUN AND GAMES -- The Diagram Group, Sterling Publishing, NY, NY, 1992. -- A lavishly illustrated volume featuring 800 games for the family group. Board games and ones requiring dice, dominoes, words, music, pencil and paper, target shooting, scavenger hunting, and much more.

FAMILY GAME BOOK, THE -- Robert Masters -- Doubleday & Co., Garden City, NY, 1967. -- Truly great volume that divides all the games according to age groups. No fancy equipment needed in order to have some great fun.

GREATEST JOKE BOOK EVER, THE -- Mel Greene -- Avon Books, NY, NY, 1999. -- A good sized collection of family-friendly humor, including the requisite gaggle of lawyer jokes.

HOLIDAY DECORATING FOR DUMMIES -- Kelley Taylor -- Publishing by Wiley, Hoboken, NJ, 2003. -- Breezy writing style with loads of illustrations. Oriented toward seasons like Christmas and New Year's, Valentine's, and Easter; yet most of the projects can be used in decorating for any or no special occasion. Simple, easy to locate materials, and many helpful hints provided. Great for the entire family, not just for mothers and daughters. Allows all the "macho men" of the family to show their tender side.

HOYLE'S RULES OF GAMES -- Morehead & Mott-Smith -- A Signet Book, NY, NY, 2001. -- Should eliminate a good deal of the squabbling among household game players, as this is the last word from the "according to" expert.

LITHGOW PALOOZA, A -- John A. Lithgow -- A Broadthink Book, A Fireside Book, Simon & Schuster, NY, NY, 2004. -- A treasure from a really huge celebrity who has derived much more satisfaction--according to him--from playing with his children than he has ever gotten from doing movies or T.V. shows. Lots of creative and whimsical fun, and lavishly illustrated. Projects feature the likes of theater, music, crafts, dance, arts, word games, food, and vacation amusement.

LITTLE GIANT ENCYCLOPEDIA OF CARDS AND MAGIC TRICKS, THE -- Diagram Group, Sterling Publishing, NY, NY, 1996. -- This title just about says it all. Covers the gamut from the well known to the obscure. The only thing to criticize may be the oxymoron in the title.

MAGIC FOR BEGINNERS -- Walter B. Gibson -- Frederick Fell Publishers, Hollywood, FL, 1999 . -- Lots of illustrations. Mental tricks as well as ones using cards, rope, coins, string, and various other household materials.

MORE TEAM BUILDING ACTIVITIES FOR EVERY GROUP -- By Alanna Jones -- Rec Room Publishing, Richland, WA, 2002. -- Outdoor games for groups like work teams, but is also appropriate for family groups whenever adjustments are made for different age levels. Builds cooperative bonds.

100 IDEAS FOR STATIONERY, CARDS, & INVITATIONS -- Laura McFadden -- Quarry Books, Gloucester, MA, 2006. -- Easy-to-complete projects, simple materials, great for parents and children of all ages. Book written in plain language and pleasantly illustrated.

100 OTHER GAMES TO PLAY ON A CHESSBOARD -- By Stephen Addison -- Peter Owen Publishers, London, 1983. -- Most suitable for adults and older youngsters, and features many games you are not likely to find elsewhere.

WORLD'S BEST INDOOR GAMES, THE -- Gyles Brandreth -- Pantheon Books, NY, NY, 1981. -- Very similar to "Family Fun & Games," but with fewer illustrations.

YEAR 'ROUND FUN -- Bill Stephani -- Krause Publications, Iola, WI, 1999. -- 101 crafts projects for children, parents, and other groups. Gorgeously illustrated, splashed with vibrant colors throughout. On the easy side, and using mostly common household materials. A really fun volume.

OTHER RECOMMENDED READINGS

ART OF LOVING, THE -- Erich Fromm -- Harper Brothers, NY, NY, 1956. -- A classic volume that examines how love flows between man and woman, and between parent and child. Ties the capacity for loving to one's inner strength, love for oneself, and personal productivity.

BETWEN PARENT AND CHILD -- Haim G. Ginott -- MacMillan & Co., NY, NY, 1965. -- Stresses the importance of listening skills. Deals with issues like sex education, jealousy, and serious emotional problems.

BLACK CHILD CARE -- James P. Comer & Alvin F. Poussaint -- Simon & Schuster, NY, NY, 1975. -- A question and answer guide covering the facts of life for African-American parents. Addresses the impact of racism, aggression, and self-esteem in bringing up children in these homes.

CHILD UNDER SIX, THE -- James Hymes, Jr. -- Prentice Hall, Englewood Cliffs, NJ, 1963. -- Easy to read book helping parents to understand young ones and their psychological needs.

CHILDREN THE CHALLENGE -- R. Dreikurs -- Hawthorne Books, NY, NY, 2004. -- Getting to emotional levels in family relationships while maintaining personal stability. Using natural consequences in response to youngsters' unacceptable behavior.

CLIENT-CENTERED THERAPY -- Carl R. Rogers -- Houghton-Mifflin Co., Boston, MA, 1951. -- A basic text on client-centered therapy. Theory and practice, foundations for research, and applications to group.

CREATIVE AGGRESSION -- George Bach & Herb Goldberg -- Doubleday, NY, NY, 1997. -- Talks about repressed and expressed aggression. Delves into a number of suggestions for uncovering suppressed aggression.

FREE TO BE YOU, FREE TO BE ME -- Marlo Thomas -- McGraw Hill, NY, NY, 1974. -- A delightful book (and also a record album) that delves into feelings, prejudices, and the joy and gentleness of living one's life.

LIBERATED PARENTS, LIBERATED CHILDREN -- Adele Faber & Elaine Mazlish -- Grosset & Dunlap, NY, NY, 1974. -- With humor and candor, this volume tells that when they acquire skills, parents can shed self-defeating habits and help themselves and their families to live together in dignity.

PEOPLE MAKING -- Virginia Satir -- Science & Behavior Books, Palo Alto, CA, 1972. -- Describes coded interactions during our communication. Offers suggestions and exercises for opening up true lines of communication.

PLAY THERAPY -- Virginia Axline -- Houghton-Mifflin, Boston, MA, 1947. -- The first book describing the application of the client-centered approach to therapy with youngsters. Demonstrates the use of active listening. Deals with the concept of imposing limits.

Techniques might be applied by parents in their home. Axline is a pioneer in play therapy.

SELF-ESTEEM TEACHER, THE -- Robert Brooks -- American Guidance Service, Circle Pines, MN, 1991. -- Includes exercises for building youthful self-image and self-acceptance.

SENSE OF WONDER, THE -- Rachel Carson -- Harper and Row, NY, NY, 1965. -- A beautiful book with pictures and ideas for parents and youngsters concerning the essence and importance of the sense of awe and wonder in children's learning experiences.

SUMMERHILK -- A. S. Neill -- Hart Publishing, NY, NY, 1960. -- The report of a pioneering English school where an attempt was made to incorporate into an educational institute the principals of democracy and the elements of a therapeutic community.

TAKING CARE OF A.D.H.D. -- Russell A. Barkley -- Guilford Press, NY NY, 1999. -- A complete, authoritative guide for parents of impulsive, inattentive, and hyperactive children.

TOWARD A PSYCHOLOGY OF BEING -- by Abraham Maslow -- D. Van Nostrand, NY, NY, 1952. -- Excellent presentation of a positive, optimistic philosophy outlining how people have an urge to mature and actualize their potential, which gets facilitated when they are accepted as they are.

TRANSPARENT SELF, THE -- Sidney M. Jourard -- D. Van Nostrand, NY, NY, 1964. -- Offers a hypothesis that we can be healthier, more functional, and more helpful if we gain the courage to be our truest selves around others. Concealing thoughts and emotions can interfere with intimate relationships. Self-disclosure begets more self-disclosure in family dialogue.

WHY AM I AFRAID TO TELL YOU WHO I AM? -- John Powell -- Argus Communications, Chicago, IL, 1959. -- A beautiful, easy-to-read book about the risks of revealing our true selves to others in open communication.

YOUR ADOLESCENT -- Lawrence K. and Mary Frank -- Viking Press, NY, NY, 1956. -- Is also a Signet Key Book published by New American Library. -- This paperback will be helpful to parents in their desire to understand the dynamics of adolescence.

YOUR CHILD'S SELF-ESTEEM -- Dorothy D. Briggs -- Double-day, NY, NY, 1976. -- Focuses on children's self-esteem and its importance for emotional and physical welfare. Offers to parents methods for fostering self-esteem.

YOUR INNER CHILD OF THE PAST -- Hugh W. Missildine -- Simon and Schuster, NY, NY, 1993. -- Excellent for understanding the effects of various parental patterns on children's personalities and their future adult ways of coping with relationship issues.